DUAL-CAREER COUPLES

Edited by

Fran Pepitone-Rockwell

 SAGE PUBLICATIONS Beverly Hills London

"Three Generations of Dual-Career Couples" by Rhona and Robert N. Rapoport is reprinted from *Marriage & Family Review*, Vol. 1 No. 5, 1-12 (September 1978), by permission of the Haworth Press. © 1978 by Rhona and Robert N. Rapoport.

For information address:

SAGE Publications, Inc.
275 South Beverly Drive
Beverly Hills, California 90212

SAGE Publications Ltd
28 Banner Street
London EC1Y 8QE, England

Printed in the United States of America

Library of Congress Cataloging in Publication Data
Main entry under title:

Dual-career couples.

   (Sage focus editions; 24)
   Bibliography: p.
   1. Married people—Employment—United States—
Addresses, essays, lectures. I. Pepitone-Rockwell,
Fran. II. Series.
HQ536.D797   306.8'7   80-15747
ISBN 0-8039-1436-9
ISBN 0-8039-1437-7 (pbk.)

FIRST PRINTING

CONTENTS

*To Don, my extraordinary husband,
and Grant and Chad, my delightful sons,
as we continue to negotiate and love*

ACKNOWLEDGMENTS

Because of the devotion of the staff of the Women's Resources and Research Center at the University of California, Davis, this book has become a reality. Ann Altamirano, Tamara Gravelle, and Alyshia Patrick all took turns in typing, making phone calls to authors, and, most importantly, they gave their loving support to this project. These three are dual-career women and dedicated feminists, and I thank them enormously for their assistance.

—F. P.-R.

INTRODUCTION

It has been only "right" that women be at home and that men work. This assumption has been based on the notion that there is a "natural order of sexual division of labour." This "natural order" has been partly based on what Oakley (1974) described as the "myth of motherhood":

> The myth of motherhood contains three popular assertions. The first is the most influential: that children need mothers. The second is the obverse of this: that mothers need their children. The third assertion is a generalization which holds that motherhood represents the greatest achievement of a woman's life: the sole true means of self-realization [1974: 186].

This myth has been the basic definition for women's roles and has been the normative standard for women; it indirectly asserts that men do not have the same needs with respect to their children, and that perhaps children do not need their fathers in the same way they do their mothers. Ultimately, the clear message was that women did not work outside the home. When women were employed outside the home, it supposedly was only on a temporary basis: to get extra "pin money," to help tide over the family in a financial squeeze, or to assume the breadwinner role in the event of death or divorce of the husband.

Most women who lived this myth therefore naturally became part of the "two-person career couple" (Papanek, 1974). Wives in the "two-person career couple" adapted their lives to accommodate their high-commitment husbands' careers, and consequently did not gain any formal acknowledgement. The phrase "Behind every successful man, there is a woman," testified to the fact that wives were honored by how successful *their* husbands were.

The "two-person career couple" and its natural outgrowth, the contemporary nuclear family, has had drawbacks. Veroff and Feld (1970) identified deleterious consequences for the family members. Husbands have been obligated to be breadwinners, and wives have been removed from a major sector of the society because of what Safilios-Rothschild (1974: 18) calls the "motherhood cult":

> The 'Motherhood Cult' has throughout history enslaved women more than all other beliefs and values. The idea that only children brought up with twenty-four-hours-per-day care by their natural mothers can have a normal development has cut women off from a large number of educational, occupational, political, and social options.

These role restraints imposed on both sexes clearly have had little flexibility, and the prescribed lifestyles have been based on one's gender, rather than on preference or choice. Both men and women have been locked into these stereotypical, socially defined roles with both sexes having been denied access to alternative ways of being in the world. There are hazards intrinsic to this unipolar view. The hazards are distributed unevenly, however. Gove (1972) found that marriage had an insulating effect against mental illness for men, but the opposite effect on women. Women who were divorced, widowed, or single had lower rates of mental illness than did married women. Gove attributed this phenomenon to role restrictions for women, the low status and boredom of housework, and the lesser status granted a position even if the married woman worked.

Married women are also more apt to seek psychiatric help (Gove and Tudor, 1973; Seiden, 1976), attempt suicide, report somatic symptoms demonstrating psychological stress (Seiden, 1976), seek out physicians more, get more prescriptions, and use more psychotropic drugs (Weissman and Klerman, 1977). Women who have never married or who are widowed report a lower incidence of depression than do married women. Weissman and Klerman (1977: 107) dispute the notion that biology is the cause:

> Furthermore, the data that unmarried women have lower rates of mental illness than unmarried men, but that married women have higher rates than married men, are cited as evidence that the excess of

symptoms noted currently are not entirely due to biological factors intrinsic to being female, but are contributed to by the conflicts generated by the traditional female role.

Radliff (1975) suggests that never-married women "have been less indoctrinated in the helplessness stereotype than those who marry." Seligman (1974) has argued that hopelessness, helplessness, and low self-esteem are not the manifest symptoms of depression, but in fact are the causes of the depression itself. Typically, women have been socialized into femininity, which—when translated—means dependency on others, and low aspirations and self-esteem (Weissman and Klerman, 1977). This socialization process is a prototype of Seligman's "learned helplessness" model, which is consistent with the development of depression, or what Chesler (1972) has called the "devalued female role." Being devalued as a result of being female is in contrast to being male and therefore highly valued. It is no wonder then that the phrase the "opposite sex" is so common: Men and women are prisoners in their sex-roles and to adopt behaviors of the other sex is to diminish one's "femininity" or "masculinity." Only recently have the benefits of androgyny become clear: The freedom to behave as one chooses regardless of one's gender is associated with positive mental health (Neville, 1977):

> The androgynous individual was shown to be capable of living in the here-and-now, of holding values of the self-actualizing person, of being sensitive to self needs and feelings, of being able to express feelings in spontaneous action, to like and accept one's self and to develop meaningful relationships with others. In addition the androgynous individual was shown to have far fewer signs of psychopathology than the sex-typed individual.

It is clear then that the two-person career couple has taken its emotional toll on women, yet may have a buffering effect on men. The emotional toll, aside from the consequences of devaluation and depression, has also appeared as "the problem that has no name" described by Friedan (1963: 11):

> The problem lay buried, unspoken, for many years in the minds of American women. It was a strange stirring, a sense of dissatisfaction,

a yearning that women suffered in the middle of the twentieth century in the United States. Each suburban wife struggled with it alone. As she made the beds, shopped for groceries, matched slipcover material, ate peanut butter sandwiches with her children, chauffeured Cub Scouts and Brownies, lay beside her husband at night—she was afraid to ask even of herself the silent question—"Is this all?"

The "stirring" eventually became part of the basis for the radical shift away from the acceptance of the two-person career couple. The stirring was to be transformed into an active struggle for women's rights and an escalation of women into the labor force. The stirring and the struggle have set the stage for the intense interest in the dual-career couple.

Before Rapoport and Rapoport (1969) created the term "dual-career families," others had described similar concepts. Blood and Wolfe (1960) addressed the "dual parenting family" which encompassed the effort of both the husband and wife to parent. Parnes et al. (1970) discussed women's efforts to negotiate both work and family roles. But Rapoport and Rapoport reported on five dual-career families (1976: 9), clearly identifying a major transition:

> The term "dual-career families" was coined to designate a type of family structure in which both heads of household—the husband and the wife—pursue active careers and family lives. 'Career' is sometimes used to indicate any sequence of jobs, but in its more precise meaning it designates those types of job sequences that require a high degree of commitment and that have a continuous developmental character.

Dual-career families are distinct from a two-person career couple in their attitudinal support of the equalization of power and domestic responsibilities, and in their belief in career advancement. Some studies have shown, however, that in reality these goals are not achieved and that women continue to be responsible for the home (Bryson et al., 1976; Epstein, 1971). Women may hold onto this role in order to avoid guilt for not being like the majority of women in our society (Epstein, 1971). Men may not assume the executive responsibility for the home because it is "outside of ordinary male responsibility or even consciousness" (Johnson and Johnson, 1976: 72):

The fact that a green pepper is undergoing autolytic changes in the refrigerator may be interesting to the husband in terms of the type of fungus it produces; it even may arouse anger about his wife's neglect. The wife on the other hand might be much more susceptible to the fantasies of her husband and children getting "food poisoning" or of her reputation as a housecleaner.

Men's early socialization, which typically has not included domestic responsibility, since this was "women's work," has logically spared them from this arena of guilt. Simultaneously, they have been denied the chance to discover personal preferences within the home. Because of what Rapoport and Rapoport (1976: 369) call "cognitive maps" men and women have not questioned early socialization contracts: "The husband simply forgets once he has left the house, wiping his mind clean of domestic concerns because he has been programmed by his society to shift his attention to external concerns." Lein (et al., 1974: 163) found that in non-dual-career couples, where both partners were employed nonetheless, the men discovered to their amazement that rewards were to be had at home:

> Several of the husbands in our sample have discovered, sometimes to their own surprise, that they enjoy the extra time with the children and the added sense of more actively participating in their development. In fact, some have found that they are skilled and competent in these tasks.

There are other benefits and psychological advantages for the dual-career couple. Women who work report greater self-esteem, effectiveness, well-being (Astin et al., 1971; Bernard, 1972), and more marital satisfaction (Safilios-Rothschild, 1970) than do unemployed women. The advantages carry over for husbands, too. Husbands whose wives work full time report happier marriages, have fewer infectious diseases, and are less prone to psychiatric impairment than husbands married to housewives (Booth, 1976). In a later study, Booth (1979) found that when women are employed there is considerable benefit for the marital relationship: "If anything, a husband whose wife is employed enjoys a happier marriage and is under less stress than a man married to a housewife."

Despite the inherent complex issues involved, the dual-career family may well become the norm. Dual-career couples attest to the benefits which sustain their efforts. The marital relationship is strengthened, self-esteem increases, and the adjective "happy" applies to dual-career couples.

This book is an in-depth examination of dual-career couples from the perspective that the traditional family model no longer meets the needs of couples in the 1980s. The dual-career family represents a search for new ways and options to gain a different kind of fulfillment. Rapoport and Rapoport (1978) have described this new structure as the "enabling family," attesting to the desire to break out of stereotypic roles so that family members may actively strive for personal accomplishment. The dual-career phenomenon underscores the notion that family members can direct their lives based on options and not rely just on tradition. The dual-career couple, then, embodies the concept of choice, not obligation to traditional roles.

In order to fully assess the complexities of the dual-career family, this book has been separated into four main sections, and various related subsections. We hope the reader will be easily able to integrate microcosmic views and macrocosmic perspectives.

Rapoport and Rapoport, dual-career theorists who coined the phrase "dual-career family," painstakingly review the major research studies in the field. Many of the articles they report on are spin-offs of their own original work. They summarize and highlight the salient points in their chapter entitled "Three Generations of Dual-Career Family Research," which is no doubt a pioneer paper in its own right.

Pepitone-Rockwell's chapter examines the parallel antecedents of the civil rights and women's movements. She further points out that attachment theories, embodiments of motherhood myths like civil rights, were divisive with respect to women. But because of the core issues inherent in civil rights endeavors, the women's movement emerged as a significant and powerful social phenomenon.

Lynn reviews the literature on women's intellectual development and concludes that as a result of sex role socialization, women often do not strive for independence. When either parent fosters the struggle for intellectual and/or artistic creativity, the woman blossoms in these areas.

Hawkes, Nicola, and Fish's chapter is the first in the section on marriage of the dual-career couple. Using interviews, they describe life and dyadic themes of 15 working couples who are also new parents. Additional information along the egalitarian-traditional continuum is also described.

Nadelson and Nadelson, both practicing psychiatrists and a dual-career couple in the same field, examine the psychological costs and rewards of the dual-career couple. They cite some clinical examples noting the dynamics of guilt, anxiety, depression, and self-esteem in dual-career couples with respect to work.

Lopata, Barnewolt, and Norr's impressive sample of 996 Chicago women tells us how much domestic responsibility employed women carry. They also examine kinds of helping behaviors within these couples.

Beginning the section on families, Johnson and Johnson assume a clear sociological stance as they uncover the components of role strain, most notable in women and offer adaptive strategies.

Seiden covers the crucial variable of time and its management in the dual-career family. She offers suggestions for its use and examines related issues of dominance, sex role demands, and interpersonal relationships.

Lawe and Lawe have addressed the more personal facets of negotiation in the dual-career relationship. They point out to us the importance of clarifying and identifying interpersonal communication, using conflict resolution as a main theme.

In the section on careers, Butler and Paisley describe four forms of career coordination of couples in the same field and in different fields with a major focus on publication.

Moore, as an Affirmative Action officer, identifies the major laws affecting dual-career couples. She also points out the advantages and disadvantages of alternative work patterns for the couples and employers.

Bryson and Bryson's survey of professional psychologist pairs and psychologists not married to each other reveals important data on advancement constraints, job satisfaction, and salary differences. They also examine egalitarian issues within the pairs.

Matthews and Matthews describe some methods for effective employment searches based on their own experience and a survey of more than 200 couples.

What becomes clear in this book is that there is considerable value in being a dual-career couple, despite the fact that the dual-career woman's workload is greater than the woman in the two-person career couple. The extensive analysis of the joys and disadvantages of the dual-career family that follows will underscore the search for "equity" in marriage, family, and career.

—*Fran Pepitone-Rockwell*

REFERENCES

ASTIN, H. S., N. SUNIEWICK, and S. DWECK (1971) Women: A Bibliography on Their Education and Careers. Washington, DC: Human Service Press.

BERNARD, J. (1972) The Future of Marriage. New York: World.

BIRD, C. (1973) Everything a Woman Needs To Know To Get Paid What She's Worth. New York: David McKay.

BLOOD, R. D. and D. M. WOLFE (1960) Husbands and Wives: The Dynamics of Married Living. New York: Free Press.

BOOTH, A. (1976) "A wife's employment and husband's stress: a replication and refutation." Journal of Marriage and the Family 39: 645–650.

——— (1979) "Does wives' employment cause stress for husbands?" Family Coordinator 28, 4: 445–449.

BRYSON, J., R. BRYSON and B. LECHT (1976) "The professional pair: husband and wife psychologists." American Psychologist 31: 10–16.

CHESLER, P. (1972) Women and Madness. New York: Avon.

EPSTEIN, C. (1971) "Law partners and marital partners." Human Relations 24: 549–564.

FRIEDAN, B. (1963) The Feminine Mystique. New York: Dell.

GOVE, W. R. (1972) "The relationship between sex roles, marital status, and mental ilness." Social Forces 51: 34–44.

——— and J. F. TUDOR (1973) "Adult sex roles and mental illness." American Journal of Sociology 78: 812–835.

JOHNSON, F. and C. JOHNSON (1976) "Role strain in high-commitment career women." Journal of American Academy of Psychoanalysis 4: 13–36.

LEIN, L. et al. (1974) "Final report: work and family life." National Institute of Education Project 3-3094. Cambridge, MA; Center for the Study of Public Policy.

NEVILLE, D. (1977) "Sex roles and personality correlates." Human Relations 30: 751–759.

OAKLEY, A. (1974) Housewife. London: Allen Lane.

PAPANEK, H. (1974) "Men, women, and work: reflections on the two-person career." American Journal of Sociology 78: 852–872.

PARNES, H. S., J. R. SHEA, R. S. SPITZ, F. A. ZELLER and Associates (1970) Dual Careers, Vol. 1: A Longitudinal Study of Labor Market Experience of Women. Manpower Research Monograph 21 Washington, DC: Government Printing Office.

RADLIFF, L. (1975) "Sex differences in depression: the effects of occupation and marital status." Sex Roles 1: 249–269.

RAPOPORT, R. and R. RAPOPORT (1969) "The dual career family." Human Relations 22: 3–30.

—— (1976) Dual-Career Families Re-Examined. New York: Harper Colophon.

—— (1978) Working Couples. New York: Harper & Row.

Roper Organization (1975) "A survey of the attitudes of women on marriage, divorce, the family and America's changing sexual morality." Virginia Slims American Women's Opinion Poll 3.

SAFILIOS-ROTHSCHILD, C. (1970) "The influence of the wife's degree of work commitment upon some aspects of family organization and dynamic. Journal of Marriage and the Family 32: 681–691.

—— (1974) Women and Social Policy. Englewood Cliffs, NJ: Prentice-Hall.

SEIDEN, A. (1976) "Overview: research on the psychology of women II. Women in families, work and psychotherapy." American Journal of Psychiatry 133: 1111–1123.

SELIGMAN, M. (1974) "Depression and learned helplessness," in R. Friedman and M. Kutz (eds.) The Psychology of Depression: Contemporary Theory and Research. Washington, DC: V. H. Winston.

SHAEVITZ, M. and M. SHAEVITZ (1976) "Changing roles, changing relationships: implications for the mental health professional." Psychiatric Annals 6.

VEROFF, J. and S. FELD (1970) Marriage and Work in America. Princeton, NJ: Van Nostrand Reinhold.

WEISSMAN, M. and G. KLERMAN (1977) "Sex differences and the epidemiology of depression." Archives of General Psychiatry 34: 98–111.

WILSON, K. M. (1974) "Today's women students: new outlooks, options." Findings 1: 1–4.

PART I

DEVELOPMENT OF DUAL-CAREER COUPLES

1

THREE GENERATIONS OF DUAL-CAREER FAMILY RESESARCH

Rhona Rapoport
Robert N. Rapoport

The phenomenon of the dual-career family was originally defined as "the type of family in which both heads of household pursue careers and at the same time maintain a family life together" (Rapoport and Rapoport, 1969, 1971: 18). The terms "career" and "family" are both somewhat imprecise, but the former was used to indicate sequences of occupational jobs which were developmental in character and which required a continuous and high degree of commitment. The latter was arbitrarily defined as involving at least a marital pair and one child living as a domestic unit. Because of the particular character of the initial definition, it was impossible to provide quantitative assessments of its prevalence. It is, by the same token, difficult to provide assessments of its increase. It was estimated that under 5 percent of the British population qualified at the time of the study, taking it as a lifelong continuous structure, but that it was likely to increase in frequency as women's rates of higher education increased to approximately those of men, as equal opportunities for employment increased, and as barriers to the realization of sex equality eroded.

Despite difficulties in making precise definitions, it is possible to document two shifts, one statistical, the other normative. The proportions of British households in which both husbands and wives were at work outside the home ("two-income families") increased from under 30 percent in 1960 to well over 40 percent in the early 1970s. Diverse motivational factors have produced these increases, but survey data on women's motivation to work show an increase in rationales other than economic, despite the fact that economic pressures have increased. Parnes et al. (1970), for example, report that "three in five American working wives would work even if they had enough money to live comfortably without working." We assume that these responses reflect both the response of women to the actual experience of occupation outside the home and the general normative shift toward legitimation of the pattern. The current situation is that most families are dual-worker families at some point in the family cycle, and that the pattern is becoming "normalized." This contrasts with the picture in the 1960s, when the early studies were being made, and the families were not only statistically rare, but often were made to feel or felt themselves to be deviant, or were conceptualized in the research as "pioneers."

PRECURSOR STUDIES

The precursors to the conceptualization of dual-career families are multilineal. Taking the proximate precursors as a "generation," there are several studies in the 1960s that were particularly influential.

Our initial formulation (1969) was rooted in a national study of highly qualified women and their careers (Fogarty, et al., 1968, 1971). Although this was a British study, it was explicitly placed in an international perspective. It drew into consideration the Scandinavian works on the subject of changing roles of women (Dahlstrom and Liljestrom, 1967; Myrdal and Klein, 1956). The work of East European sociologists was also considered. Directly influential in concept formation were the American studies, particularly those of

Alice Rossi (1964). The work of Nye and Hoffman (1963) and of Yudkin and Holme (1963) was influential in clearing the way for new thinking in relation to the impact on children. The work of Hannah Gavron (1966) provided a *cri de coeur* that has reverberated through a number of studies in the past decade. Her work, concentrating as it did on the presence of unhappiness in a role that was mythologized as joyous in our culture, linked to other studies using happiness as an outcome variable (Orden and Bradburn, 1969).

Essentially, the precursor generation focused attention on changes going on in sex roles. But this generation of studies contributed to the formulation of the concept of dual-career families partly through their omissions—of concepts to comprehend *linkages* between men's and women's roles, between parents' and children's roles, between work and family roles. They made it clear that such a formulation was needed.

THE PIVOTAL GENERATION

The pivotal generation is distinctive in this context in giving rise to a concept explicitly linking men's and women's roles and work and family domains. The concept of "dual-career family" was coined in 1969 (Rapoport and Rapoport, 1969). A number of studies using it or a very similar concept were conducted shortly thereafter. The terms "two-profession family," "two-career family," "two-income family," and "two-breadwinner family" are also versions or special cases of what is a general category of "dual-worker" family. The dual-worker family refers to family households in which both spouses are gainfully employed.

The idea of studying dual-career families as a structural type, defined in terms of system linkages and emerging out of larger social trends, arose in the context of an appraisal of issues confronting highly qualified women. Building to some extent on the Rossi (1964) study at the National Opinion Research Center, the survey of British university graduates conducted by Political and Economic Planning (PEP) delineated a subgroup of career-oriented women who were married to men who had careers as well. This was considered distinctive and worth special study because it seemed to be a modern pattern which was both difficult to operate in a society geared to more traditional family role models, and because it was likely to increase with equality of opportunity. Previously, women who developed full-fledged careers tended to do so instead of having a family, or as a response to being married to someone who was disabled. The decision to concentrate on dual-career families entailed the use of the holistic, family case study method as a fruitful methodological approach. In the opinion of some reviewers, the work also had a theoretical importance in its radical assault on the prevailing paradigm of the family itself. The Skolnicks (1974: 530) wrote:

> The variant pattern discussed here [dual-career family] . . . may be both more widespread in the future and more of a break with the conventional family that has prevailed until recently. As the studies of communes and swingers show, far-out sexual behavior can co-exist with traditional sex-role ideologies and a conventional division of labor in the sexes. The commitment of a mother-wife to a career strikes at the heart of this division of labor.

Overlapping with the British studies of dual-career families, and to some extent influenced by them, several American studies adopted a similar stance. They will be treated together here as a set of pivotal studies, standing for the emergence of the dual-career family formulation. Four studies in the set, then, are the Rapoports' studies (Rapoport and Rapoport, 1969, 1971); Epstein's study (1971), Holmstrom's study (1972), and the studies of Poloma and Garland (Garland, 1972; Poloma, 1972; Poloma and Garland, 1971). These studies had the characteristics shown in Table 1.1.

The objectives of the four studies were similar but distinct. The Rapoports' studies were part of a national study of highly qualified women's careers, sponsored by the Leverhulme Trust Fund and conducted by Political and Economic Planning (PEP). The aim was to provide a comprehensive description of how educational, economic, and social-psychological factors combined to motivate women to and to constrain women from participation in the occupational world in ways commensurate with their abilities. The studies were also con-

TABLE 1.1   Pivotal Generation: Dual-Career Family Studies

Study	No. of Families	Method	Context
Rapoport and Rapoport (1969–1971)	18	Intensive Collaborative case study, (cf. Laslett and Rapoport, 1975)	Part of larger study[a]
Epstein (1971)	12	Interviews (semi-structured)	Part of larger study[b]
Holmstrom (1972)	27	Interviews (semi-structured)	Ph.D. dissertation
Garland (1972) Poloma (1972)	53	Questionnaire (structured)	Two linked studies[c]

[a]Study of careers of highly qualified men and women; cf. Fogarty et al. (1971). Three national surveys provided the framework. The intensively studied cases were drawn separately from selected organizational contexts.
[b]Part of a Ph.D. dissertation study of sixty-nine women lawyers in the New York area. The twelve were a random subsample.
[c]Two doctoral dissertations were based on materials from the same series of families, one (Garland, 1972) concentrating on the males; the other (Poloma, 1972), on the females.

cerned with the family consequences of patterns chosen, particularly marital satisfaction. Strains in making dual-career families "work" were analyzed in terms of such dilemmas as role overload, environmental social sanctions, personal identity and self-esteem, social-network functioning, and the fitting together of demands on husbands and wives as they moved through their diverse cycles of occupational as well as domestic role demands. Contrapuntally to these "strains" were "gains" in family income, range of interests, and role models for each spouse. In working out the particular balance of strains and gains, dual-career couples were seen as "creative variants." Unlike persons and families who reject conversion roles in a negativistic "copout" way, these couples worked at creating a new form of family and career structure which they felt to be in some sense better. But they evolved their innovative patterns and sustained them without the help of norms which defined what was acceptable. Instead, they had to rely on a responsiveness in the relationship to one another's tensions and limits.

The study by Cynthia Epstein (1971) concentrated on a specific type of dual-career family, the married-couple law partnership. This was part of a larger study of women lawyers, financed by the Manpower Administration of the U.S. Department of Labor. Focusing on this form of linking family and occupation among dual-career couples, Epstein noted that husband-wife law partnerships in New York had both old and new elements: "old in the sense that it is an extension of the family enterprise . . . new in the sense [of] a special case of . . . the dual-career family" (Epstein, 1971: 550). Turner (1971) has made a similar point in likening the dual-career family to some extent with the semisubsistence agricultural family of preindustrial times. Epstein's analysis, therefore, included the concept of family-occupation linkage, and the creative attempt at implementation of an egalitarian ideology. Her analysis centered more on the process of integration. Hers was the study in the pivotal generation that gave the greatest attention to the division of labor in the workplace as well as the home. She was concerned with how the particular form of work-family integration and compromise with initial career aspirations suited the marital partners. She concluded that in most instances the husbands and their firms benefited from this particular form of nepotism. Nor was the marital relationship necessarily placed under inordinate strain. Compared with the situation where wives worked in other firms, the husbands were arguably more able to empathize with the problems of combining domestic and work tasks, and to make themselves helpful, though still in a relatively conventional pattern. As for the wives themselves, there were some who emphasized the advantages in having a husband who could facilitate their career development in contrast to their fellow women lawyers who had to withdraw. Others felt that their assignment to less prestigious roles as professional helpmates restricted the realization of their individual professional potentials. In prospect, Epstein expected that husband-wife partnerships might increase if ways could be found to allow them to take form within larger organizations. Increased specialization, which promotes the formation of larger organizations, militates to some extent against this, but the satisfactions in "greater communication and sense of [shared] purpose in the marital bond and in one's life work" which many young people feel provides the impetus (Epstein, 1971: 563).

Holmstrom's (1972) study was concerned with understanding the difficulties of attempting to operate what she termed a "two-career family." She compared a group of twenty-two career families who were "bucking the system" with seven traditional couples of comparable social status. Barriers encountered by the couples included the pressures on each member and the difficulty in coordinating the requirements of the two professional careers, the inflexible and demanding requirements of organizations and professional roles, the current definition of masculinity as superior and thus to be favored in such decisions, and the isolation of the small nuclear family, especially in relation to the task of child rearing, were investigated. When two-career families fail, there may be a breakdown of the marriage, sacrifice of the wife's career aspirations, or the deterioration of the quality of the marital relationship.

The linked studies by Poloma (1972) and Garland (1972) were concerned with the ways in which role conflicts for both husbands and wives in adopting the pattern of dual-professional family were resolved. Working with professional couples, Poloma examined the women's resolutions of role strains, and Garland examined the men's. Poloma delineated four techniques of tension management for the wives: favorable definition of the dual-career situation—i.e., emphasizing the advantages rather than the pitfalls of working wives; value clarification—i.e., that in conflict situations the family demands take precedence; compartmentalization; and compromise—e.g., in level of career aspiration. Impediments to achieving a tolerable level of tension management include the wife's achievement to a level that is felt to be a threat to her husband, her failure to clarify her own value hierarchies, and his disinclination to be supportive. Like Epstein and Holmstrom, Poloma was impressed with the women's willingness to compromise their initial career aspirations to be able to achieve even a small movement toward the valued egalitarianism.

Garland (1972), on the other hand, was concerned with the impact on the male side of the marital relationship. Analyzing his materials on fifty-three couples using a stimulus-response framework, he found no support for the idea that "the American male will automatically resent having a wife who is practicing a high status profession and that he will, by definition, be emasculated and dominated by her" (Garland, 1972: 213). Some twenty-three of the fifty-three retained traditional attitudes about who was the head of the household, while a further twenty-seven, the "neotraditionals," saw the women's contributions as important but secondary. Only three were truly egalitarian. The majority of the men emphasized the benefits in the patterns they adopted. Although there were complaints of being too pressed to pursue leisure interests, these were not linked to feelings of personal inadequacy.

EARLY DETERMINANTS

Some early personal experiences predispose individuals to seek combinations of domestic and occupational involvements. The pivotal generation of dual-career family studies suggested that, at that time in history, there was some, but not too much tension. For women, the sources of tension were rooted in family background— e.g., being an "only-lonely" child; parental conflict during childhood; or where mother felt unfulfilled in a domestic role. These, combined with certain elements in the husband's early background, including having a close relationship with his mother and thus making him perhaps more empathetic and responsive to the needs of women, predisposed couples to move into the dual-career pattern.

SUPPORTS

The "fit" between the husband's attitudes and the wife's aspirations was relevant. Men who valued self-expression in work, were ambitious, and who could sympathize with the wish to fulfill the potentials of one's training and competence fit well with women who were potential career wives. The concentration in these studies was on intact dual-career marriages. The findings in most of the studies was that the wives were the more active in pressing for the pattern. Where comparison groups were examined, wives were found to relinquish their side of the dual-career pattern when there was stress and the lack of supports. This was not found to be due to low or unstable convictions, as some earlier studies had implied.

STRAINS

All the studies emphasized the stressful character of maintaining the dual-career family pattern under the circumstances prevailing in the 1960s. The conceptualization of these stresses, as distinct from any stresses that the individuals brought to the pattern by virtue of their personal and interpersonal tensions, were differently conceptualized by the researchers. These concepts include *dilemmas,* overload, normative, cycling, network, and identity; *conflicts* between earlier and later norms, home and work expectations; ideals and feelings; *barriers,* domestic isolation, sex role prejudices and stereotypes; and *problems* such as the wife finding an appropriate job, getting a work situation with flexibility to accommodate to domestic requirements, competing with members of the opposite sex (particularly if marriage partners), keeping personal aspirations within limits that the marriage can tolerate, and arranging domestic help and child-care services.

GAINS

Most of the studies also emphasized the advantages of dual-career marriages. Financial gains were a consideration, but because the couples in most of the families studied were in highly skilled occupations, there was no economic necessity of gainful occupation. Most paid highly for services. Most of the studies emphasized the finding that the gains felt by the wives were more in terms of self-realization. Husbands, in contrast, valued having wives who were developing and fulfilling themselves as well as manifesting a pattern of which they approved as egalitarians.

BALANCE

Most of the researchers analyzed not only the strains and gains, but their tradeoffs. Outcome variables ranged from satisfaction through marital dissolution. But the investigators emphasized the importance of avoiding simplistic thinking. Dual-career couples recognized the difficulties they confronted, and they formulated their state of satisfaction as the best balance possible in an environment that was not particularly supportive of their aspirations.

TENSION LINES

Tension lines, a new concept, are marked by points beyond which individuals feel that they cannot be pushed except at risk to themselves or the relationship. Tension lines are inevitable given that most of the couples studied felt they were doing something new, something not patterned on established and socially supported lines. They created their own patterns, partly through their sensitivity to the tension lines indicating what they and their partners found feasible.

TRANSITIONAL STUDIES

There are three transitional studies between the pivotal and the current generation. They were undertaken during the time of the pivotal studies, but have the characteristics of the next generation of studies. They use cross-sectional samples and were designed to test hypotheses rather than to formulate them, as in the exploratory studies. These are the studies of Bailyn (1970), Bebbington (1973), Rapoport (1974) and Rapoport, et al. (1974). All three were conducted under the aegis of the PEP project and used cross-sectional materials from the national surveys. (Fogarty et al., 1971; Rapoport and Rapoport, 1971).

Bailyn (1970) analyzed the orientations of 217 husbands of British women eight years out of college. Classifying the husbands as well as the wives in terms of career and family orientations, Bailyn evolved a classification of the 223 couples on which she had these data. She described six couple types, as shown in Table 1.2.

TABLE 1.2   Bailyn's Couple Types: British University Graduates (in percentages)

Wife's Orientation	Husband's Orientation	
	Emphasis on Family	Emphasis on Career
Traditional	29	17
Mixed	25	9
Integrated	13	7

Bailyn asked whether dual-career couples showed a lower level of marital satisfaction than conventional couples. Her data indicated that a lower level of marital satisfaction was associated primarily with the specific subtype of dual-career pattern where an "integrated" wife is married to the type of husband who is very career oriented and who derives his primary satisfactions from his work. It is this combination, and not the pattern of dual-career family per se, that is a conspicuously unsatisfying one for the couple. Though proportionately small, only 5 percent of the couples, the experiences of this subtype may get generalized in popular stereotypes.

Bebbington (1973), using the same data base, asked why individuals and couples take on this apparently stressful pattern when not driven to do so by circumstances. His analysis supports an emphasis on the socialization experiences of the individual partners in dual-career families, particularly the wives. Many dual-career wives were reared in families where there was a relatively high level of tension and correspondingly low reinforcement for the culturally prescribed idealization of conventional marriage. Such individuals become acclimatized to a relatively high stress level and do not operate according to a principle of stress minimization. They confront the dual-career family's dilemmas as a challenge and visualize that they would be bored with the more conventional lifestyles. But, as with the formulation in the Rapoport and Rapoport (1971) study, Bebbington noted that each couple had its own structure of "tension lines" beyond which it was risky to push.

Bebbington also noted a further factor specific to the cohort of dual-career couples studied in the 1960s. Many of them came from homes in which their mothers not only worked but were expected to work because of wartime exigencies. For people growing up in this cohort, the idea of wives remaining at home was the stress-provoking discontinuity, not (as with other generational cohorts) the idea of women going out to work.

The study by Thiessen and the Rapoports (Rapoport et al., 1974) also uses the cross-sectional couple data to test the hypothesis that enjoyment of everyday activities was positively rather than negatively associated with "symmetrical" family structure. (Young and Willmott, 1975, used Gorer's [1971] term "the symmetrical family." Their use of the term is distinctive, however, highlighting a social goal or value. They did not study symmetrical families as such, though their definition is similar to that of the "dual-worker family.") They found a positive correlation, supporting the view that despite the disturbances associated with current social changes in family structure, there were perceived benefits as indicated by enjoyment patterns.

THE THIRD GENERATION

The *current* generation of studies of dual-career families differs in some respects from earlier ones. Current studies are more diverse in method and objectives. To some extent they show the emergence of specialized interests: academic, policy, feminist, therapeutic. The studies to be described have in common an explicit reference to the pivotal generation's work as at least partially setting their stage conceptually. In most instances, this was but one of several precursors, others being theoretical formulations such as those of Parsons (1949) or sexist cultural stereotypes.

Seventeen papers will be described. Ten of them are published in a book of papers entitled *Working Couples* (Rapoport and Rapoport, 1978). But these ten, as well as the seven others, are based on independently conducted empirical studies. In addition, three primarily aimed at therapists or counselors will be described, based on clinical experience and an appreciation of the relevant literature rather than on social science field investigations.

In relation to the conceptual issues highlighted in the pivotal generation, these studies concentrate very heavily on the strains with particular reference to *management of the strains* of the dual-worker family pattern. The papers by Rosen, Jerdee, and Prestwich (1975), by Handy (1978), and by Bailyn (1978) emphasize the impact of the occupational system's rigidities, demandingness, and male bias. Rosen and his colleagues (1975) emphasize the strain put on the marital relationship. Handy (1978) emphasizes the near impossibility of sustaining a dual-career pattern in families of British managers because of the managerial role's heavy demands. Bailyn (1978) provides a detailed analysis of the dynamics of accommodation of work to family at different stages of the family life cycle.

The studies of the current generation are generally more focused, either by testing a particular hypothesis—e.g., that productivity will be increased (Bryson et al., 1976); that advancement will be enhanced (Martin et al., 1975); that mobility patterns will be affected (Duncan and Perrucci, 1976)—or by exploring in depth a specific concept highlighted by the pivotal generation studies—e.g., that asymmetries (Safilios-Rothschild and Dijkers, 1978), separations,

TABLE 1.3 Empirical Social Research Using the Dual-Career Family

Researchers	Date	Couples	Method	Study Concentration
Arkin and Dobrofsky	1978	21	survey	job sharing
Bailyn	1978	1300	survey	accommodation of work-career to family
Berger et al.	1978	175	survey and interviews	joint job seeking
Bryson et al.	1975	200	documentary analysis (prof. soc. rec.)	professional productivity of d.c. wives
Burke and Weir	1976	186	psychological tests	couple personality patterns
Douvan and Pleck	1978	4	case studies	separations
Duncan and Perrucci	1976		reanalysis of survey and census data	geographic mobility and employment
Farris	1978	10	interviews	commuting couples
Gronseth	1978	16	case studies	work-sharing couples
Handy	1978	23	interviews	demanding ("greedy") occupation (managers)
Martin et al.	1976	86	professional association records	career advancement of d.c. wives
Rosen et al.	1975	1442	survey	stresses from external (occupational) discrimination
Safilios-Rothschild and Dijkers	1978	350	survey	unconventional status asymmetries
St. John-Parsons	1978	10	case studies	continuous patterns
Sundby	1980	20	interviews	compatibility of decision style
Weingarten	1978	54	interviews	interdependence
Lein et al. (Working Family Project)	1978	14	intensive case studies	domestic division of responsibility

commuting (Douvan and Pleck, 1978), or job-sharing (Arkin and Dobrofsky, 1978) can be handled without destroying the marital relationships (Farris, 1978).

The authors have tended to be positively disposed toward the pattern, and to emphasize ways in which the difficulties can be managed, but not all are in this mold. Handy (1978), for example, makes it plain that among the couples he studied at the London Business School this was considered a much more unworkable pattern than in less demanding, less "greedy" occupational careers.

Using two bodies of national cross-sectional data (the 1970 U.S.

Census data, and the 1964/68 NORC college graduates data), Duncan and Perrucci (1978) examined the hypotheses put forward by Fogarty et al. (1971) and by Holmstrom (1972) that geographical mobility problems present a critical area of difficulty for many dual-career families. They note that this formulation is consistent with the Parsonian hypothesis (Parsons, 1949) that a wife's employment will be an inhibiting factor for the husband's geographical mobility. Duncan and Perrucci concluded, further, that geographical mobility had, overall, a deleterious effect for occupation-minded wives, but that their wishes and interests were ineffectual in the situation. Mortimer et al. (1976), in a review of research on geographical mobility in relation to marriage roles, come to the same conclusion.

These findings reflect in America what Trost and Nordlund (1974) had already noted in Scandinavian countries, a stage of "lip service" democracy in sex roles. At this point in the history of the United States, the phenomenon of dual-career families exists as a pattern congruent with expressed egalitarianism. But it should not be taken to be a uniform situation, as is often implied in summary statements of statistical tendencies. Many couples, even within the cohorts of American couples described in this way overall, did not conform to the general conclusion. And in some special cases, the overall pattern itself was different.

Martin et al. (1975), also basing their formulation on a hypothesis inferred from Parsons' (1949) theories—i.e., that an occupational role for the wife would be dysfunctional because it would place the couple on an intrafamilial competitive basis to the disadvantage of one or both—studied eighty-six sociologist couples who held appointments in the same academic departments. They found that over a five-year period, sociologist wives were more successful, proportionately, to women sociologists generally; they obtained more higher degrees, more promotions, and continued with their careers for a greater portion of their professional life spans. The authors reject the general validity of the Parsonian formulation, seeing these effects as the result of a kind of "professional marital-endogamy, which enhances rather than constrains professional developmental opportunities through intellectual cross-fertilization" (Martin et al., 1975).

The Brysons and the Lichts (Bryson et al., 1976) studied 200 psychologist couples who were members of the American Psychological Association. In comparing them with controls of both sexes who were not married to fellow professionals, they found that psychologist pairs produced more publications than their same-sex controls, but the professional wives were more likely to have suppressed their own career development in other respects. They interpret this as due to institutional constraints in the form of nepotism rules and to familial constraints in the form of women's greater responsibility in domestic work than their husbands. In conclusion, the Brysons and Lichts note, as did Epstein (1971) in her earlier study of lawyer couples, that though psychologist wives of professional psychologists were dissatisfied with the constraints they experienced, they were more productive than same-sex control psychologists. Like Epstein's lawyers' wives, they were less satisfied with their careers than were their husbands, whose satisfactions and productivity may in many cases have been enhanced by the supports they received from their wives. The wives were simultaneously exploited and facilitated.

Farris's (1978) paper is on "commuting couples" who maximized both partners' career interests by arranging a split-household situation and commuting over long distances to be together periodically. She found that this pattern suited couples who were determined to implement their egalitarian ideals but who found it possible to do so only by responding to occupational opportunities in different locations. The study, though based only on a tiny sample, demonstrated that the pattern is a viable one for some people. There are even hints that for some it may be a preferable option rather than a second-choice resolution.

Safilios-Rothschild and Dijkers's (1978) analysis is of Greek couples with "unconventional asymmetries" in income and education—i.e., the wives were superior in these respects to their husbands. They found that middle-class couples were more able to accommodate to asymmetries than the more conventional-minded and lower-resource working-class couples. Weingarten's (1978) paper on interdependence delineates a structural variable of interchangeability contributing to this flexibility. Conceptual papers by Safilios-Rothschild (1976), Pleck (1976), Bailyn (1964), and Rapoport and Rapoport

(1976) emphasize the importance of values—e.g., "equity"—as intervening variables in the acceptance of unconventional patterns.

The papers by Berger et al. (1978), Douvan and Pleck (1978), and Bailyn (1978) introduce life-cycling stage into their formulations. They also provide greater depth of understanding of subpattern differentiation.

Berger et al. (1978) found that young professional couples in the earliest stages of career development in the early 1970s had a fairly high degree of responsiveness to one another's interests and requirements. In a sample of 427 young American science Ph.D.s, they found that nearly 80 percent preferred to find jobs which optimized the occupational opportunities of both partners. In the 107 who had actually searched for jobs jointly, they found that only 25 percent of spouses made egalitarian decisions based on a strategy of both looking for jobs and actual decisions being made on the principle of joint optimization. About one-third of the sample made nonegalitarian choices despite the fact that other options were available; and about 40 percent chose the male's preference only in the absence of their preferred egalitarian option.

The analysis by Berger and his colleagues (1978) clarifies some of the dynamics underlying the discrepancy between ideals of behavior. While this discrepancy had been observed, it was earlier assumed that rising generations would show a radical change toward greater consistency, particularly among the more highly educated. Berger et al. show that frequently what appears to be this kind of discrepancy with behavioral measures is a "forced choice" due to constraints in the occupational situation.

Bailyn (1978), in developing another generation of American studies following her participation in the pivotal British studies of dual-career families, has noted that in occupations such as engineering and business management, the choices overwhelmingly favor male career development. But she points out how this may build up pressure for a shift in favor of the wives later in the family cycle.

Douvan and Pleck (1978) also describe this phenomenon and report a series of cases where coming out from under the husband's shadow may be served later in the family cycle by a temporary geographical separation, a circumstance usually negatively valued. The wife makes the move into a new environment and establishes herself with an autonomous occupational identity, and the husband follows.

Further light on distinctive characteristics of dual-career couples is suggested in the study by Burke and Wier (1976). Concentrating on personality factors and the fit between husbands and wives, they compared traditional couples with dual-career couples within a set of 186 couples drawn from Ontario professional registers. Using the Fundamental Interpersonal Relations Orientation Inventory (FIRO) (Schutz, 1957, 1967), they found that working wives scored significantly lower than did conventional wives in five of the six scales used. They wanted less affection and inclusion toward others. They showed higher scores on expressed control. Husbands of working wives showed significantly lower scores than husbands of traditional housewives in that they wanted less affection and inclusion from others, and expressed less inclusion and control. They did score higher on *wanting* control. The authors conclude that although their data are plausible and in the expected direction, they provide suggestive but not conclusive evidence on such issues as how much these personality measures reflect stable traits and how much they are situationally induced, or are responses to the interactions with their spouses in relation to their specific lifestyle.

The studies by Laura Lein and her colleagues at the Working Family Project (Lein et al. 1978) have concentrated on domestic division of labor and responsibility, rather than on power and decision-making as in many of the other domestic role studies. These two areas have also been foci of study by others using a "woman-centered" approach—e.g., Andree Michel's (1974) study of professional and conjugal activities of women in France. The WFP study resembles the pivotal generation studies in method and overall formulation but provides new materials in two regards: First, they look at dual-worker families in a broader range of occupations; second, they give focal attention to responsibility as well as behavioral patterning of domestic participation. The alteration of a "sense of responsibility" is, according to the Rapoports in their reexamined analysis (1976), one of the key bottlenecks in sex role change. It requires an alteration not only of behavioral habits and patterns but of "maps in the head."

By this cognitive entity, something more complex is meant than cognitive maps. Also implied are the layers of feeling which are laid down in successive life experience to form a set of mental strata, conscious or unconscious. According to the person's psychological makeup, these maps in the head will be entrenched or amenable to redrawing. At this point in history, it is more likely to be the former in relation to sex roles; Gronseth's (1978) study is intermediate between the new data-based analyses of dual-career families and emphasis on applications in action. In a Norwegian study of eighteen work-sharing couples, all of whom were in "part-time" occupations, he did not find the high levels of strain which have been hallmarks of the dual-career family. Gronseth's argument is that part-time work is not only a more equitable arrangement but also a more emotionally tolerable one. Arkin and Dobrofsky (1978) document the viability of a related pattern, "job sharing," in the academic setting. Bailyn (1978), in tracing the vicissitudes of the accommodation process between work and family life, makes useful distinction between husbands who adopt an accommodative, sharing pattern as a "primary" value, and those who do so as a "secondary adjustment" to unsatisfactory experiences in the world of work.

APPLICATIONS: COUNSELING AND POLICY

Within the applied science fields, including psychotherapy, there are two kinds of reactions to the idea of dual-career marriage: an "old-style" and a "new-style" reaction. The old-style reaction consists of stereotypes which have been outlined as barriers to setting up the pattern in the first place. One article, by a professor of psychiatry, in *The Times* of London dated April 26, 1977, under a heading "Getting to the Root Cause of Delinquency" stated the following:

> The fact that anti-social behaviour by juveniles increases year by year indicates that the causes are not properly appreciated . . . . Juvenile anti-social behavior—vandalism, break-ins, mugging, violence, hooliganism were rare 30 years ago. Scientific logic leads to the

questions: what environmental factors affecting the development of personality have changed over the past 30 years? One such factor is the parent-child relationship, as the result of the increasing number of mothers who take up full-time employment [Krebs, 1977].

Professor Krebs goes on to say that parents who work often spoil their child out of guilt and fail to provide the necessary discipline. This is on top of not being there to give the warmth and comfort that a growing child needs. He cites the influential British psychiatrist John Bowlby, who attached such crucial importance to early mothering, and suggests tackling the problems at their roots. He implies, but does not actually advocate, a return to the conventional patterns which keep mothers at home.

"New-style" approaches are seen in the writings of university counseling personnel. Dr. Ellen Berman (cited in Meyers, 1976) at the University of Pennsylvania, states the couples who adopt the dual-career pattern are not destined to experience marital dissolution, despite the difficulties that arise in relation to the wife's becoming more assertive as she becomes established occupationally and the husband comes more under threat. She notes the possibility that some men may be attracted to strong and successful women in the same way that women have been attracted to such men in the past, and that couples may cultivate the capacity to assess their needs and deal constructively with stresses in their lives. The application of management techniques is also advocated as a useful device (Berman, cited in Meyers, 1976).

Shaevitz and Shaevitz (1976), at the University of California at San Diego, apply Festinger's (1957) concept of cognitive dissonance in their therapeutic work. Seeing new patterns of family role structure as disturbing because of the dissonances set up with conventional expectations, they suggest that the work of therapists is usefully directed toward the reduction of dissonance (Shaevitz and Shaevitz, 1976). Unlike "old-style" therapists, however, they do not imply by this that the resolution would be in favor of the conventional pattern. In their new book, Shaevitz and Shaevitz (1980) describe their personal accounts as a dual-career couple, giving practical perspectives on the day-to-day functioning of the dual-career family.

The Group for the Advancement of Psychiatry (GAP, 1975)

monograph on the educated woman has a section on changes in the
marital relationship in which the concept of the dual-career family is
discussed as a form of egalitarian marriage. They note that this concept is a "natural outgrowth of the movement for equality for women"
(1975: 226) and cite an unpublished paper of Paul Rosenkrantz in
which he notes that the lack of role models for such marriages,
together with the objective problems of arranging a division of labor
to cope with the demands of child rearing put a very great strain on
such marriages. Rosenkrantz, like the other "new-style" therapists,
notes, however, that in his experience this need not lead to a negative
outcome. Such couples can emerge with a strengthened bond if they
can tolerate ambiguities and manage conflicts. The GAP committee
concludes that, in this period of history, when men and women are
changing their role conceptions more rapidly than new social structures are evolving to provide the necessary supports, it is to be expected that there will be conflicts and difficulties to deal with, and
that flexibility will be required both of individuals and of their social
environments, including the helping professions.

Erik Gronseth's (1978) research is designed directly to influence
policy. Impressed with the strains imposed on dual-career families by
the assumption that having a career must entail taking on the occupational world's definition of full-time career demands, Gronseth and
his colleagues sought out couples who developed lifestyles with part-
time jobs. Such persons sought jobs that enabled them to share domestic work as well as "breadwinning." Impressed with the high
levels of satisfaction of the couples studied, Gronseth has recom-
mended a series of policy innovations which would make it possible
for all couples to practice work sharing, particularly at the stage of
early family and child rearing. Similarly, Hall (1979) emphasizes
policy implications for employers.

DISCUSSION

The concept of "dual-career family" is an imprecise one, and it
covers a constellation of family types rather than representing a single
homogeneous or uniform type. Nevertheless, as a concept it has had
heuristic value both in social research and in social action.

In social research, it has provided a framework for analysis that
extends beyond the individual. A good deal of analysis of changing

sex roles had tended to be limited to the analysis of individuals, even when family contexts for motivations, interactions, and ramifications have been considered. Much less has been done on the level of systems analysis of whole family structures, of which the dual-career family is one structural type among several now recognized in our society.

The first generation of dual-career studies charted many of the structured strains, the rewards, and the processes through which the pattern was sustained. It also pointed to some of the determinants in specific cases, and to factors in the normalization process of social change that might alleviate strains in the future. The second generation of studies expanded the data base to encompass families in different life-cycle stages, different social classes, and different national-cultural settings. It also sought answers to some questions raised in the first generation of studies—e.g., whether professional women in dual-career marriages did as well in terms of productivity and advancement as did their solo counterparts. Finally, applications were made in terms of applying the concept to therapeutic and social-policy goals revising underlying assumptions about the motivation and status of individuals and families in this pattern toward a more accepting, more normalized orientation.

Many of the studies of dual-career families to date have been sympathetic, biased toward a sensitivity to favorable aspects and to possible resolutions of difficulties encountered. But the counter-ideological position is firming up, not only among "reactionary" male chauvinist portions of the ordinary population, but within the scientific disciplines concerned with the study of sex roles. A psychiatrist argues that there is a causal relationship between the fact that we are experiencing rising divorce and delinquency rates at a time when employment rates of mothers is also rising (Krebs, 1977). An educator argues that working mothers produce neglected children who underperform in school and create numerous problems for teachers (Smithies, 1977).

We need more systematic studies which examine, in the context of carefully defined variables and delineated control groups, through time, the consequences of having a dual-career family structure.

How is the personal experience of men and women living in this form of intimate household structure different from the personal experience in other structures? If the women, for example, are more assertive, whether because more assertive women opt for this pattern or because the husbands like and facilitate assertiveness in their wives, how does this affect the quality of family life? We know several things from the early studies: that marital satisfaction in the pattern is determined in part by whether the pattern was chosen or thrust upon the couple; that marital satisfaction among dual-career couples requires a more refined and differentiated assessment than is ordinarily summed up in response to survey questions on marital happiness. But we know much less about the quality of the marital relationship where there have been significant shifts in the power base for control of resources, decision-making, and division of labor. Sexual and other expressive aspects of the relationship need to be assessed in greater detail, and studies need to be conducted of how other qualities in the relationship are altered. Safilios-Rothschild (1977) has done some pioneering work in this area of the study of emotional aspects of men's and women's relationships with one another. Care, respect, consideration, and assistance need further study in the context of different marital/occupational structures.

A third major area has to do with the implications of dual-career marital structure as compared with other structures for the kind of child that is socialized in such a setting. Its opponents claim that the structure creates confusions of sexual identity, deprivations of continuously available warmth and closeness, and so on. Those in favor of the pattern argue that children from such families are more independent, more resourceful, more able to draw on a wide repertoire of role models and information—i.e., are more self-sufficient. For example, St. John-Parsons (1978) found that the children in his study of ten continuous dual-career families experienced no disadvantages. Similarly, Sundby (1980) found that female children in dual-career families had relatively high self-esteem. There are data to support both contentions, but further research is required to specify the conditions under which one or another set of concomitants prevails.

Finally, the issue of how dual-career families relate to other social institutions requires further study. Rosabeth Moss Kanter (1977) has outlined some of the issues in relation to occupation, and similar work is required in relation to educational health and to other social institutions. Most of the social institutions in our society are arranged on the basis of assumptions that participant families will fall into the conventional mold. Initial responses to change have tended to be resistant. We are, however, in an era of experimentation in a number of these areas. It may be possible actually to stimulate "experiments of nature" which can be monitored and evaluated. What is the impact on productivity, as well as on families, of flexible work schedules? How does the redefinition of home/school relationships affect the caring functions of the schools and the teaching function of facsimiles (Leichter, 1974)?

There are other areas still to be explored, such as the part played by children in creating or sustaining different forms of dual-career family. What part is played by "moral communities," neighborhoods, and voluntary caring groups of different kinds in altering the viability and experience of dual-career families? The basic issues are now clear, and considerable evidence is available to remove the discussions to increasingly rational levels of discourse.

REFERENCES

ABERLE, D.F. and K.D. NAEGELE (1952) "Middle class father's occupational role and attitudes towards children." American Journal of Orthopsychiatry 22: 366–378.

ARKIN, B. and L. DOBROFSKY (1978) "Job sharing," in R. Rapoport and R.N. Rapoport (eds.) Working Couples. New York: Harper & Row.

BAILYN, L. (1964) "Notes on the role of choice in the psychology of professional women." Daedalus 93: 700–710.

———— (1970) "Career and family orientations of husbands and wives in relation to marital happiness." Human Relations 27, 2: 97–113.

———— (1978) "Accommodation of work to family," in R. Rapoport and R.N. Rapoport (eds.) Working Couples. New York: Harper & Row.

BEBBINGTON, A.C. (1973) "The function of stress in the establishment of the dual-career family." Journal of Marriage and Family (August): 530–537.

BERGER, M., M. FOSTER and B.S. WALLSTON (1978) "Finding two jobs," in R. Rapoport and R.N. Rapoport (eds.) Working Couples. New York: Harper & Row.

BLOOD, R.D. and D.M. WOLFE (1960) Husbands and Wives: The Dynamics of Married Living. New York: Free Press.

BROZEK, J. [ed.] (1966) "The biology of human variation." Annals of New York Academy of Sciences 134: 467–1066.

BRYSON, R., J. BRYSON, M. LICHT and B. LICHT (1976) "The professional pair: husband and wife psychologists." American Psychologist: 10–16.

BURKE, R.J. and T. WEIR (1976) "Some personality differences between members of one-career and two-career families." Journal of Marriage and Family 138: 453–460.

DAHLSTROM, E. and R. LILJESTROM [eds.] (1967) The Changing Roles of Men and Women. London: Duckworth.

DOUVAN, E. and J. PLECK (1978) "Separation as suport," in R. Rapoport and R.N. Rapoport (eds.) Working Couples. New York: Harper & Row.

DUNCAN, R.P. and C.C. PERRUCCI (1976) "Dual occupation families and migration." American Sociological Review 41: 252–261.

DYER, W.G. (1956) "The interlocking of work and family social systems among lower occupational families." Social Forces 34: 230–233.

EPSTEIN, C.F. (1971) "Law partners and marital partners: strains and solutions in the dual career family enterprise." Human Relations 24: 549–563.

FARRIS, A. (1978) "Commuting," in R. Rapoport and R.N. Rapoport (eds.) Working Couples. New York: Harper & Row.

FESTINGER, L. (1957) A Theory of Cognitive Dissonance. Evanston, IL: Row, Peterson.

FOGARTY, M.P., R. RAPOPORT and R.N. RAPOPORT (1968) Women and Top Jobs: An Interim Report. London: P.E.O.

——— (1971) Sex, Career, and Family. Beverly Hills: Sage.

GARLAND, N.T. (1972) "The better half? The male in the dual profession family," in C. Safilios-Rothschild (ed.) Toward a Sociology of Women. Lexington, MA: Xerox.

GAVRON, H. (1966) The Captive Wife: Conflicts of Housebound Mothers. London: Routledge & Kegan Paul.

GLAZER, B.G. and D. MOYNIHAN (1963) Beyond the Melting Pot. Cambridge, MA: MIT Press.

GORER, G. (1971) Sex and Marriage in England Today. London: Nelson.

GRONSETH, E. (1978) "Work sharing," in R. Rapoport and R.N. Rapoport (eds.) Working Couples. New York: Harper & Row.

Group for the Advancement of Psychiatry (1975) The Educated Woman: Prospects and Problems. Report 92. New York: Author.

HALL, F. and D. HALL (1979) The Two Career Couple. Reading, MA: Addison-Wesley.

HANDY, C. (1978) "Going against the grain: working couples and greed occupations," in R. Rapoport and R.N. Rapoport (eds.) Working Couples. New York: Harper & Row.

HOLSTROM, L.L. (1972) The Two-Career Family. Cambridge, MA: Schenkman.

KANTER, R.M. (1977) Work and Family in the United States: A Critical Review and Agenda for Research and Policy. New York: Russell Sage.

KOESTLER, A. (1964) The Act of Creation. London: Hutchinson.

KREBS, H. (1977) "Getting to the root cause of delinquency." The Times (London), April 26.

LASLETT, B. and R. RAPOPORT (1975) "Collaborative interviewing and interactive research." Journal of Marriage and Family 2 (November): 968–977.

LEICHTER, H.J. (1974) Family as Educator. New York: Columbia Teachers College Press.

LEIN, L., H. WEISS, and G. HOWRIGAN (1978) "Parenting," in R.R. Rapoport and R.N. Rapoport (eds.) Working Couples. New York: Harper & Row.

MARTIN, T.W., K.J. BERRY and R.B. JACOBSEN (1975) "The impact of dual-career marriages on female professional careers: an empirical test of a Parsonian hypothesis." Presented at the annual meeting of the National Council on Family Relations, Salt Lake City, August.

MEYERS, M.A. (1976) "Like husband, like wife." Pennsylvania Gazette (October): 37–40.

MICHEL, A. (1974) Activite professionelle de la femme et vie conjugale. Paris: Editions du Centre National de la Recherche Scientifique.

MILLER, D. R. and G. E. SWANSON (1958) The Changing American Parent: A Study in the Detroit Area. New York: John Wiley.

MORTIMER, J., R. HALL and R. HILL (1976) "Husbands' occupational attributes as constraints on wives' employment." (unpublished)

MYRDAL, A. and B. KLEIN (1956) Women's Two Roles. London: Routledge & Kegan Paul.

NYE, F. I. and L. W. HOFFMAN (eds.) The Employed Mother in America. Chicago: Rand McNally.

ORDEN, S. R. and N. M. BRANDBURN (1969) "Working wives and marriage happiness." American Journal of Sociology 74: 382–407.

PARNES, H. S., J. R. SHEA, R. S. SPITZ, F. A. ZELLER and Associates (1970) Dual Careers. Manpower Research Monograph 21. Washington, DC: U.S. Department of Labor.

PARSONS, T. (1949) Essays in Sociological Theory: Pure and Applied. New York: Free Press.

PLECK, J. (1976) "The male sex role: definitions, problems and sources of change." Journal of Social Issues 32, 3: 155–164.

POLOMA, M. M. (1972) "Role conflict and the married professional woman," in C. Safilios-Rothschild (ed.) Toward a Sociology of Women. Lexington, MA: Xerox.

———— and T. GARLAND (1971) "The married professional woman: a study of the tolerance of domestication." Journal of Marriage and Family 33: 531–540.

RAPOPORT, R. and R. N. RAPOPORT (1965) "Work and family in contemporary society." American Sociological Review 30: 381–394.

———— (1969) "The dual-career family." Human Relations 22: 3–30.

———— (1971) Dual-Career Families. Harmondsworth, Eng. Penguin.

———— (1976) Dual-Career Families Re-Examined. New York: Harper & Row.

———— [eds.] (1978) Working Couples. New York: Harper & Row.

———— and V. THIESSEN (1974) "Couple symmetry and enjoyment." Journal of Marriage and Family 46: 558–591.

RAPOPORT, R. N. (1974) Career development at three stages of the life cycle." Social Science Research Bulletin (June).

ROSEN, B., T. H. JERDEE and T. L. PRESTWICH (1975) "Dual-career marital adjustment: potential effects of discriminatory managerial attitudes." Journal of Marriage and Family 37: 565–572.

ROSSI, A. (1964) "Equality between the sexes: an immodest proposal." Daedalus 93: 638–646.

SAFILIOS-ROTHSCHILD, C. (1976) "A macro- and micro-examination of family power and love: an exchange model." Journal of Marriage and Family: 355–361.

———— (1977) Love, Sex and Sex Roles. Englewood Cliffs, NJ: Prentice-Hall.

———— and M. DIJKERS (1978) "Handling unconventional asymmetries," in R. Rapoport and R. N. Rapoport (eds.) Working Couples. New York: Harper & Row.

SCHUTZ, W. C. (1957) FIRO: A Three Dimensional Theory of Interpersonal Behaviour. New York: Holt, Rinehart & Winston.

———— (1967) The FIRO Scales. Palo Alto, CA: Consulting Psychologists.

SHAEVITZ, M. H. and M. H. SHAEVITZ (1976) "Changing roles, changing relationships: implications for the mental health professional." Psychiatric Annals.

———— (1980) Making It Together as a Two Career Couple. Boston: Houghton Mifflin.

SKOLNICK, A. and J. H. SKOLNICK (1974) Intimacy, Family and Society. Boston: Little, Brown.

SMITHIES, F. (1977) Teacher Education and Training. Brimingham, Eng.: National Association of School Masters and Union of Women Teachers.

ST. JOHN-PARSONS, D. (1978) "Career and family: a study of continuous dual-career families." Ph.D. dissertation, Columbia University.

SUNDBY, D. Y. (1980) "A psychological look at some divergent dual-career families," in B. Derr (ed.) Individuals, Organizations and Careers. New York: Praeger.

TILLER, P. O. (1971) "Parental role division and the child's personality," in E. Dahlstrom (ed.) The Changing Roles of Men and Women. Boston: Beacon.

TROST, J. and A. NORDLUND (1974) "Sex roles and lip service: some Swedish data." Presented at the Eighth World Congress of Sociology, Toronto, August.

TURNER, C. (1971) "Dual-work households and marital dissolution." Human Relations 24: 535–548.

WEINGARTEN, K. (1978) "Interdependence," in R. Rapoport and R. N. Rapoport (eds.) Working Couples. New York: Harper & Row.

WHYTE, W. F. (1951) Pattern for Industrial Peace. New York: Harper & Row.

YOUNG, M. and P. WILLMOTT (1975) The Symmetrical Family. New York: Pantheon.

YUDKIN, S. and A. HOLME (1963) Working Mothers and Their Children. London: Michael Joseph.

2

CATALYTIC MOVEMENTS: CIVIL RIGHTS AND WOMEN

Fran Pepitone-Rockwell

Despite the fact that World War II hurled women into the work force, the meaning of their numbers did not become substantially obvious until twenty years later as an offshoot of the civil rights movement. What set the stage for the civil rights movement worked likewise for the rise of the women's movement: the recognition and acknowledgement of oppression manifested by economic and cultural deprivation for minorities and women. Schetlin (1979) has pointed out that the concepts of racism and sexism are intertwined:

> Racism and sexism, to put it simply, are so similar that it would seem sensible for those opposed to sexism also to oppose racism, and for those opposed to racism also to oppose sexism.

In time, women discovered that the civil rights movement was as oppressive for them as exemplified in Stokeley Carmichael's 1966 statement: "The only position for women in SNCC is prone." The struggle for women's rights was in some sense more pervasive because it cut across race and class lines. Women as half the population were in a minority, but not a minority in terms of sheer numbers. Civil rights issues helped to promote the women's movement, but it did not represent its goals or its pulse.

The prelude to the women's movement was unique when compared to any other social movement. Its origins were shrouded in sexism, male dominance over women emanating from all males, regardless of race, as evidenced by Allport's (1958) perspective:

> women are viewed as a wholly different species from men, usually an inferior species. Such primary and secondary sex differences as exist are greatly exaggerated and are inflated into imaginary distinctions that justify discrimination.

Male theorists in the psychiatric and psychological literature postulated that children could not endure lengthy separations from their mothers because of the likelihood that early psychological trauma would ensue. Bowlby (1951) is an example whose attachment theory perpetuated the motherhood myth: "The mother of young children is not free, or at least should not be free, to earn." He believed that only mothers could provide the attention and nurturance children needed, and essentially ignored the issue of good "parenting" which would have taken into account the value of fathers. Fogarty et al. (1971) address this point:

> Recent research lays increasing stress on the importance of the role of the father for both boys and girls, but for boys in particular. Where a mother's work appears to be damaging to the boys in her family the right diagnosis may be that the root of the damage is not the mother's work but the absence of the father or his inadequacy in his role either in the family or in his job. A father's absence or inadequacy may lead, among other things, to over-dependence on the mother, and this in turn to 'compensatory masculinity.'

Bowlby's theory assumed that all women, regardless of their preferences or capabilities, should be at home because they were *women*. His theory has been consistent with most people's view of what men and women do. In other words, our customary sex role socialization patterns have ascribed certain personality traits to women (nurturing, like children, stay home) and men (do not stay at home with children, are employed outside of the home). Bowlby was merely addressing the prescribed gender roles of Western society.

Since women were expected to be at home, and men were to provide financial support, women were not at all expected to be career oriented. Fogarty, et al. (1971) take issue with this set of assumptions:

> The common assumption of Western society that a wife has a right to be supported by her husband must be combated, for it discourages her from making the serious commitment to a career which is needed for her own and her family's welfare.

Mitchell (1973) similarly argues that women who stay at home are not in the mainstream of society because of the inequity of consumption and production:

> Women as housewives are seen as the main agents of consumption. The ethic of consumption (spending money) is counterposed divisively to that of production (creating wealth)—the province of the husband.

Therefore, women must work in order to attain the status and economic independence that employment affords. It is not possible to seek equality and be unemployed, unless there is a concomitant trend for men. As things are now, power is achieved through economic holdings and as long as women have less economic power they will have less power in general.

The civil rights movement opened women's eyes to the issues of power and oppression by underscoring the importance of financial autonomy and career achievement. Women began to evaluate the effects of marriage and motherhood on their careers, or lack of careers. The concept of either/or with respect to marriage and a career no longer seemed useful or appropriate. Women began thinking along a both/and dimension: Career and marriage can be compatible, as it always had been for men. In fact, a 1975 Roper survey of 3000 women disclosed that women want a cooperative partnership in the family and household, including an active voice in the financial,

goal-setting, and decision-making aspects within the marital relationship. Similarly, Wilson (1974) found that women students are a "new
breed" when compared to students of less than ten years ago. The
"new breed" wants smaller families, open options for career development and is more liberal in assessment of women's roles.

Russo (1979) states that nearly one-half of all women are employed. Employed women now have fewer children (Thornton and
Camburn, 1979), and there are increasingly more women entering the
professions (Astin, 1967; Bernard, 1971; Hunt, 1968). Professional
women are more likely to marry professional men (Astin, 1967), and
these types of couples, which we can entitle dual-career, are expected
to increase in Western industrial societies. These efforts to find acceptable career patterns for both women and men are at least partly
based on three rationales described by Fogarty, et al. (1971):

1. "The manpower rationale" is based on the notion that when job and
   person are matched, the society will benefit.
2. "The human rights rationale" encourages society to help people
   have equal access to engage in social activities.
3. "The social change rationale" supports equal participation of both
   women and men at all levels of life.

These rationales support the belief that people can make voluntary
changes in their roles. This will not be easy, and there is apt to be
considerable confusion now that the options will be more varied.
What has been normative and usual in the past will no longer hold
true. Women and men will find themselves in a cafeteria approach to
their life choices, and although it will be liberating it will also require
the responsibility to choose.

The women's movement has started to identify oppression, and the
oppressors are marked as well. No longer will male dominance be
taken for granted by either women or men. All of the assumptions
about work, family, and education will be questioned, examined, and
dissected. The queries will address role preferences, and not necessarily role obligations alone. The civil rights movement helped to
bring us to this point; it did women a favor, perhaps inadvertently.

REFERENCES

ALLPORT, G. W. (1958) The Nature of Prejudice. Garden City, NY: Doubleday Anchor.

ASTIN, H. (1967) "Factors associated with the participation of women doctorates in the labor force." Personnel and Guidance Journal 46: 240–246.

BERNARD, J. (1971) Women and the Public Interest. Chicago: Aldine.

BOWLBY, J. (1951) Maternal Care and Mental Health. Geneva: World Health Organization.

FOGARTY, M. P., R. RAPOPORT, and R. N. RAPOPORT (1971) Sex, Career and Family. Beverly Hills: Sage.

HUNT, A. (1968) Survey of Women's Employment. London: Government Social Survey.

MITCHELL, J. (1973) Woman's Estate. New York: Vintage.

Roper Organization (1975) "A survey of attitudes of women, on marriage, divorce, the family and America's changing sexual morality." Virginia Slims American Women's Opinion Poll 3.

RUSSO, M. F. (1979) "Overview: sex Roles, fertility and the motherhood mandate." Psychology of Women Quarterly 4: 7–15.

SCHETLIN, E. M. (1979) "Racism and sexism: similarities." Journal of National Association for Women Deans, Administrators, and Counselors. 43: 37–42.

THORNTON, A. and D. CAMBURN (1979) "Fertility, sex roles, attitudes, and labor force participation." Psychology of Women Quarterly 4: 61–80.

WILSON, K. M. (1974) "Today's women students: new outlooks, options." Findings 4: 1–4.

3

INTELLECTUAL DEVELOPMENT OF WOMEN

David B. Lynn

Some mothers would have been frantic about those days of cactus, rattlesnakes, and cocoamud. Not Grace [mother]. She thought her orphans were smart: they could avoid snakes and digest anything.

In turn, Grace's children knew that in any emergency she would be with them and for them. They believed that this woman who could not swim a stroke would conquer a rip tide to rescue them, were they carried out to sea. They believed that this woman who feared mice and did not even like a cat to look her in the eye would strangle a mountain lion barehanded if necessary to save them. Of Eldo [father] they expected the possible; from Grace they expected the impossible.

Grace was never one to lecture. Or to say, "I told you so." And she was the last person in the world to think that "mother knows best." She sometimes thought that Grace knew best; but she hadn't the least idea that motherhood in itself was a source of wisdom. *Jessamyn West*[1]

During all these years my father spent a great deal of time watching and listening to the people who actually did the things about which he taught and wrote. My first experience of field work was through my mother's work among the Italians living in Hammonton, New Jersey,

EDITOR'S NOTE: This chapter is reprinted from *Daughters and Parents: Past, Present, and Future*, by David B. Lynn. Copyright© 1979 by Wadsworth, Inc. Reprinted by permission of the publisher, Brooks/Cole Publishing Company, Monterey, California.

where we had moved in 1902 so that she could study them. But Father's vivid accounts of how a street railway in Massachusetts had failed and of the fate of a pretzel factory also gave me a sense of the way theory and practice must be related. And it was his knowledge both of the concrete sequences of activities necessary to carry out any process and of the men involved—the workmen, for example, who alternately cursed and made the sign of the cross over the recalcitrant machinery used to dredge the "creek"—that gave me a sense of how important it was to link together the concrete and the abstract. *Margaret Mead*[2]

Liv: . . . Who gave you your interests, Erica?
Erica: I have no idea. I think I got a lot from my mother, from her unfulfilled dreams, which in a way I fulfilled for her, and a great deal from my father, with whom I identified, and a lot from the fact that they both had a great deal of pride in my talent from the time I was very small. *Liv Ullmann and Erica Jong*[3]

The previous chapter critically analyzed parental influences on traditional femininity. That discussion forms the basis for the present chapter, which inquires into some parental influences on daughters' scholastic aptitude and style of thinking, achievement, vocational choice, and creativity. In previous chapters these intellectual attributes and achievements of daughters were discussed in relation to working mothers, in relation to single-parent families, and in relation to diverse groups within our society. In the next chapter, we look at three women whose creative achievements set them apart and who are examples of how far women can go in breaking away from traditional roles.

Discussing women's intellectual development in the last part of this book—on the future—does not imply that women have not developed in this area up to now. Women have, however, been hampered in intellectual areas by their parents' and society's emphasis on traditional femininity. What are some of the characteristics of people who demonstrate any or all of the following: high scholastic aptitude, analytic thought processes, powerful motivation to achieve, high achievement, the choice of a challenging vocation, and creativity? All of these require, in varying degrees, self-confidence, assertiveness, considerable autonomy, and intellectual curiosity if not a sense of adventure—all attributes which Grace, in the quotation that began this chapter, tried to foster in her daughters. The person who develops any of these traits cannot be overly passive and dependent on others to solve her problems. But, by society's definition, the traditional feminine girl or woman is dependent on others and cannot be too assertive. In the future, all women should be freed from these constraints so that they can develop their intellectual and creative powers to the fullest.

INTELLECTUAL DEVELOPMENT AND TRADITIONAL FEMININITY

From the perspective of our discussion of traditional femininity, let us examine what, in their relationships with their mothers and fathers, can dampen or foster the intellectual attributes and achievements of daughters.

MOTHER/DAUGHTER RELATIONSHIP

The mother is usually the first model for both boy and girl infants. Since our society distinguishes sharply the roles of each sex, when the boy discovers that he belongs in a different sex category from that of the mother, he is powerfully motivated to differentiate himself from her. Albeit with much anxiety and ambivalence, he separates himself and explores widely in trying to establish his masculine identity; and society encourages and supports his efforts. He often painfully overcomes his fear of separation and of the unknown in his explorations and develops considerable autonomy, a sense of competence, and self-confidence—essential characteristics for developing intellectual aptitudes and for later achievements.

As the girl is of the same sex as the mother, no shift in identification is required, and society does little to encourage autonomy. We have seen that mothers often urge their young girls to stay close and to maintain physical contact, perhaps motivated by that special bond between mothers and daughters. The danger in the mother/daughter relationship is that the mother will not help her daughter differentiate herself and independently explore the environment so that she will develop skills in coping and confidence in her ability to do so.

Apparently girls who are bold and daring become intellectually oriented women (Kagan and Moss, 1962). If a girl does not explore on her own, she will not develop the necessary resources to cope. In that case, situations that demand that she be autonomous will frustrate and sometimes frighten her. The less she faces such situations and overcomes her fears, the less she develops the autonomy essential for growth of intellectual aptitude and the motivation for high achievement (Hoffman, 1972; Lynn, 1969). For the mother's love and nurturance of her daughter not to dampen her intellectual development and achievement motivation, the love must be expressed at least in part through encouraging her autonomy and high achievement.

FATHER/DAUGHTER RELATIONSHIP

In the father/daughter relationship, the risk is that the father will relate to his daughter in such a way that to reciprocate she has little choice but to play the traditional feminine role. That role is by definition incompatible with high intellectual development and achievement. "Daddy's" traditional feminine little girl is not among the bold and daring ones who become intellectually oriented women.

PARENTAL STANDARDS OF ACHIEVEMENT

From the above discussion we would predict that parents who hold high standards for their daughters and urge them on to their best achievement would have daughters with high intellectual attributes who do in fact achieve well. That is indeed what the research shows. The setting of high standards for their daughters by parents and the urging of their daughters to achieve have been associated with their daughters' scholastic aptitude, achievement motivation and high achievement, positions in top management in business and industry or as professionals, and creativity (Alper and Greenberger, 1967; Balazs, 1975; Berens, 1972; Biller, 1973; Christopher, 1967; Froiland, 1970; Goertzel and Goertzel, 1962; Hennig and Jardim, 1977; Kagan and Moss, 1959a, 1959b; Kandel and Lesser, 1972; Lipman-Blumen, 1972; Patrick, 1973; Ringness, 1970; Solomon et al., 1971).

Both parents likely set higher standards for daughters who are first-borns than for those who are later-borns, especially in small families.

At least until another child comes along, all the hopes and aspirations of the parents may rest on that one child. We do have evidence that mothers, at least, exert greater pressure for achievement on their young first-born daughters. Rothbart (1971) observed mothers super-vising 5-year-old girls' and boys' performances on several tasks. Mothers of the first-born children, especially first-born girls, put greater pressure on their children to achieve than did mothers of the later-born children.

Evidence indicates that this pressure on first-born girls to achieve pays off. A disproportionate number of first-born females from small families were found among high school students earning high verbal achievement scores, entering college freshmen, women with Ph.D.s holding the rank of assistant professor or above, Swedish medical students, women holding top management positions in business and industry, and college women judged by their professors to have cre-ative potential (Altus, 1965; Breland, 1974; Helson, 1968; Hennig and Jardim, 1977; Monson, 1973; Shaver et al., 1970).

Parents may be especially likely to set high standards for the eldest daughter who has no brother. This tendency seems particularly likely for fathers. Were there a son in the family these fathers would invest their hopes and aspirations in his achievements. Lacking sons, they turn instead to their eldest daughters. Hennig and Jardim (1977) found that all the 25 women they studied who were in top manage-ment positions in business and industry were either only children or the eldest in all-girl families of no more than three children. To their fathers they could do much more than girls ordinarily did. Similarly, Helson (1971) found that few of the creative women mathematicians whom she studied had a brother, and the father/daughter relationship was of special importance. The creative women mathematicians, however, were not necessarily first-born children.

PARENTAL ENCOURAGEMENT OF INDEPENDENCE

We postulated that a mother who urges her daughter to differenti-ate herself and independently to explore the environment fosters intellectual development and encourages achievement. We also pro-posed that the father who relates to his daughter as a person rather than as the embodiment of the feminine role enhances intellectual

attributes and achievement. In the research, the offer or encouragement of independence by parents has been associated with their
daughters' being curious, eager to explore, logical, and analytical in
approaching problems (Worell and Worell, 1971); being high in
achievement motivation (Berens, 1972); and reaching top management positions in business and industry (Hennig and Jardim, 1977).

PARENTAL ENCOURAGEMENT OF TRADITIONAL FEMININITY

When parents set high standards for their daughters, urge them
toward achievement, and encourage their independence, they are
guiding them toward androgyny, not traditional femininity. An assumption here is that parents who encourage traditional femininity
discourage the development of intellectual attributes and achievement. The mother who believes in sharp differences between boys
and girls on such characteristics as obedience, dependence, and
thoughtfulness is likely going to encourage traditional femininity in
her daughters. If she does so, her daughters would not be expected to
achieve the intellectual development of the daughters of a mother
who does not believe in such sharp differences between boys and girls
and who probably is not encouraging traditional femininity. Domash
and Balter (1976) found an inverse relationship between mothers'
beliefs that there should be large differences in boys and girls and the
analytic ability of their daughters in nursery school and kindergarten:
the more sharply the mother differentiated by sex, the poorer the
daughter's analytic ability. The child's analytic ability was measured
by having her find figures that were embedded in a background with
many other figures or designs (the Embedded Figures Test) and by the
complexity of her drawings of human figures.

Another way in which a mother can influence her daughter toward
the traditional feminine role is by herself being a model of that role. If
the daughter patterns herself after such a model, we would expect her
to be less developed intellectually and to have less drive for achievement than she would had her mother been a less traditional model. We
would not expect a daughter modeling a traditionally feminine
mother to have broad vocational interests. In this regard, Heilbrun
(1969) reports that college women who view themselves as similar to
a traditionally feminine mother have a more narrow range of voca-

tional interests than those who think they are similar to the father or to a less traditional mother.

PARENTAL MODELS OF INTELLECTUAL DEVELOPMENT AND ACHIEVEMENT

Evidence indicates that both parents do serve as models for their daughters of intellectual style, achievement, and vocational choice (Bieri, 1960; Constantinople, 1974; Helson, 1971; Lawrence, 1969; Long, et al., 1967; Lovett, 1969; Plank and Plank, 1954; Ringness, 1970; Schaffer, 1969; Sostek, 1963). An example of a mother who is a model of achievement to her daughter is the working mother. As we saw in Chapter 7, daughters of working mothers more often consider work as something they will want to do when they are mothers, and they are, in fact, more likely to be employed themselves than are daughters of nonworking mothers (Hoffman, 1974).

Women choosing challenging careers may be, to some extent, modeling working mothers. Almquist (1974) compared the family backgrounds of college women who chose careers in fields with a predominance of men (biological research, advertising, personnel management) and those who chose careers more typical of women (high school teacher, dietician, social worker). Those who chose careers with a predominance of men had mothers who were better educated and who were much more likely to have worked while their daughters were growing up and in college.

The surprisingly specific modeling of fathers by daughters is revealed in a study by Werts and Watley (1972). Daughters as well as sons excelled in high school in the kinds of skills that their fathers used in their occupations. For example, if the father were a physicist, his daughter was 3.5 times more likely than the average to excel in science. (Sons of physicists were 2.7 times as likely to excel in that discipline.) If the father were a clergyman, his daughter was almost 1.5 times more likely than the average to excel in drama and speech. If the father were an architect, his daughter was almost 2.5 times as likely to achieve in art. Daughters of fathers who were writers were twice as likely to achieve in literature.

Mothers will doubtless become more salient models of intellectual style and achievement as they increasingly achieve prominence in the vocational world and in public life generally.

PARENTAL INFLUENCE ON DAUGHTERS' CREATIVITY

Several studies suggest that fathers often have the predominant influence on the development of creativity in their daughters (Anastasi and Schaefer, 1969; Helson, 1967, 1971; Long et al., 1967). It might be tempting to speculate that fathers' influence in this area is a function of male dominance in intellectual and creative pursuits, that fathers are in a better position than mothers to be influential in the development of creativity in their children of either sex. That would seem a reasonable explanation except that several studies suggest that mothers are the main influence on the development of creativity in sons (Dauw, 1966; Long et al., 1967; MacKinnon, 1962). If the father is in a better position to influence the development of creativity of children of either sex, then he should be the prime influence on the creativity of sons as well as daughters. Special dynamics may occur in the parent/child relationship of highly creative individuals. Be that as it may, Dewing and Taft (1973) did not find the opposite-sex parent to be the more influential one in their study of creativity in seventh-grade children. They found that the mother's personality was more related to creativity in daughters; the father's personality, to creativity in sons. We also know of many examples in which the same-sex parent has been the more influential in the development of creativity in the child (for example, Isadora Duncan, Maria Montessori, John Stuart Mill).

Before examining the influence of parents on the creativity of their daughters further, let us consider what we mean by creativity. *Creativity* is difficult to define, but it usually connotes a genuinely new and meaningful input into society. It does not refer only to artistic productions; it may refer to technological breakthroughs, to scientific theories that lead to dramatic advances in knowledge, to philosophical innovations, or, for that matter, to new forms in almost any dimension of life. Although when one thinks of creativity, works of genius usually come to mind, creativity can occur on a scale from the mundane and commonplace to the highest level of originality, to advances that change the course of human life (such as in religion or science).

One can conceive of a creativity scale for specific acts: The builder following a blueprint is engaging in a less creative act than the architect's. The technician testing a hypothesis derived from a valid scientific theory is performing an act not as creative as that of the constructor of the theory. A musician faithfully following printed notes is engaging in a less creative act than the composer's.

As with most significant aspects of life, creativity is not easily measured. One way is to ask people in the same field (physics, for example) to rank their colleagues on a creativity scale. An obvious problem here is that the most creative person may lack the charisma of someone who is less creative and be ranked too low by colleagues. Another method is to use creativity tests that measure such aspects as flexibility of thought, fluency of ideas, unusual use of common objects, and originality. The problem with such tests is that although people who have demonstrated their creativity through their inputs to society do well on such tasks, other people who may not perform in a creative fashion in daily life also do well on them. Therefore, when creativity tests are administered to children, it is impossible to predict which of them will in fact grow up to be highly creative adults. Despite these problems, creativity is such an important aspect of life that we must examine parental influence on the creativity of daughters.

Helson (1971) discovered that half the fathers of the creative women mathematicians she studied were foreign born and that most of the fathers were professional men, whereas most of the fathers of less creative women mathematicians were businessmen or skilled workers. Typical of many other findings, the fathers of the creative women tended to have more education than the fathers of the comparison group. In this study, a disparity in education between father and mother was more frequent in the creative group, with the father better educated than the mother. Such a disparity does not appear with parents of daughters who have reached top management positions in business and industry (Hennig and Jardim, 1977). Also typical of the families of many creative men and women (Goertzel and Goertzel, 1962), the socioeconomic position of the families of the creative women mathematicians was poor or insecure relative to the education and professional status of the father. The lawyer could not collect his fees, the engineer was unemployed, the professor had died.

Typically, the homes in which creative daughters grow up have a higher cultural level than the homes of their less creative counterparts. Anastasi and Schaefer (1969) found, for example, more musical instruments played in the families of creative high school girls, and the fathers of the girls who were creative in writing tended to have more hobbies, often of a literary nature. Dewing and Taft (1973) discovered that the mothers of creative seventh-grade girls had more interests than did mothers of less creative girls and their interests were more unusual. Joesting (1975) found that fathers of highly creative college women tended to play musical instruments, and the mothers' frequent hobbies were writing and the other arts. The less creative women's mothers often had no hobbies.

Let us look more closely at the mothers of creative daughters. As we mentioned earlier, one study found the mother more influential than the father in the creativity of seventh-grade daughters as measured both by tests and by performance. Dewing and Taft (1973) report that, compared with the mothers of the less creative girls, the mothers of the more creative daughters had more formal education, were more likely to work outside the home, and were more egalitarian in child rearing.

In considering one extreme of the creative continuum, the genius, Besdine (1971) postulates that it is typical of women geniuses, along with their male counterparts, that their mothers devote themselves almost exclusively to them, force precocious development, and generate unusual drive to create and perform. The performance is first for the mother, later for the chosen love, and finally for an audience. This often occurs in a home with a weak or absent father. The daughter remains attached to the mother in a fusion of love, hate, and lust.

Besdine illustrates this relationship with the dancer Isadora Duncan. Isadora's mother divorced her older husband and earned a living for herself and her four children by giving piano lessons and moonlighting at odd jobs. She introduced her gifted daughter, Isadora, to the best in music, poetry, and philosophy early in life and had the highest ambitions for her. Isadora recalled that she was placed on the table as a baby and performed by moving her arms and legs in rhythm, greatly amusing her audience of family and friends. Her mother took a strong hand in her education, read to her constantly in the evenings, and played the piano for her endlessly. To her mother's gratification, her gifted daughter responded to the playing by developing dances to the music. Her mother was Isadora's first accompanist and introduced her to the wonders of music, so vital to her creativity during her entire life.

Whether it be the mother or the father, intense focus on the development of the daughter by one parent or the other is typical in the childhood of creative women.

TWENTY-FIVE MANAGERIAL WOMEN

Hennig and Jardim (1977) studied in depth twenty-five women who successfully held or still hold positions as presidents or divisional vice-presidents of nationally recognized firms. These women have high intellectual development, achievement, a most challenging vocational choice, and a higher than average degree of creativity.

Most women going into management (although not these twenty-five women) have been raised to think that they can become nurses but not doctors, secretaries but not bosses, and that another person, their husband, will support them. The authors state that when men go into management, they bring with them a sharper, more definitive understanding of where they are going, what they will have to do to get there, how they must act, and what they must take into account to achieve their goals.

All but three of the fathers of the twenty-five managerial women themselves held management positions in business; the three who did not were college administrators. All but one of the mothers were housewives; the one who worked was a teacher. The mothers were, however, generally as well educated as their husbands, and half of them were better educated. The parents' education ranged from high school up to the doctorate (two fathers earned that degree).

These women remembered happy childhoods and close, warm relationships with their parents. They all felt that they were special in the eyes of their parents, and they all were only children for at least the first two years of their lives; those who became eldest children were the eldest of no more than three girls.

These women all experienced a special relationship with their fathers. Fathers and daughters shared interests and activities traditionally considered the domain of fathers and sons. They engaged in vigorous physical activities. Their fathers taught them outdoor skills and offered them unusual early learning experiences, a means for expanding their horizons. They shared eagerly in their daughters' wish to achieve and willingness to compete. Often the father's approval was contingent on the daughter's success, but even so the means of success was enjoyable as it was shared with the father. The daughters drew attention and approval and they gained rewards and were confirmed as persons through the father/daughter relationship. Their fathers were models with whom they could identify. Despite this special relationship, they were always girls to their fathers, but girls who could do as much as or more than boys could.

Here is one woman's recollection of her relationship with her father:

> As I think back Father was really something special. As far as I can recall, I was Daddy's special girl. There were always special times set aside for him and me to be alone. When I was very young, he would take me places on Saturday afternoons. He was a very active man and I was always expected to be active with him. In the winter we would go sledding and skating. He taught me to skate when I was four and he used to show me off to all his friends who had sons older than me. "See," he would say, "you may think she is just a girl, but watch her outskate those boys of yours." I always enjoyed these sessions, and afterward we would go to a soda fountain and have hot cocoa and he would praise me and brag about me to the druggist or anyone else who would listen [p. 78].[4]

Another of these fathers, a railroad executive, took his five-year-old daughter with him as he walked several miles along railroad tracks under construction, stopping to talk with work crews. She rode with him in work trains full of sweaty, dirty men, and she loved it. Another father took his little daughter with him to a fishing club on weekends. She was the only female there and slept in a crib.

The twenty-five managerial women's recollections of their relationships with their mothers were not specific. The mother was characterized as a quiet person who once in a while exerted influence but who usually submitted to her husband's wishes. She provided the socially sanctioned, warm, caring, feminine model the daughter shared with her girlfriends. She also allowed the critical relationship with the father to flourish.

The fathers taught their daughters that the feminine model was not binding and backed them up when they acted on this belief. When these women began school, they were virtually unaware that some behavior is "appropriate" for boys and not for girls and vice versa. They didn't know, for example, that certain sports are only for boys. They didn't know that it is unacceptable for girls to excel in some activities; they had been taught to always try their best. Because of their beliefs, friction with the school was bound to arise, and when it did the girls held firm and so did their parents (especially their fathers). The fathers' position was essentially "if anybody has a right to do it, so does my daughter."

In adolescence, the daughter found it difficult to be sustained by the support their families had given them because the attitudes and opinions of their peers loomed more and more important to them. They were in conflict between the temptation to submit to the restricted, confining definition of femininity and the drive to be themselves. In their determined struggle during adolescence not to be submerged by the traditional feminine role, they began to feel anger and resentment toward their mothers. They came to view their mothers as having relinquished the struggle and as trying to force them to do the same. They felt betrayed by mothers who they felt were attempting to sacrifice them to the demands of a patriarchal society (see also Chesler, 1972; Rich, 1976).

The sense of betrayal might have been much worse had there been a son in the family to whom their mothers give privileges they would not allow them. But there were no sons in these families. It might also have been worse had they seen themselves as competing with their mothers for their fathers' affection or had they viewed their mothers as threatening their special relationships with their fathers. They did not think their fathers needed any special winning over during adolescence as they had been won over years before and continued to support them now that everything seemed to give way around them. Their mothers, of course, had allowed the special relationships with the fathers to develop in the first place. When they became interested in boys and in their appearance, their mothers relaxed and supported their achievements once again. The daughters had never rejected being female, nor had they rejected the mother either with finality. They had only rejected the constricting societal definition of femininity that she attempted to impose. These twenty-five women excelled academically but they also dated and had full social lives.

Their first jobs were mainly as secretaries—it was during the Depression—and most of their positions were created as favors to their fathers. When they found the right firm, they didn't job-hop but stayed with the same company for the next thirty years, finally reaching top managerial positions. It was clear to these women that a woman could advance only by proving herself more capable than any man who might qualify for the position. Since it took much time and energy to establish good working relationships and a reputation in a company, it would have been to their disadvantage to move to another.

At age twenty-five or so each made the decision to give up social life; none of them married until they were at least thirty-five, and then half of them married. Instead of a social life each woman focused on her job and on her relationship with her boss, who played much the same role that her father had earlier. He supported her, and finally an explicit understanding was reached that she would move upward with him through the company.

Can a woman without such a unique background as these twenty-five women had also succeed in a managerial career? The authors recognize that no one can redo their birth order or rework their early relationships with their parents. They nevertheless believe that women without this special background can succeed with time and much effort; they have seen it done. It is deplorable that so much more thought, energy, planning, and support seem necessary for a woman than for a man to reach managerial status.

NOTES

1. From *The Woman Said Yes: Encounters with Life and Death,* by J. West. Copyright 1976 by Jessamyn West. Reprinted by permission of the publisher, Harcourt Brace Jovanovich, Inc.

2. From *Blackberry Winter: My Earlier Years,* by M. Mead. Copyright 1972 by Margaret Mead. Reprinted by permission of William Morrow & Company, Inc.

3. This and all other quotations from this source are from "Two Women—Liv Ullmann and Erica Jong: An Intimate Conversation," *Redbook Magazine,* August 1977. Reprinted by permission.

4. From *The Managerial Woman,* by M. Hennig and A. Jardim. Copyright©1976,1977 by Margaret Hennig and Anne Jardim. Reprinted by permission of Doubleday & Company, Inc.

REFERENCES

ALMQUIST, E. M. (1974) "Sex stereotypes in occupational choice: the case for college women." Journal of Vocational Behavior 5: 13–21.

ALPER, T. G. and E. GREENBERGER (1967) "Relationship of picture structure to achievement motivation in college women." Journal of Personality and Social Psychology 7: 362–371.

ALTUS, W. D. (1965) "Birth order and academic primogeniture." Journal of Personality and Social Psychology 2: 872–876.

ANASTASI, A. and C. E. SCHAEFER (1969) "Biographical correlates of artistic and literary creativity in adolescent girls." Journal of Applied Psychology 53: 267–273.

BALAZS, E. K. (1975) "Psycho-social study of outstanding female athletes." Research Quarterly 46: 267–273.

BERENS, A. E. (1972) "The socialization of need for achievement in boys and girls." Proceedings of the 80th Annual Convention of the American Psychological Association 7: 273–274.

BESDINE, M. (1971) "The Jocasta complex, mothering and women geniuses." Psychoanalytic Review 58: 51–74.

BIERI, J. (1960) "Parental identification, acceptance of authority, and within-sex differences in cognitive behavior." Journal of Abnormal and Social Psychology 60: 76–79.

BILLER, H. B. (1973) "Paternal and sex-role factors in cognitive and academic functioning," in J. K. Cole and R. Dienstbier (eds.) Nebraska Symposium on Motivation. Lincoln: University of Nebraska.

BRELAND, H. M. (1974) "Birth order, family configuration, and verbal achievement." Child Development 45: 1011–1019.

CHESLER, P. (1972) Women and Madness. Garden City, N.Y.: Doubleday.

CHRISTOPHER, S. A. (1967) "Parental relationship and value orientation as factors in academic achievement." Personnel and Guidance Journal 45: 921–925.

CONSTANTINOPLE, A. (1974) "Analytical ability and perceived similarity to parents." Psychological Reports 35: 1335–1345.

DAUW, D. C. (1966) "Life experiences of original thinkers and good elaborators." Exceptional Children 32: 433–440.

DEWING, K. and R. TAFT (1973) "Some characteristics of the parents of creative twelve-year olds." Journal of Personality 41: 71–85.

DOMASH, L. and L. BALTER (1976) "Sex and psychological differentiation in preschoolers." Journal of Genetic Psychology 128: 77–84.

FROILAND, D. J. (1970) "Parental attitudes: a predictor of academic achievement." Dissertation Abstracts International 31: 1618–1619.

GOERTZEL, V. and M. G. GOERTZEL (1962) Cradles of Eminence. Boston: Little, Brown.

HEILBRUN, A. B., JR. (1969) "Parental identification and the patterning of vocational interests in college males and females." Journal of Counseling Psychology 16: 342–347.

HELSON, R. (1967) "Personality characteristics and developmental history of creative college women." Genetic Psychology Monographs: 205–256.

———— (1968) "Effects of sibling characteristics and parental values on creative interest and achievement." Journal of Personality 36: 589–607.

———— (1971) "Women mathematicians and the creative personality." Journal of Consulting and Clinical Psychology 36: 210–220.

HENNIG, M. and A. JARDIM (1977) The Managerial Woman. Garden City, N.Y.: Doubleday.

HOFFMAN, L. W. (1972) "Early childhood experiences and women's achievement motives." Journal of Social Issues 28: 129–155.

———— (1974) "Effects on child," in L. W. Hoffman and F. I. Nye (eds.) Working Mothers. San Francisco: Jossey-Bass.

JOESTING, J. (1975) "The influence of sex roles on creativity in women." Gifted Child Quarterly 19: 336–339.

KAGAN, J. and H. A. MOSS (1959a) "Parental correlates of child's IQ and height: a cross-validation of the Berkeley Growth Study results." Child Development 30: 325–332.

———— (1959b) "Stability and validity of achievement fantasy." Journal of Abnormal Psychology 58: 357–364.

———— (1962) Birth to Maturity: A Study in Psychological Development. New York: John Wiley.

KANDEL, D. B. and G. S. LESSER (1972) Youth in Two Worlds. San Francisco: Jossey-Bass.

LAWRENCE, G. L. (1969) "Behaviors and attitudes of college females differing in parent identification." Dissertation Abstracts International 30: 1362.

LIPMAN-BLUMEN, J. (1972) "How ideology shapes women's lives." Scientific American 226: 34–42.

LONG, B. H., E. H. HENDERSON, and R. C. ZILLER (1967) "Self-social correlates of originality in children." Journal of Genetic Psychology 111: 47–57.

LOVETT, S. L. (1969) "Personality characteristics and antecedents of vocational choice of graduate women students in science research." Dissertation Abstracts International 29: 4287–4288.

LYNN, D. B. (1969) Parental and Sex-Role Identification: A Theoretical Formulation. Berkeley, CA: McCutchan.

MacKINNON, D. W. (1962) "The nature and nurture of creative talent." American Psychologist 17: 484–495.

MEAD, M. (1970) Culture and Commitment. Garden City, NY: Doubleday.

MONSON, R. (1973) "The relationship between nuclear family structure and female achievement." Dissertation Abstracts International 34: 3578–3579.

PATRICK, T. A. (1973) "Personality and family background characteristics of women who enter male-dominated professions." Dissertation Abstracts International 34: 2396.

PLANK, E. H. and R. PLANK (1954) "Emotional components in arithmetical learning as seen through autobiographies," in R. S. Eissler (ed.) Psychoanalytic Study of the Child. New York: International Universities Press.

RICH, A. (1976) Of Woman Born: Motherhood as Experience and Insitution. New York: W. W. Norton.

RINGNESS, T. A. (1970) "Identifying figures, their achievement values, and children's values as related to actual and predicted achievement." Journal of Educational Psychology 61: 174–185.

ROTHBART, M. K. (1971) "Birth order and mother-child interaction in an achievement situation." Journal of Personality and Social Psychology 17: 113–120.

SCHAFFER, M. C. (1969) "Parent-child similarity in psychological differentiation." Dissertation Abstracts International 30: 1888.

SHAVER, P., J. R. P. FRENCH, and S. COBB (1970) "Birth order of medical students and the occupational ambitions of their parents." International Journal of Psychology 5: 197–207.

SOLOMON, D., K. A. HOULIHAN, T. V. BUSSE, and R. J. PARELIUS (1971) "Parent behavior and child academic achievement, achievement striving, and related personality characteristics." Genetic Psychology Monographs 83: 173–273.

SOSTEK, A. B. (1963) "The relation of identification and parent-child climate to occupational choice." Dissertation Abstracts International, 24: 1690.

WERTS, C. E. and D. J. WATLEY (1972) "Paternal influence on talent development." Journal of Counseling Psychology 19: 367–373.

WORELL, J. P. and L. WORELL (1971) "Supporters and opposers of Women's Liberation: some personality correlates." Presented at the meeting of the American Psychological Association, Washington, D.C., September.

PART II

MARRIAGE AND FAMILY ISSUES

4

YOUNG MARRIEDS: WIVES' EMPLOYMENT AND FAMILY ROLE STRUCTURE

Glenn R. Hawkes
JoAnn Nicola
Margaret Fish

INTRODUCTION

In the study of social change, scientific objectivity is a difficult, if not impossible, goal. We are caught up in the same social milieu as are our subjects. Our views change, just as our subjects' views change. One way of obtaining objectivity is to utilize simple descriptive statistics which reflect specific changes in social practices—mobility, fertility, income levels. Unfortunately, this way of studying change tells us little if anything about the dynamics of change.

In this study, we centered on the sociopsychological forces underlying social change. We sought to "know" people so that we might detect how their views of the world influenced their behavior. We wanted to see how they changed with the passage of time. We were particularly concerned with the interplay within the family as it changed over time.

We were especially interested in the effects of increasing opportunities for women to move into different areas of the world of work;
we also wanted to study the influence of birth control technology.
Thus, we looked at young married couples in which the wife had
chosen to be employed after marriage. By looking at these young
people at a time when their lives had changed—that is, after the birth
of the first child—we hoped to gain a better understanding of the
factors that went into such specific decisions as whether or not the
wife would continue her career. We could examine the interactions
within the families as they made such decisions.

We also looked for comparison purposes at couples in which only
one person was employed as well as those in which both were employed. Previous studies of dual-career families, such as those of the
Rapoports (1971) and Holmstrom (1973) had examined social-
psychological aspects of a limited number of families, nothing the
successes and conflicts generated by dual careers. We were influenced by their approaches, but we wanted to look at a wider
spectrum of families, and we particularly wanted to examine the
antecedents of attitudes toward work in both husbands and wives.

Our study sample is composed of young couples in which (a) the
wife had been employed for at least thirteen postmarriage months; (b)
there was one child between the ages of one and three years; and (c)
the wife had either interrupted her career to become a full-time
mother, modified her career to accommodate her new family roles, or
returned to her career after a short maternity leave. We imposed these
requirements because we wanted the families to be well enough
established to imply commitment through the birth of a child; we also
wanted the child to be old enough for the newness of the experience of
parenthood to have worn off, yet not so old as to signify a decision to
have only one child. In addition, we wanted our women subjects to
have had employment that required specialized training; this would
indicate that they had initially had some career commitment.

The first subjects were obtained through advertisements in local
newspapers. The sample was filled out by asked respondents to recommend other potential families they knew. By using these combined methods, we eventually generated a list of names from a four-
county area in Northern California.

Tables 4.1–4.4 outline the characteristics of our population. Almost two-thirds of the women interrupted their careers after the first child was born. Average age was twenty-eight for the wives and thirty for their husbands; they had been married an average of five to six years. Husbands of wives who interrupted their careers tended to have higher incomes than husbands of wives who continued working after the birth of a child (see Table 4.3). Educational level among our subjects ranged from high school (about 10 percent of the women and 3 percent of the men) to a graduate degree (about 12 percent of the women and 39 percent of the men; see Table 4.4). Equal proportions of women who interrupted their career and those who continued working had completed a bachelor's degree or higher.

TABLE 4.1   Population Description

	Interrupted Career[a] Women _n_	Continuing Career[a] Women _n_	Total _N_
Wives originally interviewed	46	28	74
Husbands interviewed (of above wives)	23	17	40
Couples reached in 2 year call-back	44	25	69
Couples in thematic analysis	6	9	15
Divorced/separated since original interview	2	4	6

a. The wife had worked since marriage, had not worked after the birth of the child and was not working at the time of the interview. Her first child was 1–3 years old when she was first interviewed.
b. The wife had worked since marriage and had returned to part-time or full-time work before the interview. She was either currently working when interviewed or had worked for some time after the birth of the first child.

TABLE 4.2   Demographic Information

Mean Characteristics of Subgroups	Interrupted Career Women	Continuing Career Women
Child's age (months) when wife first interviewed	21.7	27.3
Mother's age (years) at time of interview	28.1	28.5
Father's age (years) at time wife was interviewed	30.0	30.5
Number of years married as of interview	5.3	6.5
Number of years mother worked before pregnancy	5.0	5.6
	(S.D. = 3.32)	(S.D. = 3.95)

TABLE 4.3   Income Information

Husband's Income at Time of Initial Interview	Interrupted Career Women n = 44		Continuing Career Women n = 25	
	%	(n)	%	(n)
Less than $7,000	4.3	(2)	10.7	(3)
$7,000 to $8,999	21.3	(10)	3.6	(1)
$9,000 to $11,999	12.8	(6)	35.7	(10)
$12,000 to $14,999	10.6	(5)	14.3	(4)
Percentage of husband's earnings under $15,000	49.0		64.3	
$15,000 to $19,999	29.8	(14)	17.9	(5)
$20,000 to $29,000	10.6	(5)	7.1	(2)
over $30,000	4.2	(2)		
Percentage of husband's earnings over $15,000[a]	44.1		25.0	

a. Percentages may not add to 100 due to missing information.

INTERVIEW AND ANALYSIS

Our interview schedule has undergone numerous revisions in order to increase its utility, reliability, and ease of administration. It now holds the respondent's attention while quickly getting to central issues.

We had originally planned to work from typed protocols taken from the tape-recorded interviews, but we realized that typed protocols failed to communicate the rich background of information that came from changes in vocal tone and emphasis, pauses, and environmental sounds—all the nuances of the setting in which the interview took place. Not wanting to miss this, we modified our method, using the tape-to-analysis procedure.

The tape-to-analysis method has many advantages that should be recognized. There need be no lengthy time lag between interview and analysis caused by the time-consuming process of having the protocol typed. Much of the total response, as mentioned, is preserved. This method also allows for the continuous monitoring of interviewers for consistency and reliability and permits almost immediate sharing of information with the research team.

TABLE 4.4   Educational Information

	Interrupted Career Women n = 44		Continuing Career Women n = 25	
	%	(n)	%	(n)
WIFE'S EDUCATION				
High school	8.7	(4)	10.7	(3)
Attended college	19.6	(9)	14.3	(4)
Associate of Arts degree	2.2	(1)	10.7	(3)
Vocational/trade school	-0-	-0-	-0-	-0-
Bachelor's degree	43.5	(20)	39.3	(11)
Teaching credential	13.0	(6)	7.1	(2)
Attended graduate school	2.2	(1)	-0-	-0-
Graduate degree	8.7	(4)	17.9	(5)
HUSBAND'S EDUCATION				
High school	4.3	(2)	-0-	-0-
Attended college	10.9	(5)	17.9	(5)
Associate of Arts degree	6.5	(3)	3.6	(1)
Vocational/trade school	2.2	(1)	-0-	-0-
Bachelor's degree	30.4	(14)	17.9	(5)
Teaching credential	-0-	-0-	3.6	(1)
Attended graduate school	6.5	(3)	14.3	(4)
Graduate degree	39.1	(18)	39.3	(11)

The final interview schedule took from one to two hours to administer. Schedules were developed for both husband and wife which paralleled each other. In all cases, the wife was interviewed first. She served as our entree into the family.

Six researchers conducted the interviews over a two-year period. Each interviewer listened to the tapes of other interviewers, until all were convinced that the method was as consistent as possible across interviewers. As soon as each interview was completed, the project director listened to it on tape in order to insure that the method was consistent and to give the interviewers immediate feedback.

After we had completed 114 interviews, we selected fifteen couples (thirty interviews) for thematic analysis. We believed these fifteen couples represented the range of attitudes found in our larger group. They represented a diversity of socioeconomic statuses and relationship types, and we believed an in-depth analysis of these fifteen couples would give us a reasonably accurate picture of the group as a whole.

We approached the thematic analysis as a cumulative process, with each taped interview building upon the others. Our method was to have two researchers listen to the tapes at the same time, commenting on the themes. Then the project director listened to the tapes and either agreed or disagreed with the analysis. A free-flowing discussion ensued until consensus was reached.

Our thematic analysis had two main subdivisions. First, we analyzed themes in the lives of subjects as individuals and related this analysis to our knowledge of the subjects' socioeconomic status, birth order, religion, and related demographic information. The other subdivision contained themes that appeared in the dyadic relationship. We examined how the couple related to each other and how the themes surrounding their life as a couple had developed. During this analysis, we would listen to the tapes of a husband and wife in tandem.

Our interests were focused on differences and similarities between individuals in the goals, values, and attitudes they expressed. As we listened to tapes of the interviews and heard what these people had to say about work, parenting, and marriage, the following themes seemed to emerge and recur.

As couples talked about dividing household tasks and integrating career with home roles, we began to construct a continuum of marital types, with traditional, sex role-stereotyped marriages at one end and modern, egalitarian marriages at the other. A second continuum evolved as we noted some people seemed to be able to integrate roles of career employee, spouse, and parent, while others appeared to lead very compartmentalized and fragmented lives. Another continuum that in some way affected each person we talked to was that of acting-reacting. Those who planned and controlled their lives were at one end, and those who seemed to allow random events to shape their lives were at the other end. Independence or dependence was revealed in relationships with parents, children, and spouses. Some subjects appeared to us to have transferred unmet dependency needs from childhood and adolescence to their spouses and/or children. And as parents, some clearly fostered their child's dependency on them, while others encouraged independence. Power versus cooperation, illustrated by interpersonal relations at work and at home, was a dimension along which respondents seemed either to desire influence and control over others or to help and cooperate with others. These dimensions characterized the dyadic relationship of each couple. We also identified four main themes describing influences on the lives of our subjects as individuals: (1) socioeconomic status, (2) religion, (3) birth order, and (4) family of orientation.

Finally, both the husbands and the wives in the fifteen couples used for thematic analysis were telephoned three years after the original interviews and were asked several open-ended questions. By analyzing their own accounts of how their lives had changed or not changed, how satisfied they were about their life situations, and what contributed to their satisfaction, we confirmed or revised our assessments of individuals and relationships. We found those changes that did occur—marital separation, change in job or return to work, or a geographic move—were often predictable from listening to the early tapes. These data will be discussed in a subsequent publication.

What follows is a section of the study dealing with the theme of egalitarianism versus traditionalism in the marriage relationship. We have used the subjects' own words as much as possible to allow the reader to judge the validity of our interpretations. Names and revealing details have been changed in order to protect the anonymity of our subjects.

THEMATIC ANALYSIS: EGALITARIAN VERSUS TRADITIONAL MARITAL ROLES

We were eager to explore the extent to which couples followed an egalitarian pattern, particularly regarding an equal division of household chores and child care. Current literature indicates a trend toward shared household and child care roles when both husband and wife assume the provider role, though, so far

> women have not been able to get men to participate in those household duties to the same significant extent as women had been able to get themselves involved in the provider duty [Scanzoni, 1978: 82–83].

We found várying degrees of egalitarianism among the couples we interviewed. Several couples had egalitarian attitudes and practices concerning career and home roles. The wives in the more egalitarian relationships had true careers, defined by Rapoport and Rapoport (1971: 18) as a "job requiring a high degree of commitment and which has a continuous developmental character." They were not working just to make money. Furthermore, the need for the wife to have her own career was recognized by both husband and wife.

For example, Roger, a laboratory technician, when asked why his wife was working responded:

> It's germane to our marriage. I couldn't be married to someone who sat home and kept the place spotless. It would be difficult for me to live with someone who didn't have something.

Robin, who has continued her career with only short maternity leaves for the birth of her two sons explained:

> Work means a lot to me. I feel I have to be doing something beneficial to others, contributing something. I feel I'm a better mother when I'm working, because I'm happier and more tolerant with the kids.

Karen, a biochemist, said: "I think I would go mad if I had to sit home day after day." She explained the decision of household labor she and her husband have agreed on:

> We split all the work at home with respect to housework and child care. I see him as doing more housework and child care than he sees himself doing.

When her husband Ken, a college professor, was interviewed, he said:

> I think we would continue child care even if she weren't working. She does not see the housewife role as satisfying . . . . I feel more secure and confident if she is working. I think the kinds of questions that would arise just don't need to arise.

One other couple, Everett and Elaine, indicated that they divided household responsibilities—laundry, vacuuming, dishes, and cooking—equally, and he also assumed the responsibility of taking their daughter to the day care center. Everett, an attorney who is employed as a public defender, feels that Elaine's career

> gives a dimension to her life that she wouldn't have. She is satisfied personally and professionally, and this makes her a more stable person and helps our relationship.

In talking about how she was able to integrate her work as a high school teacher with home and family, Elaine explained:

> The thing that has made it easiest for me to do all this is the kind of husband I have . . . the support he gives me . . . he is not stuck into any traditional role.

Both partners in these three couples gained psychic as well as monetary rewards from the wife's career and were willing to structure other areas of their lives to accommodate dual careers.

Current research continues to indicate that shared roles are negatively linked to level of husband's income and positively linked to wife's education (Ericksen et al., 1979). Husbands who earned high incomes felt justified in letting their wives do the majority of housework and child care, whereas wives with higher education were more likely to be employed in higher-paying jobs. These wives were in a better bargaining position to obtain role-sharing with their resources of education and income.

One couple, Leonard and Lynne, are an example of this exchange of resources as they traded off housekeeper and provider roles during their early years of marriage. Lynne had a graduate degree and a high-paying career as a speech therapist, while Leonard was first an unemployed writer and then a student. When we interviewed Leonard, who is now a college professor, he told us:

> When she was working I would shop, cook meals, clean the house and do all that sort of thing. At one time I was trying to be a writer and living off her salary . . . then later I was in grad school and in a sense living off her, keeping house while she was working . . . I still prepare dinner 2 nights a week and we've always shared laundry.

After their first child arrived, though, Lynne described her husband as being "adamant" about her not working full-time. By then Leonard was a professor, earning more than his wife. In her own words: "He would just as soon I stayed home. I think his fantasy before I had the baby was that I would stay home and be the perfect mother." She feels her husband now has accepted her working part-time because, "He sees me as being a lot happier and a better mother when I do work." Leonard acknowledged: "She couldn't exist without working. She's happier and feels better about herself when she is not just keeping the floor free from lint."

However, in order to work only part-time, Lynne had to modify her career in speech therapy by going into private practice, and she sees this as a disadvantage. (Helen, another woman in our group works three days a week as a dental hygienist. She finds this part-time arrangement ideal.)

For several other women, the ambivalence between a career and motherhood was resolved in favor of being a full-time mother. These women found more rewards in unshared child rearing than in work, and some who had to work out of financial necessity resented turning their children over to another caretaker, even their husband. In these women, the commitment to the traditional nurturing role was stronger than their desire to continue a career.

Some mothers reiterated the belief that they could not entrust the rearing of their children to other people. As one mother, Diane, said, "I realized there was a lot more to raising a child that I didn't want to give to someone else. I didn't want someone else raising him and felt this was my responsibility."

Betty, a former teacher, who said her husband would actually like her to go back to work, explained:

I wouldn't give up the experience of mothering for anything. It enriches your whole life with new experiences. People are missing a whole lot if they don't have a child. People who don't want children haven't matured.

Cathy, also a former teacher, considered going back to work but said she literally had nightmares about leaving her son with a sitter:

I dreamt I had to go back to work and I had to find a babysitter and I was crying in my dream 'cause I didn't want to do it. I woke up from the dream actually crying tears, as I didn't want to leave him with a babysitter all day. If it happened that's probably how I would feel . . . . I really didn't know my feelings were that strong.

Nancy, who returned to work three months after her son was born because "financially there didn't seem to be any alternative" no longer obtained the same gratification from her job:

It made me unhappy that there was somebody else taking care of my kid who was so little. A lot of the stimulation from work just wasn't as stimulating because there was something else that was important to me.

Nancy, however, continued to work intermittently, and at the time we interviewed her husband, Ned, he appeared to the research team to have assumed the role of primary psychological parent. Ned's profession, illustrating, allowed him to work principally at home while Nancy was employed in a neighboring city.

Ned described caring for his son and daughter as:

the most important thing I do and will probably be the most important thing I ever do so it is worth the time . . . . I don't look at it [child care] as a contribution to my wife. It's a responsibility and what I like to do . . . . In most families the parents have different roles but I really like the role I have. Her working enables me to have that role . . . dominant parent although I don't like the value judgment of that word . . . when the kids fall down or wake up in the middle of the night it's me they cry for. It's a natural response as the person who is with them most becomes most responsive to their needs.

Ned even reported that he enjoys participating at his son's parent cooperative nursery school and having been the only father to host a weekly play group session in which his toddler daughter participated. He explained:

I was in a play group last year where eight of us "housewives" all met on Tuesday or Thursday morning . . . . I could arrange my job 8–5 and work at the office but that's not what I want. I have turned down promotions that would have taken me away from the family in terms of time at home.

Ned was the only father in our group to take on the role of primary caregiver.

In contrast, several couples expressed the belief that their marriages had been more egalitarian in sex roles and division of labor before they had children. Some husbands professed incompetence and/or unwillingness to care for infants. The shifting of domestic tasks and child care to the wife was therefore reported by some couples when the wife stopped working, and there was a young infant to be cared for.

For example, Roger, whom we saw as having a largely egalitarian philosophy toward marriage and as being strongly supportive of his wife's career, admitted making less than an equal contribution to domestic chores after their second child was born. In response to the question, "Do you share household duties?" he replied:

I'm not nearly as good as I used to be. It used to be a lot more equitable around here. It's deteriorated lately; I don't really do a whole lot around the house. I take care of the yards, of course, and I take care of the cars, but not the cleaning. Also I'm not too big on babies so as a general rule I don't spend a great deal of time with Ray [the infant].

This pattern of behavior would support Nye's (et al., 1970) findings that with increasing family size there seems to be more role specialization, toward a more traditional model.

The most clear-cut example of a shift in roles toward a more traditional pattern with the birth of a child occurred with Don and Diane. Don is a physician. Diane formerly worked as a reference librarian; she now stays at home with their two children.

In Don's words:

I think we shared responsibilities much more before children were born and that's because Diane worked. The fact that she is now home most of the day obligates her to do most of these things . . . . I spend no more than one-half hour with the baby. He always needs to be held and since my wife is breastfeeding there is nothing I can do . . . . I do probably less than 30 percent of the obligations around the house—the ones that Diane can't or doesn't want to do—maintenance, gardening, garbage. Dishwashing, cleaning, ironing are Diane's responsibility.

Diane, though, did not complain about Don's lack of involvement in household and child care, giving further support to Ericksen's et al. (1979) research that when a husband has the earning capacity of a physician, he can justify not doing housework or child care which might intrude on his career.

Don said he did not expect fatherhood to be nearly as time-consuming as it is, nor did he realize how severely it could, "cut into the time I was using for myself." He both resented the time he gave to his child and felt guilty at not giving enough:

I think he takes up a lot of my free time and it's difficult for me to give away some of my free time. I think I don't have enough time to myself . . . . I feel more comfortable being married than being a father. I feel fatherhood restricts me in some of the ways marriage doesn't.

It seemed to us that some of these men who left the majority of child care and housework to their wives fell into the category which Komarovsky (1973) calls "pseudo-feminists"; that is, although the husbands favored having their wives work, their approval was hedged with qualifications which few women could meet. For example, Diane told us:

He'd like for me to go back to work . . . but if I go back everything would be completely up to me—baby-sitting, housecare. He'd want me to get someone to do it. He wouldn't. If I went back to work it wouldn't affect him at all.

And Betty reported, "My husband likes for me to work. He likes that second paycheck, but he doesn't like taking care of the children."

Another couple, Gordon and Gretchen, were in strong agreement that a mother's place *was* at home. Their religion (Latter-Day Saints) gives strong legitimation to her wife and mother roles. Gordon is a grocery clerk; Gretchen had been a clerical worker. When asked about his wife working, Gordon responded, "I really didn't want her to work at all. I just wanted her to take care of the house."

Gretchen told us, "My husband wants me to stay at home but he wouldn't care if I wanted to go to school or work. I never plan on working, though."

Even though this couple held traditional attitudes regarding the roles of provider and homemaker, Gordon made a substantial contribution in the area of child care. With the first child, Gretchen reported that Gordon

> spends from when he gets home to Grant's bedtime with him. He takes him out for an hour in the evening and gives him a bath. He gets him [Grant] up in the morning and gives him breakfast so I can sleep . . . . He washes out all the dirty diapers too. I feel kind of guilty about that.

After their second child was born, Gordon told us:

> I really enjoy both kids. I don't mind getting up and taking care of them. I enjoy having the kids around . . . . I got up at night and changed them all night long, burped 'em and all. She takes care of them all day so I relieve her at night.

Although Gordon saw himself as a provider and his wife as house-keeper, he was willing to become involved in a shared child care role, unlike Don or Bill. He recognized that his continuing opportunity to father more children was related to his willingness to accept a high degree of involvement in child care. Gretchen cooperates in child-bearing (four children under five years of age) so long as she has the opportunity to be relieved of the nighttime drudge of losing sleep and of diaper-washing.

Moreover, Gordon has few resources with which to bargain in terms of "buying" off from doing the housework and child care. He has only a high school education and a low-paying job with little chance of advancement. Gretchen also has only a high school education and few job skills. Thus, her opportunity to share the provider role would be minimal. Her minimum wage would probably not pay for child care for their four children.

SUMMARY

When we examined the theme of egalitarian versus traditional attitudes and practices in marriage, our couples seemed to range along a continuum. Only two couples had consistently shared household and child care responsibilities while both partners pursued full-time careers. These two wives had graduate education which they translated into good-paying, high-status jobs. Several women gave up professional careers because they could not bear to leave their children in the care of others, even a husband. When wives gave up working, they were expected to assume the bulk of housework and child care, especially if their husbands were in high-salary careers, such as physician, professor, government analyst. Although husbands might indicate they favored their wives working, in actuality the wives saw the husbands doing nothing practical to facilitate it. Although college-educated, these wives did not have the skills they could translate into careers, so they had less bargaining power to involve their husbands in routine household duties.

REFERENCES

ERICKSEN, J. A., W. L. YANCEY, and E. P. ERICKSEN (1979) "The division of family roles." Journal of Marriage and Family 41, 2: 301–313.

FASTEAU, M. F. (1974) The Male Machine. New York: McGraw-Hill.

GLASER, B. G. and A. L. STRAUSS (1967) The Discovery of Grounded Theory. Chicago: Aldine.

HOLMSTROM, L. (1973) The Two Career Family. Cambridge, MA: Schenkman.

KOMAROVSKY, M. (1973) "Cultural contradictions and sex roles: the masculine case." American Journal of Sociology 78: 873–884.

LEVINE, J. A. (1976) Who Will Raise the Children? New York: J. B. Lippincott.

NYE, F. I., J. CARLSON, and G. GARRETT (1970) "Family size, interaction effect, and stress." Journal of Marriage and Family 32: 216–226.

RAPOPORT, R. and R. N. RAPOPORT (1971) Dual-Career Families. Harmondsworth, Eng.: Penguin.

SCANZONI, J. (1978) Sex Roles, Women's Work, and Marital Conflict. Lexington, MA: D. C. Heath.

5

DUAL-CAREER MARRIAGES: BENEFITS AND COSTS

Carol C. Nadelson
Theodore Nadelson

The past few years have seen many changes in attitudes and life patterns regarding careers and families, especially among young people. In a 1967 study, 50 percent of women college students stated that having a career was important in addition to being a wife and mother (Lozoff, 1972). By 1971, 81 percent of a sample of college students held this view. At the same time, contrary to prevailing mythology, 91 percent of male students expressed interest in a wife with a career out of the home (Lozoff, 1972). Furthermore, 60 percent of male and female students thought that fathers and mothers should spend equal time with children, 44 percent of males believed that men and women should share household responsibility, and 70 percent of females and 40 percent of males stated that both males and females should contribute equally to family financing. This latter discrepancy may represent either a realistic evaluation of the present differences in male/female earning power or a male reluctance to relinquish the privileges accompanying the role of the major "breadwinner" (Lozoff, 1972).

By 1977, three-quarters of college men said that they expected to spend as much time as their wives in bringing up children (Katz, 1978).

Another important change has been in the number of women in the work force. Currently, more than one-half of all women sixteen years old or older are in the work force or actively seeking employment. Fifty-three percent of all women in intact families are in paid employment, 41 percent of these women have children under 18 years of age and 31 percent of children under six have working mothers (Moroney, 1978; Pifer, 1978).

At this time, only 6 percent of American families fit the traditional model of two parents with husband working and wife caring for children (Moroney, 1978; Pifer, 1978). Thus, we might consider these the deviant families in our society, where dual-working families are the norm.

Marital patterns, as well as attitudes, appear to be changing. More people are now marrying later or not marrying at all than a decade ago. The divorce rate continues to rise, people are having fewer children, and more people are choosing to remain childless. In addition, there has been a striking increase in the number of adults who live alone or in nonmarital living arrangements (Frieze et al., 1978).

DUAL-CAREER AND DUAL-WORKER FAMILIES

In 1971, the Rapoports suggested that dual-career families would increase with more women in the work force, and that this change would require more child care, revisions in sex role attitudes, and reconsiderations of the organization of productive work and of family life. In their subsequent volume, Rapoport and Rapoport (1976) pointed out that while the dual-career pattern was more prevalent, many of the necessary changes in lifestyle patterns had not occurred because of the inflexibility of social systems and individuals internalized resistance to change.

Both partners of a dual-career marriage in high-commitment career activities have responsibilities which extend beyond the usual eight-hour work day. Such commitment demands modification in usual roles, tasks, and decision-making. For example, a husband cannot assume that his wife will be absent from work when a child is ill, or when household repairs are needed. It is equally the case that a wife cannot count on her husband to be available to escort her to a social engagement, or to repair the car when it breaks down. Couples must work out a variety of strategies to cope with both the ordinary aspects of life and the special circumstances which are created by the lack of availability of one partner who functions as the "wife," the partner who tackles the chores, arranges child care, schedules social activities, and buffers the other (the husband) from the demands of daily life.

In most marriages, one of the spouses tends to be able to accommodate his/her needs to those of the family or at least to rotate these responsibilities with the other spouse. Traditionally, the husband in our society has been the nonaccommodating partner with respect to domestic responsibilities, and the wife has accommodated, placing her primary emphasis on the family and not on job or career.

Couples have adapted to the dual-career situation in a number of ways. Some couples continue to function in a traditional sex role division of labor model, others choose a nontraditional or even opposite approach, and still others opt for an egalitarian alternative. This last choice implies that the couple makes decisions together about the best options for each of them as well as for them as a unit. For example, the offer of a new job in a distant place involves a cooperative effort and it may not be a unilateral decision. This model may be particularly difficult for people who have been raised in more traditional families. The husband who was brought up to believe that housework is women's work may be resentful of the demands on his time, or he may experience anxiety because of his perceived failure to live up to what he unconsciously believes to be a masculine role. Furthermore, he may find that colleagues at work are unsympathetic or even frankly hostile when he takes time off to take a child to the dentist or to attend a parent's meeting. He may even find family and friends displaying negative attitudes and withdrawing support, or he may find his job jeopardized. The wife in this situation often experiences even greater conflict and anxiety, despite her commitment to an egalitarian model. Furthermore, children exposed to a more traditionally oriented environment at school, in the community, and via the media may expect and even demand traditional behavior. They may find it difficult to invite friends to their house because neither parent is home, or to be the child whose parents are unable to assist in school activities as often as parents who have taken on family tasks along traditional lines.

Weingarten (1978) describes a typical scene which points to some of the adaptational issues faced by the dual-career couple:

> Mr. Jones is in his study finishing a speech he will be delivering in New York the next day, while making calls to the usual network of babysitters to arrange for someone to stay with his children for the evening. Dr. Jones is talking with her answering service on the other line to ascertain how high a fever Billy Smith has, while simultaneously heating up a stew for dinner. In an hour Mr. Jones will drive to the airport, the babysitter will arrive, and Dr. Jones will meet Billy Smith and his parents at a local hospital emergency room.

> Meanwhile, at Bill Smith's home, Mr. Smith is calling his wife at her law office to ask her to stop off on her way home and buy a pizza so that they will not have to prepare dinner in case Dr. Jones wants to see Billy that evening.

Clearly, dual-career marriages press both partners to make adaptations that may not be required within more conventional marriages. Modifications occur in many areas of life, but can be seen in terms of decision-making and allocation of responsibilities for family maintenance and the care of children. Couples must often redefine gender-oriented activities and adapt emotionally to the stresses of new roles and expectations, since the needs of the family may assume a different distribution than in more traditional family situations.

While there is reported to be a higher divorce rate for dual-career couples than for more traditional couples, it is important to emphasize that this pattern is newer, and deviant in terms of societal values and expectations. Models of conflict resolution are thus not established, and therefore it is difficult to evaluate such reports. Furthermore, a dual-career marriage is more complex. It is fashioned to incorporate differing individual concepts and attitudes; it offers the opportunity for growth and readaptation as well as the possibility of failure. Women and men entering this new and complex arrangement may also be different from those who choose a traditional relationship. They have defined themselves, even before marriage, as different, and they have taken on what was seen as "different" relationships in the past. They often pride themselves on not holding to traditional values. If they are careful with regard to career, they may prefer to take interpersonal risks. They often have a "why not" attitude when social dogma is questioned, and want more of a relationship and marriage than stability, which they will risk to try to attain it. In this context, divorce may not be a symptom of maladaptation but the result of a greater risk.

Those problems which occur when life circumstances make it necessary to reassess or reorient plans and expectations are particularly problematic. When decision-making must include an active consideration of the interests, career options, and so on of a partner in a more directly substantive way, there may be distress and tension. For example, the husband who is transferred to a new location may have to consider not only his wife's social adjustment and interests, his children's schooling and relationships with peers, but, to a greater extent, his wife's career possibilities. *She* may not be able to obtain a position equal to her present one or her career advancement may, in fact, be jeopardized by a change in location. Wives share a complementary dilemma. The wife may be offered a potentially gratifying career opportunity, only to recognize that this shift might put added pressure on her family, especially if a location change were required. She may decide to decline the offer, or she may seek another apparent solution: that one partner commute. This latter pattern has become frequent in recent years. The costs of these changes may be significant enough to cause a rupture in the marital relationship.

Dr. B. was a 46-year-old scientist with a tenured university faculty position. Her husband, Mr. B., was 45 and approaching the upper-management level of his company. He was offered a promotion if he relocated. Dr. B. protested, stating that there was no comparable position for her in her field, and that it might mean the end of her career. Mr. B. was angry. He resurrected many previously buried issues, complaining about her lack of interest in his career, her higher income and his many sacrifices for her. He accused her of being "castrating, selfish and uncaring." Dr. B. felt devastated. She had believed that they had made a good adaptation, and she had always been gratified by her husband's sense of internal security and support of her.

Since she saw that in this situation there was no solution that did not require considerable compromise and sacrifice, for either or both of them, she proposed that they not move and that he commute. She would then promise to take the major share of household responsibility. He was not satisfied with this solution and expected her to move. He was asking for a reward for his previous sacrifice. Dr. B. was angry, guilty and deeply hurt but she complied and the family moved. Dr. B. obtained a laboratory research position, which offered neither the challenge of her previous job nor the opportunity to be creative. She became increasingly frustrated and withdrawn from her husband and children. Within six months she decided to enter therapy because she was aware of increasing feelings of insecurity, hopelessness and intense rage. While the move itself in another individual might or might not have precipitated as profound a reaction, for Dr. B. the shift in location was a major stress, since it meant a decline in her creative work and the goals she had set for herself. During their marriage her husband had only seen her competence and had been unable to appreciate her vulnerability—and she had not been aware of her husband's unexpressed resentment.

In therapy, Dr. B. focused on her low self-esteem and her constant fears of "being discovered as a fraud." As she worked through these issues and began to "own" her competence she was able to find a position commensurate with her ability.

Both of the B.s were also seen in couples therapy, where they learned to share more and to allow themselves to trust each other. They experienced enormous relief when they were each able to acknowledge anger, fears and also their love. What emerged most prominently was that both of them most feared being exposed as vulnerable. They both struggled with dependency needs which they saw as antithetical to their ego ideals. It was their difficulty with dependency that made them guard against mutual affection.

It is important to recognize that areas of conflict and dissonance in dual-career couples stem from intrapsychic as well as sociocultural factors. Issues of competition, jealousy, and unrealized expectations or failure to resolve dependency problems from the past play a part in addition to administrative and reality-oriented concerns. Those more basic psychological aspects, while intensified in a situation where needs may not be met and many demands may be made, are not substantially and qualitatively different from those problems arising in any marital situation. They may, however, go unrecognized for long periods of time in situations where roles are diverse and there are few competitive areas, or where, because of the clearly defined structure of the relationship, envy and jealousy are less manifest.

When a previously traditional marriage evolves into a dual-career relationship, additional problems related to a role change occurs. When his wife develops new interests a husband's sense of loss, abandonment and competitiveness may lead to demanding or regressive behavior on his part. Likewise, children may also experience the changes as loss. The woman's guilt and conflict about her outside interests and the "abandonment" of her family may cause her to give up or she may overcompensate and become overly compliant or self-sacrificing. At times she may respond by displacing or projecting her anxiety and thus may be seen as overcritical, intolerant, or unresponsive. She may see her family or her work as the major source of her problems, rather than understanding her responses to the pressures, and the guilt she experiences when she moves outside her family and into a more independent position. Problems with children intensify these conflicts and may lead to inappropriate solutions, such as giving up a career. In this surrender of a hard-won goal, there is angry capitulation to the demands of family; what follows is usually against a background of continuous resentment. The woman says by her attitude and actions: "If you want or demand this sacrifice of the self *I* hold to be important I will give to you the rest of me, which is worthless." Such a solution is not solution at all. In part it also represents the woman's ambivalence regarding her need to struggle in a career. Blaming her family can thus be a way to avoid her own conflict about her role and aspirations.

Mrs. A. was a 40-year-old married mother of a 12-year-old son and a 9-year-old daughter when she resumed her career as a lawyer. Her husband, a 43-year-old engineer, was ostensibly supportive and enthusiastic. Mrs. A. negotiated what seemed to be a reasonable salary and part-time work arrangement. After two months on her job, however, it became apparent that more would be expected of her than she had anticipated, if she expected to succeed. Mr. A. betrayed his ambivalence about his wife's aspirations by his increased demands and expectations. He wanted his life to remain unchanged despite his wife's work, and he was unwilling to make compromises.

Initially, Mrs. A. blamed her field, the firm, and those who made "inhumane" demands. She felt that she was being exploited, and Mr. A. agreed. They colluded in their anger against a common enemy. Over the next several months, Mrs. A. began to become more angry with Mr. A.'s unwillingness to take a more active role in the family. She alternately expressed anger and felt guilty when she made even minimal demands, but she would fly into a rage if he didn't anticipate a problem and offer to help.

Mrs. A., however, was also unwilling to make any changes in her own expectations of herself. She felt that she should keep house, shop, cook, take the children to their lessons, etc., as she had always done, but she also wanted to pursue her demanding, time-consuming career. Her ambivalence was overwhelming. She became increasingly frustrated and depressed.

Mr. and Mrs. A. had clearly made an effective adaptation for thirteen years. They had utilized their individual styles and traits in a mutually satisfactory fashion. Mrs. A. was well-organized and able to maintain control, and Mr. A. wanted her to take care of him while he concentrated on his career goals. Neither partner had seen obstacles which would arise or the changes which would be necessary if they altered their life styles.

The A.s were very invested in the marriage and cared about each other. They were, however, unable to see alternative "unrealistic" solutions, and they began to displace their anger, disappointment and frustrations on each other. They sought marital therapy in order to work toward understanding each other. It was difficult for them to see their mutual contributions to their distress and to be willing to compromise. Slowly, Mrs. A. began to facilitate Mr. A.'s increased participation in aspects of family life that she had previously believed were her responsibility. As she dealt with her guilt, she gave up her fear of being a "bad" mother. Mr. A. was able to be more active and offer more. He could see his wife as a friend and companion. He was able to grow toward more independence and at the same time become more nurturant toward their children, without feeling compromised. He became a real support rather than an obstacle to Mrs. A. in her efforts. At the same time Mrs. A. was also able to examine her work situations more objectively, and to make decisions about how far she wanted to go. She was able to make requests for flexibility which both she and her firm saw as reasonable and realistic.

The reentry of the wife into a more active instrumental societal role is often a source of tension and conflict within each partner as well as between the partners. This is especially apt to occur when there is ambivalence experienced by both partners about the potential disruption imposed by a change in the system. It is important for a therapist in this situation to facilitate sharing of anticipated rewards as well as problems. It is often too simplistic to see only the sacrifices necessary. In treating a couple like the A.s, the therapist must be aware of the realities generated by the world in which they live, as well as those generated by their personality styles, modes of adaptation, and the defenses of each partner. While it may appear to be self-evident, therapists frequently fail to heed this basic therapeutic principle. There can be impositions of the therapist's values and lifestyle and failure to recognize and/or support those of the couples.

We have seen both sides of this issue. The therapist who is unable to support a wife who chooses a career or a couple who chooses to commute because s/he believes these patterns to be "pathological" is committing a therapeutic error. So is the therapist who is so committed to his/her own alternative lifestyle or values that s/he prematurely supports divorce for a couple with marital difficulty or presses a new mother who wants to remain at home, to return to work.

At times sexual problems are prominent in the concerns of dual-career couples. There has been much discussion and concern about increased male impotence as a result of women's greater assertive behavior and possibly increased clarity of sexual needs. However, the validity of this concern is difficult to evaluate. It does perhaps reflect men's anxiety about their masculinity when traditional roles are changed, and there are demands to perform in roles which had been considered traditionally feminine. This can lead to withdrawal, including loss of sexual interest or potency, compensatory and sometimes rigid assertions of masculinity, or a variety of other responses to restore self-confidence and diminish anxiety. Loss of potency then reinforces the sense of lack of control in a cycle of reverberating helplessness. At such a time, couples may seek sexual counseling. The therapist using an exclusively behavioral approach may miss the essential communication contained in sexual symptoms. A deeper understanding of the nature of the conflict expressed by sexual dysfunction may help to save the relationship. If it is the case, as happens frequently, that one partner cannot tolerate important developmental or motivational shifts in the other, therapy can help or allow a more intelligent or civilized separation.

COMPETITION

Competition is also an important dimension in dual-career couples. It may be intensified in dual-career marriages where many activities are shared. At times it is overt and produces conflict. Couples may find that their productivity is stimulated in this atmosphere, but at other times tension and distress result when there is overt, or even covert competition. Within a conventional marriage, some competitiveness is resolved through gender-enculturated differences which carefully relegate certain aspects of family functioning to one individual, and another portion to the other—e.g., "my wife takes care of that" or "I don't know anything about cars."

In the dual-career family, the allocation of power and responsibility creates a situation which exposes competitive striving openly. Conflict occurs if the character styles and dispositions of the partner make compromise difficult. For those couples who work in the same field, competitive issues may be even more apparent, since they may find it difficult to keep work apart from other aspects of their life, and they may also provoke enormous anxiety in colleagues when they disagree or attempt to differentiate themselves.

The C.s are a couple in major administrative roles in the same university department. They found that while colleagues would make every effort to put them on different committees, and arrange their schedules so that they did not coincide, they would nevertheless expect of each that they knew the whereabouts of the other and they would send messages with one for the other.

In order to enable themselves to work autonomously the C.s had made efforts to keep their work days separate from each other, and they indeed did not keep track of each other's schedules, papers, messages, mail, or meals. It puzzled colleagues (who suspected marital problems) when one of them would answer "I don't know" when asked the location of the other.

For many professional men, the experience of attending a social or work-related event in the role of a spouse rather than primary guest can be unsettling and uncomfortable. The man may attempt to make contact with strangers, who politely inquire about him without any real interest. The social role of husband as spouse is not really symmetrical with that of the wife.

Wives continue to find less social support for their career commitments than do their husbands. Instead, they are harshly evaluated and judged by the activities of their children or their husbands. Likewise, husbands are not socially supported in homemaking activities which continue to be seen as the wife's domain. Thus, neither partner is supported in career role or home role if the "deviant" pattern is taken.

On the other side of the ledger are the rewards of sharing with one's "best friend" and being able to trade "war stories." While at times one would rather talk than listen, or register some fear of being told "I wouldn't have done it that way," there is a real chance to share in the context of caring.

A particular male perspective has been stated:

We have had—and continue to have—a quite extraordinary experience in marriage, not one we were perceptive enough to seek when we fell in love nor even one we welcomed fully when its depth first became manifest but one with unique meaning for our own growth: the experience of living with a complete woman. We had been socialized to expect less and to settle for the creature comforts that came with the acceptance. Along the way, we may have shown some lack of grace in surrendering the customary conveniences: yet in return we have been granted a love the richer and fuller for having its roots in mutual respect and growing maturity. That, we acknowledge, we owe to our wives. Had it not been for their capacity to insist on respect for their integrity, it is doubtful we would have achieved what we now enjoy. Of course it was not unilateral; we claim our due for what we have fashioned together; but we know it would not have happened without what they brought us: gentle courage, soft strength, selfless individuality.

Our wives are our best friends. No, it is not because, as the conventional wisdom currently has it, friendship between men is difficult, at least for us as particular men. We have men to whom we are close whose friendship we treasure, with whom we can share our private thoughts, hopes and fears. It is that our wives are all that, and more. They do not replace friends or make them unnecessary. We continue to need, and be needed by friends, both men and women. But our wives, our "successful professional women," are our lovers, our friends, and our comrades in loves and lives of high adventure.

We consider ourselves the most fortunate of men [Nadelson and Eisenberg, 1977].

WORK AND TIME

Work is one way of subduing anxiety and dealing with depression. It affords expression of ambition, relief of intrapsychic guilt, and the gratitude of those who receive help, particularly when individuals are involved in service activities. For the professional, for whom hard work has brought increasing rewards, immersion in work is an automatic response to life stress. Moreover, when one is in a service field—e.g., medicine,—s/he can work late to care for needy people when marital or family pressures occur. It is a personally and socially acceptable way to avoid such problems and incorporates unique defense and attack strategies: It is more difficult to be angry at the partner's seeming altruism, even if such sacrifice results in less time with family. Moreoever, people who value hard, goal-directed work also often ignore the needs or concerns of their partners.

When a person who has been a hard-working professional is disappointed because of failure to meet internalized demands for achievement, dissatisfaction with marital or other relationships, or being overwhelmed by the needs and demands of others at work, the response tends to be what has always been relied upon—to work harder. This is related not only to the individual achievement orientation;

it is probably also related to the unique satisfactions to be gained from certain careers where hard work brings increasing rewards.
The following example is a case in point:

> Mr. and Mrs. D. had been married for two years. Mr. D. had two sons, aged eleven and fourteen, who lived with his first wife. He was forty-six years old, and well settled in his career as an artist. Mrs. D., a forty-two-year-old editor, had been married briefly, and divorced twenty years before. She had no children.

> Mrs. D. was jealous of Mr. D.'s attention to his sons. She also complained that he was too lenient and failed to set appropriate limits with them. Mr. D. felt guilty about having left his sons. In order to "make it up to them," he failed to make any demands on them when they visited. Mrs. D. saw this as a constraint on her, and a parenting failure on the part of Mr. D. He was unwilling to discuss this and reminded her that she did not understand how to raise children because she was childless. Mrs. D. was angered by Mr. D.'s attitude and by his many expectations of her. She retreated into work and began to spend less time at home. Mr. D. in turn complained about the demands of Mrs. D.'s career, which he felt relegated him to second place. He was unprepared to compete with her career, and she was unwilling to make any concessions.

> Both D.s were strong, successful people, who had each functioned autonomously in the past. They admitted to difficulty in listening, in respecting differences and in accepting that part of their commitment to each other necessitated that each relinquish some control. Neither could understand the other's perspective.

> In the course of intensive couples treatment, they learned, by repeated exposure, that there were greater rewards in yielding to understanding the other's position (as opposed to defensiveness). Mr. D. understood that his position with his wife arose in part from his use of isolation when affective issues emerged. Mrs. D. recognized her need to withdraw when she was confronted by what she saw as too many demands. It became clear that these had been lifelong defense mechanisms which had been adaptive in other situations, but were no longer effective. The D.s were able to help each other by recognizing the signals that evoked these responses, respecting the anxiety behind them, and attempting to be more supportive rather than attacking at stressful times.

Every working couple is wedded as much to time as they are to each other. When two marital partners have roughly equivalent and demanding career roles, problems of scheduling become prominent and constant. In addition to the rigors of individual work schedules, each partner must be aware of the schedules of all members of the family. Most often family scheduling around shopping, working, or recreational activities is administered and carried out by the wife. When the shift is toward an egalitarian model, both partners share an array of instrumental tasks within a family. Thus, instead of allocating a whole set of activities to one particular person, both people are potentially involved in making decisions concerning not only the schedule, but many other aspects of the activity within a family. Redundancy is balanced at times when one member is ill or absent, and the family still can remain functional. Often differences in style or emphasis can cause problems. But the loss of efficiency and redundancy is also believed to be a necessary sacrifice to equality. In practice most couples specialize in various facets of domestic maintenance, with overlap. Although the husband "does not do summer camps for the children" and the wife "does not do cars," they both may have varying proficiency in marketing or finance. There are often areas of conflict, and there are escalating complaints of "doing too much," which can be translated as sacrificing a career on the domestic altar. Traditionally, the woman has been asked to make such a sacrifice, and it takes a continuous vigilance and energy to avoid "falling into the trap."

"So I've fallen into the trap" was the opening comment of a thirty-six-year-old lawyer appearing with her husband, a physician, in a psychiatrist's office. "I swore I never would, but someone has to take care of things. He is busy. I can get away, I work part-time—but I want a full schedule." (The husband said he could try to do more.) With the therapist, the couple thrashed out the issues: social demands, the internal conflict of wishes, career versus the protection and anonymity of the homemaker, and projected blame.

Clock time spent apart is by definition the same for both partners, but experienced time may be quite different. To the extent that women are socialized into roles which are more expressive than instrumental and into greater dependence on affectionate feedback for maintenance of self-esteem, there may be differential pricing in personal cost. However, this is, in turn, offset by the way men are socialized. They are less ready to have personal needs or attention displaced by their wives' career demands. The fact that serious careers do not operate within a 9:00 a.m. to 5:00 p.m., five-day a week schedule means that evening and weekend hours are often invaded. Homework is less preemptive than away-work, because it is carried out in a common residence and can be interrupted for a bit of conversation or affection (Nadelson and Eisenberg, 1977). Time away leaves one partner homebound, left with all of the household and child care chores, and feeling lonely, perhaps even abandoned. The more professionally ambitious the spouses are, the more togetherness will be invaded this way. Yet an irreducible minimum follows inevitably from a serious commitment to a career. The very best efforts to coordinate schedules cannot change the inevitable separations. Moreover, if there are young children to be cared for, scheduling may have to be deliberately staggered, thus making less time available for a couple to be together. A spouse may be unavailable at the time when the partner may most need support, advice, or caring. Outside social activity is often curtailed, and weekends are filled with catching up with errands, chores, and each other.

This is a problem without solution in the current contemporary context. What each spouse loves, admires, and respects in the other would not be the same without all of the components, including work. Yet this commitment decreases the partner's availability and thus one has less of what one wants most. The cost comes with the benefit, both are tied together and cannot be eliminated—but they can be balanced (Nadelson and Eisenberg, 1977).

Given the demands of a career, there are on the average, fewer hours in the week for the working parent to be with the children. That statement does not translate into what is commonly taken to be its equivalent: that the child is cheated of care. When we talk of the quality rather than quantity of time spent with children, we often feel this more as a rationalization to alleviate our guilt, but we underestimate what we give out to children.

Allen's mother overhead him talking to a schoolmate about their parents' occupations. Allen proudly explained that both his parents were psychiatrists who make unhappy people feel better. His companion had no difficulty in describing his father's occupation as an orthopedist who fixed broken bones but he said his mother "didn't do anything." Allen was unable to understand this and kept insisting that she must "do something." His friend finally blurted out: "I know what she does! She yells and hollers at me and talks on the telephone all day!" After his friend had gone home, Allen ran to his mother, embraced her, and said: "Am I glad you're a doctor" [Nadelson and Eisenberg, 1977].

In a dual-career family, it is not only time constraints which lead us to say that there is more room and more need for fathering, but we become aware that perhaps what can be provided will ultimately be a more important experience for children, as well as for their parents. Children gain in the quality of the relationships they can have with both parents. For girls, wider career horizons are present as tangible possibilities; for boys, there is exposure to more egalitarian marital roles. They interact daily with both parents, who are full participants in the human activities of the work place and the home. There is less risk for the child of becoming the sole source of maternal satisfaction, with its attendant infantilization and impediments to autonomy. Of course, we speak only of potentialities rather than guarantees, because competence as a parent is not a necessary consequence of competence as a professional, but it is important to emphasize that, other things being equal, the countervailing virtues within a dual-career marriage can more than offset the constraints imposed by the competing demands on time (Nadelson and Eisenberg, 1977).

Nonetheless, a prominent feature of working women's lives is the conflict they have about the care of their children. If children develop any physical or emotional problems, women are usually quick to be blamed and also blame themselves, regardless of the etiology of the problem (Nadelson and Notman, 1973). Many working women believe their work is not in the best interests of the family. Because of this, they often overcompensate by asking for less help from other family members than does the woman who is at home (Nye and Hoffman, 1963). This dynamic overcompensation serves to bind the guilt associated with work.

There is a rapidly emerging literature which supports the idea that there are benefits for mothers, children, and families when the mother works, even if it is out of necessity rather than desire (Howell, 1973a, 1973b; Murray, 1975, Al-Timimi, 1976; Warshaw, 1976). For example, Hoffman reports that the working mother expresses more positive affect, uses less coercive discipline, and feels less hostility and more empathy toward her children, although she may be somewhat overindulgent (Hoffman, 1972). Birnbaum (1975) studied the attitudes of professional women toward their children and compared them with nonworking mothers. She found that these women experienced greater pleasure in their children's growing independence. They were also less overprotective and less self-sacrificing.

There is considerable support for the idea that having a working mother has a positive effect, particularly for her daughters (Nye and Hoffman, 1963). The daughters of working mothers have been noted to be more likely to choose their mothers as models and as the people they most admired. Adolescent daughters of working mothers, particularly in middle- and upper-socioeconomic groups, were active and autonomous and admired their mothers, but were not unusually tied to them. For girls of all ages, having a working mother contributed to a concept of the female role which included less restriction, a wider range of activities, and a self-concept relfecting these views. Girls usually approved of maternal employment and planned to work when they grew up and became mothers. Unlike the daughters of nonworking mothers, they did not assume that women were less competent than men.

Studies of daughters' academic and career achievements provides additional evidence of the positive effects of having a mother with career interests. A number of investigators have reported that achieving women, and women who aspire to careers, particularly less conventionally feminine careers, are more likely to be the daughters of educated and employed women (Nye and Hoffman, 1963; Birmbaum, 1975; Tangri, 1969; Levine, 1968; Almquist and Argrist, 1971). There are fewer data on the impact of the mother's working or a career on sons.

Data on the husbands of working women indicate that they are more actively involved in the care of their children, and that this has a positive effect on both sons and daughters (Young, 1975; Lamb, 1977). Furthermore, the husbands of professional women are more likely to respect competence and achievement in women (Rapoport and Rapoport, 1971; Nye and Hoffman, 1963; Maccoby, 1966; Birmbaum, 1975; Tangri, 1969; Levine, 1968; Almquist and Argrist, 1971; Dizard, 1968; Garland, 1972).

CONCLUSIONS

We have much to learn about the positive aspects of changing traditional role concepts. Currently, much of our concern has focused on the negative. There is positive value connected with indicating to children that any number of instrumental cognitive and emotional functions among human beings are not necessarily gender based. It is beneficial for young men not to feel as if there is something denigrating, demeaning, or strange about running vacuum cleaners, cooking, and washing dishes, just as it is important for young women to be competent mechanically. It seems reasonable to hope that children who grow up in a home where caretaking activities are shared between the father and the mother will be able to develop flexible ideas of their personal work role and family role identities. Furthermore, children can develop the idea that both parents can be readily and realistically available for all kinds of problem resolution while caring for each other for what they are and acknowledging differences without denigrating them.

REFERENCES

ALMQUIST, E. and S. ARGRIST (1971) "Role model influences on college women's career aspirations." Merrill Palmer Quarterly of Behavior and Development 17, 3: 263–279.

AL-TIMINI, S. (1976) "Self-concepts of young children with working and non-working mothers." Ph.D. dissertation, Peabody College.

BIRNBAUM, J. (1975) "Life patterns and self esteem in family oriented and career committed women," in M. Mednick et al. (eds.) Women and Achievement: Social and Motivational Analysis. New York: John Wiley.

DIZARD, J. (1968) Social Change in the Family. Chicago: University of Chicago Press.

FRIEZE, I. et al. (1978) Women and Sex Roles. New York: W. W. Norton.

GARLAND, T.N. (1972) "The better half?: the male in the dual profession family," in C. Safilios-Rothschild (ed.) Toward a Sociology of Woman. Lexington, MA: Xerox.
HOFFMAN, L. (1972) "Early childhood experiences and women's achievement motives." Social Issues 28: 129–155.
HOWELL, M. (1973a) "Employed mothers and their families." Pediatrics 52, 2: 252–263.
───── (1973b) "Effects of maternal employment on the child." Pediatrics 52, 3: 327–343.
KATZ, J. (1978) "Past and future of the undergraduate woman." Presented at Radcliffe College, Cambridge, April.
LAMB, M. (1977) "Fathers: forgotten contributors to child development." Human Development 18: 245–266.
LEVINE, A.G. (1968) "Marital and occupational plans of women in professional schools." Ph.D. dissertation, Yale University.
LOZOFF, M. (1972) "Changing life styles and role perceptions of men and women students." Presented at Radcliffe College, Cambridge, April.
MACCOBY, E. (1966) "Sex differences in intellectual functioning," in E.E. Maccoby (ed.) The Development of Sex Differences. Stanford: Stanford University Press.
MORONEY, R. (1978) "Note from the editor." Urban and Social Change Review 11: 2.
MURRAY, A. (1975) "Maternal employment reconsidered: effects on infants." American Journal of Orthopsychiatry 45,5: 773–790.
NADELSON, C. and M. NOTMAN (1973) "Medicine: a career conflict for women." American Journal of Psychiatry 130, 10: 1123–1127.
NADELSON, T. and L. EISENBERG (1977) "Successful professional woman: on being married to one." American Journal of Psychiatry 134, 10: 1071–1076.
NYE, F.I. and L. HOFFMAN (1963) The Employed Mother in America. Chicago: Rand McNally.
PIFER, A. (1978) "Women and working: toward a new society." Urban and Social Change Review 11: 3–11.
RAPOPORT, R. and R.N. RAPOPORT (1971) Dual-Career Families. Harmondsworth, Eng.: Penguin.
───── (1976) Dual-Career Families Re-examined. New York: Harper & Row.
TANGRI, S. (1969) "Role innovation in occupational choice." Ph.D. dissertation, University of Michigan.
WARSHAW, R. (1976) "The effects of working mothers on children." Ph.D. dissertation, Adelphi University.
WEINGARTEN, K. (1978) "Interdependence," in R. Rapoport and R. Rapoport (eds.) Working Couples. New York: Harper & Row.
YOUNG, S. (1975) "Paternal involvement as related to maternal employment and attachment behavior directed to the father by the one-year-old infant." Ph.D. disssertation, Ohio State University.

6

SPOUSES' CONTRIBUTIONS TO EACH OTHER'S ROLES

Helena Z. Lopata
Debra Barnewolt
Kathleen Norr

Numerous social scientists have documented the manner in which modernization, and especially its capitalistic, urbanization, and industrialization subtrends have pulled the ongoing economic and political life of Western European and American societies out of the home (Aries, 1965; Bird, 1979; Dahlstrom and Liljestrom, 1967; Easton, 1976; Laslett, 1971; Lerner, 1969; Oakley, 1974a; Rubin, 1976; Sicherman, 1975). In the eighteenth century, the world became divided into the private sphere of the home, dominated by the woman, and the public sphere, dominated by the man, while the children moved from one to the other depending on age and sex.[1] In America, the Puritan version of the Protestant Ethic, combined with a strong focus on the economic institution, accentuated this trend (Goode, 1963). The gradual removal of relatives, including older children for most of the day, and servants from the home and its immediate environs finally created the role of housewife or home-maker by focusing most rights and duties of home maintenance upon one woman in each house (Coser, 1975; Lopata, 1971). An ideology of "true womanhood" explained and justified this removal of the home from public life and the assignment of the woman to its management (Easton, 1976; Lerner, 1969; Sicherman, 1975; Welter, 1966).

> The extreme emphasis on sexual differentiation that characterized nineteenth-century American culture—variously manifested in the "cult of true woman," Victorian sexual morality, and the "doctrine of the spheres"—has been viewed in the recent past as a primary setback for women [Sicherman, 1975: 470].

Freudian psychoanalysts such as Helene Deutsch gave a psychiatric underpinning to this ideology as late as 1944, labeling a woman interested in roles outside the home as "masculine." Lundberg and Farnham (1947) titled their book on Americans with this identity *Modern Woman: The Lost Sex,* because they showed signs of wanting a fuller life space.

The 1940s, 1950s, and 1960s in America abounded with books teaching women how to be proper wives and mothers. Several of these argued that the man functioning as the "breadwinner" for the home and family needed a variety of supports only a wife working full-time as a homemaker could provide. These included the series of books for wives of men in the Armed Services by Nancy Shea, such as *The Army Wife* (1941), as well as most of the etiquette books by Emily Post and Amy Vanderbilt.

Whyte actually devoted very few lines to wives in *The Organization Man* (1956), but throughout that book runs the assumption that the wife is a full-time homemaker. He also focused an article on "The Wife Problem" (1952) (see Epstein, 1970, for an update of this thesis). Lopata (1965, 1971) found that over half the suburban and urban housewives interviewed in the years between 1956 and 1965 believed that wives influence their husbands' careers mainly through the work they do maintaining the home, the children, and the husband. In those years, *Occupation: Housewife* (Lopata, 1971) was the prime work activity of the majority of adult women. Those who took jobs outside of the home felt guilty over "deserting" the home and generally explained such action not in terms of individual gains or a commitment to a career, but as necessitated by financial need (see also Helfrich, 1961). Even as late as 1976, Mortimer et al. argued that some men's jobs acted as constraints upon the wife's employment because either they prevented sharing household management or they demanded supports which took extensive time and energy on the part of the wife.

The traditional, or at least idealized, American family in all but very recent years thus consisted of a husband whose primary identification and duties were to his job and a wife who managed the home and family full-time and who, if among the middle and upper classes, did some volunteer work (Glick, 1957). The income which the husband earned was distributed in a variety of ways by the husband or wife or through some form of shared arrangement (Bernard, 1973; Blood and Wolfe, 1960; Blood, 1969; Cardozo, 1976; Lopata, 1971). The husband "helped with" some of the household or child-rearing tasks, as if such activity were a favor to the wife rather than part of the role of family member (Bernard, 1973, 1975a; Lopata, 1971: 115–122; Rubin, 1979). The role of housewife was taken very seriously by women, as inevitable in the case of the working-class wives or as part of a two-person career, as Papanek (1973) aptly called the arrangement for middle-class wives. Although Lopata (1971) found the housewives of the Chicago area committed to this role in the 1950s and 1960s, with personal explanations and self-doubts for whatever problems they experienced within their semi-isolated lives, numerous observers detected the underlying dissonance of their situation (Bernard, 1973, 1975a, 1975b; Friedan, 1964; Riesman et al., 1950; Rubin, 1976, 1979). Furthermore, this type of family was becoming more and more atypical, although Americans continued to use it as a model and until very recently considered all other arrangements, such as the presence of a wife employed outside of the home in a two-paycheck marriage (Bird, 1979) or as the financial head of the family, as "abnormal" or problem infused. Nye and Hoffman (1963) devoted the majority of their *The Employed Mother in America* to proving that children did not suffer drastically from the absence of a mother during her on-the-job hours, if arrangements were made for their proper care and if the husband approved. Interestingly enough, the 1974 revision of the Hoffman and Nye book devotes much less space to this subject.

In spite of the strong emphasis on the occupation of housewife for women and in spite of the fact that so many women were performing it with little help from others, this occupation has not been highly valued in this society (Bernard, 1971, 1973; Lopata, 1971). As Glazer-Malbin (1976) points out, only recently have social science studies of this role been undertaken, although there are uncountable studies of the occupations of men and some jobs that women enter outside the home. Three books on the work women do in the home, containing a depressing portrayal, are *The Captive Wife* (Gavron, 1966), *The Sociology of Housework* (Oakley, 1974b), and *Worlds of Pain* (Rubin, 1976). Berk and Berk (1979) have recently published the results of a detailed study of the work involved in maintaining a home, the previous research in this area being mainly cross-cultural comparisons of time budgets (Szalai, 1972; Schultz, 1974).

Whether personally rewarding, demanding in its routine and social services, or overwhelming in the complexity and energy demands of a multitude of occupants (Lopata, 1966), the role of housewife has been undergoing some changes in modern homes in which the wife and husband are both employed, especially in situations in which the couple tries to evolve an egalitarian sharing of home care (Bahr, 1974). As many authors observe, however, the attempt to remove the role of housewife from family roles through an incorporation of its duties and rights into the roles of spouse, parent, and child has met with many problems (Hunt and Hunt, 1977). Bird (1979) and Rubin (1976, 1979) detail those problems and frustrations, and all studies of "dual career" or "two-paycheck" couples devote some section of their reports to them, as well as to methods used in attempts to avoid or alleviate them (Bryson and Bryson, 1978; Farkas, 1976; Fogarty et al., 1971; Garland, 1972; Poloma and Garland, 1970; Poloma, 1972; Rapoport and Rapoport, 1976; Veroff and Feld, 1970).

THEORETICAL FRAMEWORK

This chapter examines the wife's perception of the ways in which husbands and wives in two-paycheck marriages help each other with their occupational and home roles. Its theoretical framework is a combination of social role analysis with that of the "construction of reality" segment of symbolic interaction theory (Berger and Kellner, 1970; Berger and Luckmann, 1966). A social role is here defined as a system of interdependent relations between a social person and a social circle, involving duties and rights (Lopata, 1971, 1973, 1979; Znaniecki, 1965). The symbolic interactionist approach is used here to determine the ways in which people, in this case Chicago-area women aged twenty-five to fifty-four who are married and employed, perceive the help they give to, and receive from, their husband in both occupational and home roles, and their husband's supportiveness of their employment outside of the home.[2] The data being reported here form part of a larger study based on the same theoretical framework, of the changing commitments of women to family and work roles.[3]

In each social role, there are obligations and rights focused around the person in order that she or he is able to carry forth the role. The person must maintain a healthy self, able to carry out the duties and the rights of the role. To do this the person must eat, sleep, be assured of safety, have rights of access to resources necessary for self-maintenance, and the like (Znaniecki, 1965). These rights are complex and cannot be adequately covered here. In addition, the social person has general duties and rights of the role with no direct or apparent beneficiaries, such as maintenance of the space and equipment, upgrading role-relevant skills, and so on. Finally, there are rights and duties in relation with each of the members of the social circle: "clients" or beneficiaries, suppliers of needed resources, members of the work group, colleagues performing similar or complementary roles, those working or living in physical proximity, the administrators of the organization, and so forth. Circle members are more clearly defined in some roles, such as that of employee, than in others, such as that of housewife (Lopata, 1966, 1971; Mack, 1956). They may form an organized social group, but do not necessarily do so, as in the situation of a doctor's patients. They may, but do not need to, fall into an organization or status hierarchy (Lopata, 1964).

The study of the Chicago women, or at least the part of it being reported here, focuses on three roles of women, as perceived and defined by them, and on the association between these roles and the occupational, husband, and homemaking roles of their husband, again as perceived by the wife (see also Pleck, 1977). Figure 6.1 illustrates these three roles in general terms. Of course, if there are children in the home, the role complex becomes even more interwoven and convoluted (Holmstrom, 1972). Each social circle includes everyone to whom duties are directed or from whom rights are received in order for the basic functions of the role to be met. Circle members are as much a part of the role as is the social person whom the social role concept locates at the center of this network.

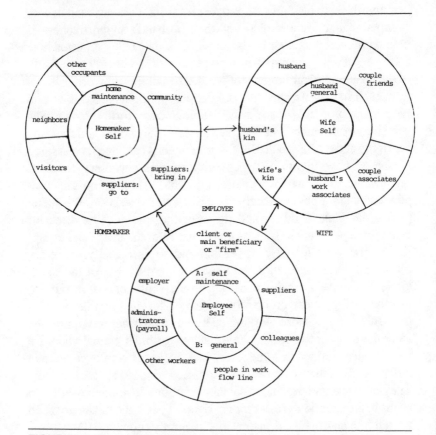

FIGURE 6.1　Three of the Major Social Roles of an American Urban, Married, Employed Women

THE CHICAGO-AREA WOMEN

The findings of this chapter are based on a larger study of the changing commitments to work and family roles of Chicago women.[4] Seventy-four percent of the women are currently married, 5 percent are separated, 8 percent divorced, 3 percent widowed, and 10 percent have never been married. Women who are currently married tend to have entered that relation later in life than women who have been, but are no longer, married. The divorced, separated, and even the widowed women, of whom there is a weighted total of 304 in the sample, disproportionately entered a first marriage at the age of eighteen or younger (34 percent) or between nineteen and twenty-one (36 percent; the gamma between age at first marriage and marital status is −.43). Young age when the first child is born also relates to marital dissolution. Not surprisingly, in view of national statistics, only 54 percent of the nonwhites, compared with 80 percent of the whites, are now married (gamma = .55). Interestingly enough, we find that a woman's education bears no statistical significance on whether or not she is married (gamma = .01), although the very uneducated are the most apt to be no longer married.

In fact, there is a high level of homogeneity within the marriages, with a gamma of .70 between education of the wife and the husband and between the husband's and wife's occupation. The wife's education does not translate into Duncan prestige as well as does the husband's, a pattern typical for American society. In spite of this, there is a strong relation between the husband's and wife's Duncan score. Twenty-eight percent of the couples have a 5-point or less difference between Duncan scores. In addition, women who married young are not apt to have highly educated husbands or to be as highly educated themselves, and the pattern repeats with late marriage and high level of schooling.

Married women in our sample are living on a higher family income than are the currently unmarried women (gamma = .75 between family income and marital status). Reflecting national figures, the women whose marriages ended in separation, divorce, or widowhood and who have not remarried tend to be the most disadvantaged in terms of background and current financial situation. They also tend to have been married to men with little schooling and low-status jobs.

Forty-eight percent of the marrieds are full-time homemakers, 15 percent work less than thirty-five hours on the job, and 37 percent are full-time workers outside the home (gamma between employment and marital status is .46). Ninety percent of the women who are not currently employed and prefer this labor force status are married. Currently married women are also disproportionately represented among women who are working part-time by preference. The combination of marital and employment status and preferred employment status leaves a large number of women in an incongruent preference and behavioral situation. A full 40 percent of the married women are unhappy with the amount of their involvement in the labor force. This fact reflects the inflexibility of the labor market as well as the problems of women with families who try to organize their homemaking and job demands in a satisfactory manner.

HELP WITH THE OCCUPATIONAL ROLES

Although activities defined as work have become organized into occupational roles in complex social systems outside the home for which an individual is hired, regardless of his or her other commitments, there is in many such jobs an awareness by employed women of possible role conflict. This conflict is expected within the American economic system to be solved by the worker by giving highest priority to occupational duties and sometimes even by the use of circle members from other roles. As discussed briefly in the first part of this chapter, many employers actually include duties and rights in the job which must be performed with the help of people outside the work organization. In the past, wives were often assumed to help a man with a job, and the argument against hiring or promoting a woman to executive positions has been not only the probability that she will face higher role conflict than experienced by a man but also that she would lack backup supports. Syfers (1977) complained that women need wives to perform all the services such nonemployed partners provide for men. Such supports may range from help with work brought home from the job, with telephone or correspondence, with keeping accounts or entertaining work associates, to the home-maintenance tasks of providing food and clothing, to very passive but personal ways, such as being a sounding board or listening (Lopata, 1971).

We asked the women in the study of role commitments not only how the wife helps the husband, but also, in the case of employed women, how the husband helps the wife. The 1977 respondents consistently present themselves as giving more help to the husband in his job-related work than receiving it from him in all areas except providing transportation (see Table 6.1). Interestingly enough, there are few, if any, differences between employed wives and those who are full-time homemakers when it comes to the areas of help supplied to the husband. Listening and acting as a sounding board is the most frequently acknowledged support to the husband, as well as the most frequent support flowing from him. This is followed by "helping prevent or ease problems in other roles," which is a restatement of the concept of role conflict (see Hunt and Hunt, 1977; Mortimer, 1980; Mortimer et al. 1976; Pleck, 1977). The most important influences upon the amount of help a wife gives her husband in connection with his job are his occupation itself, followed by, in interdependent fashion, its Duncan prestige score, his education, her education, her occupation, and its Duncan score. The husband's occupation affects especially the wife's assistance with take-home work, secretarial tasks, entertaining and preventing or easing role conflict (see Table 6.2).

Help with entertaining work-connected associates varies by social class variables more than does such assistance as "listening or acting as a sounding board," reflecting social class variations in lifestyle and occupational demands. Professional men, managers, and some sales-persons are much more apt to be involved in entertaining, whether in the home or in public places, than are men in manual or other blue-collar jobs (Kanter, 1977; Vandervelde, 1979; Whyte, 1952, 1956). As many observers have pointed out, working-class people seldom entertain anyone other than relatives in their homes (Berger, 1970; Bott, 1955; Cohen and Hodges, 1961; Komarovsky, 1967; Rainwater

TABLE 6.1 Wives and Husbands Who Help Each Other with Jobs Outside the Home

| | Wife Assists Husband | | | | Husband Assists Wife | |
| | Employee | | Homemaker | | (Employee Only) | |
Forms of Assistance	%	(n)	%	(n)	%	(n)
1. Help with take home work	20	(106)	20	(104)	10	(50)
2. Secretarial, typing	32	(171)	34	(176)	15	(77)
3. Entertaining	53	(281)	56	(287)	41	(204)
4. Transportation	24	(127)	29	(151)	40	(203)
5. Preventing or easing problems	85	(452)	84	(431)	83	(419)
6. Advice	66	(350)	63	(326)	66	(332)
7. Listening, acting as sounding board	94	(499)	91	(470)	85	(426)

TABLE 6.2 Employed Wives Who Help their Husband with His Job in Selected Ways, by Husband's Occupation

	Husband's Occupation									
	Profes-sional		Other white collar		Crafts		Other blue collar		TOTAL	
Forms of Assistance	%	(n)	%	(n)	%	(n)	%	(n)	(n)	gamma
1 Help with take home work	28	(34)	29	(58)	6	(7)	10	(9)	(108)	.40
2. Secretarial, typing	39	(48)	39	(80)	23	(26)	21	(19)	(173)	.26
3. Entertaining	58	(71)	73	(148)	25	(29)	36	(33)	(281)	.37
4. Transportation	24	(30)	28	(56)	21	(24)	19	(17)	(127)	.10
5. Preventing or easing problems	95	(117)	87	(177)	67	(77)	91	(83)	(454)	.30
6. Advice	61	(75)	70	(141)	68	(78)	63	(57)	(351)	−.02
7. Listening, acting as sounding board	92	(113)	94	(191)	95	(109)	96	(87)	(500)	−.16

et al., 1959; Rubin, 1976). The findings of Bird (1979) and Rubin (1979) that entertaining is the first thing to be given up by women when they reenter full-time employment are not fully supported by our figures. Fifty-six percent of the full-time homemakers and 53 percent of the employed wives help their husband with entertaining his job associates.

Interestingly enough, family income, with or without the wife's earnings, and her earnings alone do not influence the forms of help she gives her husband. Thus, the only significant variable besides occupation is race. However, this subject is so complex that it cannot be examined at this point.

Returning to Table 6.1, we now must look at the ways in which the husbands of married women help them with their jobs outside the home. As stated before, the help is more frequent than the assistance given to him by her only when it comes to transportation. The wife is less apt to be assisted by her husband in the entertainment of work-associated people, quite possibly because so many women do not have the kind of job that demands such behavior on their part. Few husbands provide secretarial help, again possibly because the wives do not receive job-related correspondence or phonecalls in their homes. Most frequent help is in listening to job-related problems and in decreasing role conflict, probably through homemaking or child-rearing activities.

The type of help a woman receives is influenced not only by the negotiated arrangement she has with her husband but also by her occupational demands. Table 6.3 documents not only the occupational differences but also the variations among types of supports. Professional women do not need assistance with the work they bring home any more often than do women in managerial, sales, or high clerical jobs, or else their husbands do not have the skills needed to contribute such help. The same is true of secretarial help. Women in higher-status jobs tend to talk about work-related problems more often than do high clerical or service women, but the differences here and in advice-giving are not large. Interestingly enough, it is the managers, more often than the professionals, who get help from their husbands in entertaining work associates. Only in the provision of transportation are the women in lower-prestige occupations receiving

TABLE 6.3 Employed Wives Whose Husbands Help with Their Jobs Outside the Home in Selected Ways, by Her Occupation

| | Occupation | | | | | | | | | | | | | |
| | Professional | | Managerial | | Sales | | High Clerical | | Low Clerical | | Manual | | Service | | |
Forms of Assistance	%	(n)	%	(n)	%	(n)	%	(n)	%	(n)	%	(n)	%	(n)	gamma
1. Help with take home work	15	(14)	16	(10)	14	(6)	17	(12)	4	(4)	6	(4)	4	(2)	.33
2. Secretarial, typing	28	(26)	25	(16)	10	(4)	18	(13)	10	(12)	6	(4)	7	(4)	.38
3. Entertaining	54	(50)	62	(40)	29	(12)	50	(36)	39	(44)	19	(12)	18	(10)	.35
4. Transportation	36	(33)	34	(22)	43	(18)	39	(28)	42	(48)	48	(30)	43	(24)	−.10
5. Preventing or easing problems	83	(77)	84	(54)	81	(34)	87	(63)	93	(106)	68	(42)	77	(43)	.10
6. Advice	75	(70)	81	(52)	43	(18)	69	(50)	63	(72)	61	(38)	61	(34)	.15
7. Listening, acting as sounding board	94	(87)	81	(52)	100	(42)	81	(58)	79	(90)	90	(56)	76	(43)	.20

more assistance than are their more highly placed counterparts. Thus, occupational differences operate mainly in the type of help received.

Education of both the respondent and her husband relate to many of the forms of assistance she receives from her husband. The higher her education, the more likely it is that she will receive help from her husband in the active forms of assistance such as secretarial work and entertaining work associates. Women with more education are more likely to be in occupations that require this type of help. In addition, husbands of college graduates are much more likely to act as a sounding board than husbands of women with less education. Ninety-seven percent of the college graduates say their husbands listen and act as a sounding board compared to 73 percent of those women with less than a high school education. Husbands with more education are more likely to help their wives with their jobs in all ways except providing transportation. However, husbands with some college are more apt to help with the wife's take-home work and prevent and ease problems than husbands who have graduated from college.

In spite of the internal differences in the type of help given to, and received from, the husband, summary statistics make the patterns of variation by relevant characteristics clearer. In spite of expectations that homes in which both the husband and the wife were gainfully employed and in which there were young children would require a greater exchange of job-related services than homes where there were no young children, we found no such patterns. High levels of assistance by the husband with the wife's job came both in families where there was at least one child less than three years of age (59 percent) and in homes with no child under 18 years of age (60 percent). Husbands helped much less frequently in homes with children between the ages of three and five (37 percent were in the high category) and in homes with children between five and eighteen years of age (42 percent in the high category). The presence or age of the children in the home did not affect the variety of assistance the wife gave the husband, a surprising finding, since one would assume that she would have more time and energy to help the husband in their absence. Again, these findings reinforce the prior conclusion that it is the set of occupational characteristics rather than other life circumstances which influence the giving and the receiving of assistance with a job by either the husband or the wife.

We had speculated whether there would be more exchanges by couples accustomed to the employment of the wife because she had maintained such a status at least 75 percent of the time since finishing school than in situations in which she remained outside of the labor force for extended periods of time. The association was relatively low, but present, for the help given the currently employed wife (gamma = .24), but was totally insignificant in the amount of help she gave the husband.

Help the employed wife gives the husband is affected by his occupation (gamma = $-.32$) and his Duncan occupational prestige scores (gamma = .30), as well as by the wife's occupation (gamma = $-.33$) and Duncan score (gamma = .38).[5] The help she receives from the husband, however, is not as influenced by his occupation (gamma = $-.20$) and Duncan score (gamma = .17) as by his education (gamma = .32). It is influenced by her occupation (gamma = $-.28$), her Duncan score (gamma = .32) and her education, as seen in Table 6.4, which illustrates some of the variables influencing high and low scores on the "help gives" and "help gets" scales which combine all seven areas of assistance. Education again proves to be an important influence on the total scores, but it does not make any difference whose education we used, since the distributions are very similar. The higher the schooling, the more apt the wife is to give and get multiple forms of assistance with her job from her husband.

HUSBAND'S SUPPORTIVENESS OF WIFE'S EMPLOYMENT

Since the amount of assistance husbands and wives give each other with their occupational roles is so varied by the job, we used two other measures of role supportiveness and assistance. We asked our respondents for their perceptions of their husbands' feelings about and definitions of working wives. Of course, we do not know if the wife's perception is a projection of her wishes, a means of increasing role congruence (Arnott, 1972), or the actual stance of the husband. That is not, however, our concern in this study. We want to know what are her perceptions or definitions of the husband's feelings and how these relate to her perceptions of home maintenance responsibilities and work.

TABLE 6.4 Employed and Full-time Homemaker Wives Giving and Receiving Help, by Selected Measures (in percentages)

| | Wife Assists Husband | | | | | | Husband Assists Wife | | |
| | Employee | | | Homemaker | | | (Employee Only) | | |
Attributes	Low	High	(n)	Low	High	(n)	Low	High	(n)
RACE:									
Nonwhite	42	58	(26)	69	31	(26)	48	52	(71)
White	50	50	(489)	43	57	(489)	51	49	(426)
gamma		−.16			.50			−.06	
RESPONDENT'S EDUCATION:									
Less than H.S.	56	44	(61)	56	44	(54)	63	37	(65)
H.S. graduate	58	42	(199)	51	49	(259)	56	44	(187)
Some college	37	63	(117)	37	63	(108)	56	44	(119)
College graduate	37	63	(144)	36	64	(94)	31	69	(126)
gamma		.35			.13			.30	
RESPONDENT'S LAST OR CURRENT JOB:									
Professional	39	61	(99)	41	59	(108)	42	58	(93)
Managerial	28	72	(64)	36	64	(28)	41	59	(64)
Sales	56	44	(54)	52	48	(42)	45	55	(40)
High Clerical	35	65	(86)	30	70	(88)	37	63	(70)
Low Clerical	52	48	(112)	42	58	(148)	53	47	(114)
Manual	81	19	(52)	64	36	(44)	67	33	(60)
Service	70	30	(54)	58	42	(43)	75	25	(56)
gamma		−.33			−.15			−.28	

DUNCAN SCORE OF RESPONDENT'S LAST OR CURRENT JOB:

	%	(N)	%	(N)	%	(N)
0–19	81	19 (84)	57	43 (60)	73	27 (96)
20–39	56	44 (64)	59	41 (69)	44	56 (50)
40–59	46	54 (126)	40	60 (180)	58	42 (120)
60–69	38	62 (186)	33	67 (116)	38	62 (170)
70–96	38	62 (61)	47	53 (90)	41	59 (61)
gamma	.38		.16		.32	

HUSBAND'S EDUCATION:

	%	(N)	%	(N)	%	(N)
Less than H.S.	67	33 (60)	56	44 (78)	64	36 (62)
H.S. graduate	64	36 (169)	51	49 (164)	62	38 (165)
Some college	35	65 (102)	37	63 (76)	40	60 (88)
College graduate	37	63 (190)	36	64 (195)	40	60 (182)
gamma	.38		.25		.32	

HUSBAND'S OCCUPATION:

	%	(N)	%	(N)	%	(N)
Professional	41	59 (121)	39	61 (131)	45	55 (117)
Other white collar	35	65 (195)	36	64 (166)	43	57 (175)
Crafts	69	31 (115)	59	41 (126)	58	42 (111)
Other blue collar	63	37 (89)	46	54 (92)	62	38 (91)
gamma	-.32		-.17		-.20	

DUNCAN SCORE OF HUSBAND'S JOB:

	%	(N)	%	(N)	%	(N)
0–19	61	39 (70)	45	55 (62)	63	37 (68)
20–39	60	40 (88)	51	49 (90)	60	40 (82)
40–59	64	36 (87)	41	39 (88)	45	55 (87)
60–69	36	64 (172)	35	65 (126)	45	55 (156)
70–96	39	61 (103)	37	63 (149)	46	54 (101)
gamma	.30		.17		.17	

In this series of analyses, we will concentrate on the education of the husband as the main independent variable for both theoretical and data-based reasons. Theoretically, we hypothesized that the more education a man has, the more egalitarian would be his view of women's roles, including household management, and the more these definitions would result in actual sharing of the role of homemaker between the husband and the wife. We set up this hypothesis in spite of evidence from other studies that this is not a consistent pattern (see Mainardi, 1970).

More-educated husbands have been found to hold more egalitarian definitions, but not necessarily to convert these into the sharing of homemaking responsibilities and behavior (Axelson, 1970; Bahr, 1974; Bernard, 1973, 1975a, 1975b; Deutscher, 1966; Klein, 1965). We wanted to see which of the wives perceive their husbands to be supportive to their homemaking or employment roles, and how they perceive this supportiveness when translated into actual sharing of the homemaker role, especially in homes in which there technically is no full-time homemaker (see Dahlstrom and Liljestrom, 1967; Liljestrom et al., 1975, for the Swedish situation).

As expected, the higher the husband's education, the more the employed wife perceives her husband as much less in favor of her working outside of the home (see Table 6.5). The full-time homemaker perceives her husband as much less in favor of her working outside the home. Looking at the advantages and disadvantages of having a working wife (see Table 6.6), we found a consistent tendency for employees to state that the husband thinks that "a working wife is a big help financially" and that "it is good for a woman to work and get out of the house." These perceptions are particularly true of the wives of more-educated husbands, who, of course, themselves tend to be more educated. On the other hand, over half the full-time homemakers, whose husbands are at all levels of education, think that they would find a working life to be an economic asset. Even employed women consider their husbands as not favoring working mothers with small children. This means that, regardless of the husband's level of education, there are some women employed with children who consider the husband as disapproving the fact that they work outside the home.

TABLE 6.5 Husband's Feelings About Employment of His Wife, as Perceived by the Wife, by Selected Measures (in percentages)

	Employee					Full-time Homemaker				
	Husband's Education					Husband's Education				
Perceptions	Less than H.S.	H.S. graduate	Some college	College graduate	TOTAL	Less than H.S.	H.S. graduate	Some college	College graduate	TOTAL
HUSBAND'S FEELINGS:										
Strongly in favor	40	37	48	66	48	12	8	13	29	16
Somewhat in favor	34	46	28	31	36	25	33	34	25	29
Does not care	2	3	8	2	4	9	8	13	9	10
Somewhat opposed	19	9	13	0	9	25	22	17	25	23
Strongly opposed	5	4	3	1	3	29	30	23	12	23
(n)	(116)	(258)	(131)	(210)	(715)	(130)	(213)	(94)	(217)	(654)
gamma			-.31					-.22		
HOUSEHOLD RESPONSIBILITY:										
Respondent	64	54	58	53	56	55	69	51	70	64
Shares with husband	25	37	34	45	37	37	24	45	26	30
Husband	5	5	5	1	4	5	6	4	4	5
Other	5	4	4	1	3	3	2	0	0	1
(n)	(118)	(258)	(131)	(210)	(717)	(130)	(213)	(94)	(219)	(656)
gamma			.03					-.12		
PROPORTION OF HOUSEHOLD WORK DONE BY HUSBAND:										
None	32	23	8	7	17	29	34	8	27	27
Less than 25%	24	38	60	47	42	40	52	49	52	49
25% to 100%	44	38	32	46	40	26	19	26	30	24
(n)	(118)	(258)	(131)	(210)	(717)	(130)	(213)	(94)	(219)	(656)
gamma			.16					.04		

TABLE 6.6 Husband's Agreement with Wife's Perceptions

Definitions of Wife's Employment	Husband's Education								TOTAL
	Less than H.S.		H.S. graduate		Some college		College graduate		gamma
	%	(n)	%	(n)	%	(n)	%	(n)	
1. Husband should be breadwinner	65	(77)	55	(142)	43	(56)	55	(116)	.10
2. Women should not work when preschool children are home	65	(75)	69	(178)	63	(83)	76	(158)	-.11
3. Working makes women too independent	42	(49)	36	(92)	22	(29)	14	(30)	.39
4. Working wife is a big help financially	76	(90)	78	(200)	86	(113)	85	(178)	-.18
5. Good for women to get out of the house	77	(89)	75	(193)	74	(97)	91	(190)	-.26
6. Husband should share housework with working wife	53	(63)	57	(147)	61	(80)	75	(157)	-.25
Full-time Homemaker									
1. Husband should be breadwinner	83	(106)	76	(161)	77	(72)	63	(137)	.27
2. Women should not work when preschool children are home	92	(116)	85	(181)	85	(80)	79	(169)	.26
3. Working makes women too independent	43	(54)	35	(73)	28	(26)	17	(36)	.36
4. Working wife is a big help financially	50	(64)	53	(113)	47	(44)	56	(122)	-.06
5. Good for women to get out of the house	41	(52)	44	(94)	55	(52)	63	(136)	-.28
6. Husband should share housework with working wife	52	(68)	52	(111)	73	(66)	59	(129)	-.12

There is a very noteworthy disparity between all the definitions of working wives and the statement that the husband "feels husbands should share the household work when the wife has a job." The husband's general supportiveness of the wife's employment is strongly related to the individual definitions for both working and nonworking women, except for the statement concerning housework sharing. That definition of what the husband should do is completely disassociated from the benefits and role competition constraints. When these variables are rotated in a factor matrix, we find that they cluster very clearly around an index of employment supportiveness and an index of dependency supportiveness. The most salient item for the employment supportiveness factor is the statement that it is a good idea for the wife to get out of the house, while the dependency supportiveness factor centers on the husband's self-definition as the breadwinner. The husband's perceived supportiveness and definitions of working women are strongly related to individual items for the nonworking women. The least difference between the full-time homemakers and the employees is on the, possibly less value-laden, item that the wife is a big help financially. It thus appears that the full-time homemakers may need to defend their employment status by reference to the husband's attitudes and definitions more than the employees. If this conclusion is true, it may be a good indication of the changing commitments of women to family and work roles, or to the ability of employed women to differentiate among perceived attitudes of the husband and be less swayed by them. Of course, the more-educated women are the ones who are more apt to both be in the labor force and see their husbands as supportive of such action.

HOUSEHOLD MANAGEMENT

The supportiveness for the homemaking or employee roles of wives does not automatically transfer into a belief that the husband should share the rights and duties of the homemaking role just because the wife has maintained or added the role of worker outside the home (see also Hoffman and Nye, 1974; Klein, 1965; Myrdal and Klein, 1968; Perrucci et al., 1978; Pleck, 1977; Rubin, 1976; Shostak, 1969; Weingarten, 1978). The incongruence between stated opinion and actual behavior is maintained for those husbands who agree that a husband should share housework when the wife is employed. Of those husbands who agree with the statement and have wives who work outside the home, 42 percent are perceived as doing less than 25 percent of the housework, and 83 percent of these wives feel their husbands do less than half the work around the house.

In only 5 percent of the homes when the wife is a full-time homemaker is the husband defined as the person who has the main responsibility for running the household (see Table 6.5). In 64 percent of such homes, it is mainly the wife's duty, while in 31 percent of the cases it is shared. The employment of the woman makes little difference for the distribution of homemaking responsibility, as numerous authors have pointed out (Bahr, 1974; Bernard, 1971). The husband has the responsibility for household management in 4 percent of the households in which the wife is employed, the wife in 66 percent, and it is shared in 37 percent (see also Blood and Wolfe, 1960; Glazer-Malbin, 1976; Myrdal and Klein, 1968; Rapoport and Rapoport, 1976). Only 8 out of 656 married full-time homemakers and 23 out of the 717 employed women share household management with a child or another adult. The women most apt to take the full responsibility for household management are the unemployed wives of high school or college graduates. The employed women are less apt to claim full responsibility if the husband is highly educated, but more often if he has not finished high school. In this particular study, the wife's perception that she shares responsibility with her husband is not deeply affected by the husband's education, occupation, or the Duncan prestige score of his job, which goes against some findings of the other studies (Bahr, 1974; Berk and Berk, 1979; Weingarten, 1978). Of course, taking responsibility is not the same as the division of labor or getting "help with," which is what other studies primarily investigated (Farkas, 1976). Although not statistically significant, the relation of the locus of responsibility and the husband's Duncan scores are varied at the extremes, in the direction other research measured. Fifty-nine percent of women married to men at the bottom of the scale (0 to 19) compared to 70 percent of those married to men at the top (70 to 96) take full credit for the management of the home if they are full-time homemakers. This compares to a difference from 52 to 59 percent for the employed women.

When it comes to actual work, the women were asked: "Considering all of the cooking, cleaning, grocery shopping and child care that needs to be done each week, what percentage of this work would you say your husband does?" Because only 7 percent of the husbands did 50 percent or more of the housework, it was necessary to combine several categories for our analysis. We find, again, that the lower-educated husbands of full-time housewives or employees are the most apt to be designated as not helping at all (see Table 6.5). More than four times as many of the most-educated husbands than the least-educated do at least some work around the house if the wife is employed, but there is little difference among them if she is a full-time homemaker. For some unexplained reason, the husbands who had some college education but did not graduate are most involved in household work when the wife is not employed. Of course, this is the wife's report, and her perceptions may vary considerably by social class and the expectations resulting from other life circumstances.

In addition to these measures of the husband's behavior concerning housework, the women were asked questions concerning financial decision-making within the family. In 18 percent of the respondents' families, the wife mainly decides how to spend the family income and in 13 percent of the families that responsibility is primarily the husband's. The great majority (76 percent) share the responsibility. The financial decision-making of employed women was more affected than that of full-time homemakers by husband's and wife's education and occupation. Financial decision-making is most likely to be shared in households where husbands have some college. This tendency is more pronounced in households with employed wives than in those with full-time homemakers. When the husband has a lower level of education, the wife is more likely to take responsibility for the family's financial decisions. There is some question concerning the meaning of this responsibility for the wife. Some authors contend that it measures power within the marriage (Bird, 1979; Blood and Wolfe, 1960; Blood, 1969; Safilios-Rothschild, 1972), while others believe that wives have that responsibility primarily because a large part of the family income is going toward nondiscretionary items, usually decided upon by the person in charge of the household (Epstein, 1970; Lopata, 1971).

The employed wives were also asked who decides how to use the money they earn. Forty percent of the wives make that decision, and 57 percent of them share the decision of how to spend their earnings with their husbands. Wives whose husbands have some college are more likely than those whose husbands reached other educational levels to make the decision by themselves.

SUMMARY AND CONCLUSIONS

The image of the traditional family is based on supposed segregation between the home sphere, run by the woman, and the public sphere, run by the man. However, there is no way in actual life these can be easily separated. First, many careers have been built around two-person jobs which require both members of the marital partnership. Second, more women are becoming part of the public sphere and are requiring more assistance in the home. In addition, there is a growing ideology of sharing, as described by Pleck (1977). These factors lead to the realization that there is an interweave between the roles men and women perform both inside and outside the home. In this chapter, we have examined the woman's perception of the interdependence and the interweave between her roles as wife to an employed husband, as an employee herself, and as part of a homemaking team (Bird, 1979; Papanek, 1973). The whole analysis is dependent upon the wife's perception, in other words, the reality she has constructed about the interweave of these roles.

Both the amount of assistance and the types of help the wife gives her husband are more affected by his occupation, Duncan prestige score, and educational level. For example, it is mainly the characteristics of his occupation which influence his need for entertaining work associates in a style that often involves couple companionate interaction (Lopata, 1979; Znaniecki, 1965). In general, full-time homemakers, who assumably have more time than do full-time women employees, actually do not perceive themselves as offering more help to their husbands with their jobs. The perceptions of the women workers are more influenced by both their education and their husband's education and occupation than are those of the home-makers. This is particularly true of the women employees with a lower educational and occupational level, who are less apt than are their homemaking counterparts to perceive themselves as helping the husband. When we look at the occupations of the husbands and the working wives, and the former occupations of the full-time home-makers, we find a very interesting pattern. The former women em-ployees in all types of occupations other than managerial and profes-sional are more likely to consider that they help their husbands with their jobs than are the current women employees.

Most women who work outside the home perceive themselves as giving the husband more help with his job than he gives her with her job. The only assistance which the wives report receiving more often than giving is transportation, and this support is more frequent among the lower socioeconomic couples. Wives report giving help with entertainment and secretarial tasks much more often than receiving it. It is possible that this asymmetry in the flow of assistance is because many occupations in which men are concentrated assume a two-person career or worker situation, with the wife being expected to provide help, much as described by Coser (1974). Women tend to work in occupations which are not built upon the same set of assump-tions. The other possibility is that the marriage initially started with the flow of help going to the husband while the wife's job involve-ment was perceived as peripheral (Bird, 1979). The wife's continued employment or return to work may not modify this pattern. Occupa-tion and education of both the wife and the husband influence the type and amount of assistance she receives from him with her job. Women managers and, to a lesser extent, professionals, get help with enter-tainment and advice more than do women in other jobs. However, women in these jobs report less direct assistance with the job than wives of professional and managerial men report giving their hus-bands. However, both men and women at these occupational levels are reported as receiving the same amount of indirect support.

The higher the educational and occupational levels of the husband and the wife, the more positively the woman perceives her husband's feelings toward her working and his definitions of working women in general. One of the interesting findings is that these perceptions on the part of the wife are not associated in any significant way with his agreement with the statement that the "husband should share household work when the wife has a job." Even husbands who appear to favor the wife's work to the extent of agreeing with that statement do not carry that opinion into behavior. Very few of the wives report that their husbands carry the main responsibility for household management, but the higher the education of the husband, the more the responsibility is shared between husband and wife if both are employed. This does not hold true for the full-time homemakers. In households with a full-time homemaker, it is mainly the wife's responsibility for household management if the husband is a college graduate; it is more likely to be shared if the husband has some college. This is not true of households in which the wife is also a full-time employee, which lends some support to the two-person career theory.

Lower-educated husbands are least apt to actually help in the household, whether the wife is employed or not. The fact that wives of more educated husbands report them as helping more than wives of less-schooled men goes somewhat contrary to the current stereotype of the educated man being supportive verbally but not necessarily actually sharing in household work. However, it must be remembered that the amount of work the husbands do is minimal in the vast majority of the households. Financial management is more apt to be shared in families in which the wife is employed than if she is a full-time homemaker.

Using regression techniques, very little of the variance in assistance with job-related activities, homemaking responsibility, or husband supportiveness was explained by income or background variables such as race, education, or occupation. Cross-tabular analysis lends some interesting insights into the difference in the interweave of roles among the women in the sample. The basic contribution of this analysis of work patterns of Chicago-area women aged twenty-five to fifty-four is in showing the interweave between the roles of wife, employee, and homemaker. In examining the role of wife, we find a tendency for the traditional format in which the wife reports assisting the husband with his job more often than she reports his helping her with her job. In examining the relationship between the role of wife and homemaker, we find the woman reporting assistance given to the husband with his job while carrying the major responsibility for household maintenance. If she is working outside the home, she still reports giving the husband more help than she receives from him with the job, while the household management and work are still not shared evenly. Employed wives do not report helping their husbands less than do full-time homemakers. Education and occupation are important influences on assistance given by the husband and wife on the job, and her perceptions of his supportiveness of women's employment, but the differences are slight when it comes to household responsibilities and work.

NOTES

1. Of course, other times and societies, including those of ancient Greek, Chinese, and Islamic civilizations (see Sullerot, 1971 and numerous other histories of the status of women), have also cut the human world sharply into two spheres. We are concentrating here on the consequences of social change in the past century and a half or so in Western Europe and especially in America.

2. We are, of course, aware of Safilios-Rothschild's (1969) criticism of family sociology as being too dependent upon the study of wives and neglectful of the husband's perspectives. This study is not so much oriented at family sociology as it is on the reality constructed by American urban women. It is thus not concerned in determining "objective" reality, only the world which women have defined for themselves and in which they thus live. Capitalizing on the twenty years of past study of American women by the senior author, it focuses on the perceptions of American society, men and women, the job, the husband's definitions and feelings, and themselves. It would be interesting to examine the world construction of the husbands, but that is a different study.

The pervasiveness of the American assumption that a woman = housewife and needs support in order to work outside of the home and that a man = worker became obvious when our research team of men and women burst out in laughter when we suggested that the interview should, in order to maintain symmetry, include questions on the woman's supportiveness toward her husband's employment outside the home.

3. Research on the changing commitments of women to work and family roles has been funded by the Social Security Administration (Contract SSA600-75-0190, 1975–1979). Dr. Henry P. Brehm was the project officer, Helena Znaniecka Lopata, principal investigator, and Kathleen Fordham Norr, research coordinator. Interviews were conducted by the staff of the Survey Research Laboratory of the University of Illinois, Circle Campus, with Ron Czaja as project director. Our thanks also go to Marlene Simon, Cheryl Miller, Suzanne Meyering, and Jennifer Ettling of the Center for the Comparative Study of Social Roles, Loyola University of Chicago, for their contributions to various stages of the research.

4. The universe for this study consisted of all women aged twenty-five to fifty-four residing in the Chicago Standard Metropolitan Statistical Area. A stratified random sample with over-sampling for unmarried women was taken, and personal interviews were conducted in 1977 and early 1978 with an interview completion rate of 71.9 percent. The actual interviews total 996, and when appropriately weighted represent 1877 women. Details of samplings and findings are contained in our final report to the Social Security Administration, June 1979.

5. A Duncan occupational prestige score, developed by the social scientists at the National Opinion Research Center of the University of Chicago, is assigned to all occupations. The scale ranges from 1 to 100, with jobs of lower prestige receiving lower scores.

REFERENCES

ALDOUS, J. (1969) "Occupational characteristics and males' role performance in the family." Journal of Marriage and Family 31: 707–712.

ARIES, P. (1965) Centuries of Childhood. New York: Random House.

ARNOTT, C. (1972) "Husbands' attitude and wives' commitment to employment." Journal of Marriage and Family 34 (November): 673–684.

AXELSON, L. (1970) "The working wife: differences in perception among Negro and white males." Journal of Marriage and Family 32 (August): 457–463.

BAHR, S. J. (1974) "Effects on power and division of labor in the family," pp. 167–185 in L. W. Hoffman and F. I. Nye (eds.) Working Mothers. San Francisco: Jossey-Bass.

BERGER, B. M. (1960) Working Class Suburb. Berkeley: University of California Press.

BERGER, P. and H. KELLNER (1970) "Marriage and the construction of reality: exercise in the microsociology of knowledge," pp. 50–73 in H. Dreitzel (ed.) Patterns of Communicative Behavior. London: Collier-Macmillan.

BERGER, P. and T. LUCKMANN (1966) The Social Construction of Reality. Garden City, NY: Doubleday.

BERK, R. A. and S. F. BERK (1979) Labor and Leisure at Home: Content and Organization of the Household Day. Beverly Hills: Sage.

BERNARD, J. (1971) "The status of women in modern patterns of culture," pp. 11–20 in C. F. Epstein and W. J. Goode (eds.) The Other Half: Roads to Woman's Equality. Englewood Cliffs, NJ: Prentice-Hall.

———— (1973) The Future of Marriage. New York: Bantam.

———— (1975a) Women, Wives, Mothers: Values and Options. Chicago: Aldine.

———— (1975b) The Future of Motherhood. New York: Penguin.

BIRD, C. (1979) The Two-Paycheck Marriage. New York: Rawson, Wade.

BLOOD, R. O., Jr. (1969) Marriage. New York: Free Press.

———— and D. M. WOLFE (1960) Husbands and Wives. New York: Free Press.

BOTT, E. (1955) "Urban families: conjugal roles and social networks." Human Relations 8: 345–384.

BRYSON, J. G. and R. BRYSON [eds.] (1978) Dual-Career Couples. New York: Human Sciences.

CARDOZO, A. R. (1976) Woman at Home. Garden City, NY: Doubleday.

COHEN, A. K. and H. M. HODGES (1961) "Characteristics of the lower blue-collar class." Social Problems 10: 303–333.

COSER, L. (1974) Greedy Institutions. New York: Free Press.

COSER, R. (1975) "Stay home little Sheba: on placement, displacement and social change." Social Problems 22: 470–479.

DAHLSTROM, E. and R. LILJESTROM (1967) "The family and married women at work," pp. 19–58 in E. Dahlstrom (ed.) The Changing Roles of Men and Women. London: Duckworth.

DEUTSCH, H. (1944) The Psychology of Women. New York: Grune & Stratton.

DEUTSCHER, I. (1966) "Words and deeds: social science and social policy." Social Problems 15: 235–254.

EASTON, B. L. (1976) "Industrialization and femininity: a case study of nineteenth century New England." Social Problems 23: 389–401.

EPSTEIN, C. F. (1970) Women's Place: Options and Limits in Professional Careers. Berkeley: University of California Press.

FARKAS, G. (1976) "Education, wage rates and the division of labor between husband and wife." Journal of Marriage and Family 38: 473–483.

FOGARTY, M., R. RAPOPORT, and R. N. RAPOPORT (1971) Sex, Career and Family. Beverly Hills: Sage.

FRIEDAN, B. (1964) The Feminine Mystique. New York: W. W. Norton.

GARLAND, T. H. (1972) "The better half? The male in the dual profession family," pp. 199–215 in C. Safilios-Rothschild (ed.) Toward the Sociology of Women. Lexington, MA: Xerox.

GAVRON, H. (1966) The Captive Wife: Conflicts of Housebound Mothers. London: Routledge & Kegan Paul.

GLAZER-MALBIN, N. (1976) "Housework." Signs 1: 905–922.

GLICK, P. (1957) American Families. New York: John Wiley.

GOODE, W. J. (1963) World Revolution and Family Patterns. New York: Free Press.

HELFRICH, M. (1961) "The generalized role of the executive's wife." Marriage and Family Living 23: 384–387.

HOFFMAN, L. W. and F. I. Nye [eds.] (1974) Working Mothers. New York: Jossey-Bass.

HOLMSTROM, L. (1972) The Two-Career Family. Cambridge, MA: Schenkman.

HUNT, J. G. and L. L. HUNT (1977) "Dilemmas and contradictions of status: the case of the dual-career family." Social Problems 24: 407–416.

KANTER, R. M. (1977) Men and Women of the Corporation. New York: Basic Books.

KLEIN, V. (1965) "Women workers: a survey in 21 countries." (unpublished)

KOMAROVSKY, M. (1967) Blue-Collar Marriage. New York: Random House.

LASLETT, P. (1971) The World We Have Lost: England Before the Industrial Age. New York: Charles Scribner's.

LERNER G. (1969) "The lady and the mill girl: changes in the status of women in the age of Jackson." American Studies Journal 10: 5–15.

LILJESTROM, R., G. F. MELLSTROM, and L. L. SVENSSON (1975) Sex Roles in Transition. Sweden: Swedish Institution.

LOPATA, H. Z. (1964) "A restatement of the relation between role and status." Sociology and Social Research 49: 58–68.

——— (1965) "The secondary features of a primary relationship." Human Organization 24: 116–123.

——— (1966) "The life cycle of the social role of housewife." Sociology and Social Research 51: 4–22.

——— (1971) Occupation: Housewife. New York: Oxford University Press.

——— (1973) Widowhood in an American City. Cambridge, MA: Schenkman.

_____ (1979) Women as Widows: Support Systems. New York: Elsevier North-Holland.

LUNDBERG, F. and M. F. FARNHAM (1947) Modern Woman: The Lost Sex. New York: Harper & Row.

MACK, R. (1956) "Occupational determinateness: a problem and hypotheses in role theory." Social Forces 35: 20–24.

MAINARDI, P. (1970) "The politics of housework," in R. Morgan (ed.) Sisterhood Is Powerful. New York: Vintage.

MORTIMER, J. (1980) "Occupation-family linkages as perceived by men in the early stages of professional and managerial careers," pp. 99–117 in H. Z. Lopata (ed.) Research in the Interweave of Social Roles: Women and Men. Greenwich. CT: JAI.

_____ R. HALL and R. HILL (1976) "Husband's occupational attitudes as constraints on wife's employment." Presented at the American Sociological Association meetings.

MYRDAL, A. and V. KLEIN (1968) Women's Two Roles. New York: Humanities.

NYE, F. I. and L. W. Hoffman (1963) The Employed Mother in America. Chicago: Rand McNally.

OAKLEY, A. (1974a) Women's Work: A History of the Housewife. New York: Pantheon.

_____ (1974b) The Sociology of Housework. Bath, Eng.: Pitman.

PAPANEK, H. (1973) "Men, women and work: reflections on the two-person career." American Journal of Sociology 78: 852–872.

PERRUCCI, C., H. POTTER, and D. RHOADS (1978) "Determinants of male family-role performance." Psychology of Women Quarterly 3: 53–66.

PLECK, J. (1977) "The work-family role system." Social Problems 24: 417–427.

POLOMA, M. (1972) "Role conflict and the married professional woman," in C. Safilios-Rothschild (ed.) Toward a Sociology of Women. Lexington, MA: Xerox.

_____ and N. GARLAND (1970) "The myth of the egalitarian family: familial roles and the professionally employed wife." Presented at the American Sociological Association meetings.

RAINWATER, L., R. COLEMAN, and G. HANDEL (1959) Workingman's Wife. New York: Oceana.

RAPOPORT, R. and R. N. RAPOPORT (1976) Dual-Career Families: New Integrations of Work and Family. New York: Harper & Row.

RIESMAN, D., N. GLAZER, and R. DENNY (1950) The Lonely Crowd. New Haven: Yale University Press.

RUBIN, L. (1976) Worlds of Pain: Life in a Working Class Family. New York: Basic Books.

_____ (1979) Women of a Certain Age: The Midlife Search for Self. New York: Harper & Row.

SAFILIOS-ROTHSCHILD, C. (1969) "Family sociology or wives' family sociology?" Journal of Marriage and Family 31: 290–301.

_____ (1972) Toward a Sociology of Women. Lexington, MA: Xerox.

SCHULTZ, T. W. [ed.] (1974) Economics of the Family. Chicago: University of Chicago Press.

SHEA, N. (1941) The Army Wife. New York: Harper & Row.

SHOSTAK, A. B. (1969) Blue-Collar Life. New York: Random House.

SICHERMAN, B. (1975) "Review essay: American history." Signs 1: 461–485.

SULLEROT, E. (1971) Woman, Society and Change. New York: McGraw-Hill.

SYFERS, J. (1977) "I want a wife," pp. 91–92 in J. P. Wiseman (ed.) People as Partners. San Francisco: Harper & Row.

SZALAI, A. [ed.] (1972) The Use of Time: Daily Activities of Urban and Suburban Populations in Twelve Countries. The Hague: Mouton.

VANDERVELDE, M. (1979) The Changing Life of the Corporate Wife. New York: Mecox.

VEROFF, J. and S. FELD (1970) Marriage and Work in America: A Study of Motives and Roles. Princeton, NJ: Van Nostrand Reinhold.

WEINGARTEN, K. (1978) "The employment pattern of professional couples and their distribution of involvement in the family." Psychology of Women Quarterly 3: 43–52.

WELTER, B. (1966) "The cult of true womanhood: 1820–1860." American Quarterly 18: 151–160.

WHYTE, W. H., Jr. (1952) "The wife problem," in C. F. Epstein and W. J. Goode (eds.) The Other Half: Roads to Women's Equality. Englewood Cliffs, NJ: Prentice-Hall.

———— (1956) The Organization Man. New York: Simon & Schuster.

ZNANIECKI, F. (1965) Social Relations and Social Roles. San Francisco: Harper & Row.

7

PARENTHOOD, MARRIAGE, AND CAREERS: SITUATIONAL CONSTRAINTS AND ROLE STRAIN

Colleen Leahy Johnson
Frank A. Johnson

Today there is a widespread cultural mandate among members of the upper-middle class that bright and talented women should not bury their talents in domestic and child-rearing concerns. Instead, they should compete with men by engaging in high-commitment careers. At the same time, women are still expected to marry, to have children, and to retain their stereotypic femininity. In order to satisfy these incongruent cultural directives, increasing numbers of men and women are attempting to fashion a new family form where both partners are engaged in dual roles which demand an extraordinary expenditure of time and energy. These couples are faced not only with dissonant cultural mandates, but also with a widely publicized myth that professional opportunities are equally open to women, a belief which flies in the face of current statistics on women's entrance into high-level positions in business and the professions.

In an earlier paper, we discussed the nature of role strain women experience when they simultaneously attempt to engage in high-pressure careers as they raise their children (Johnson and Johnson, 1976). In this review, we summarized some of the social-scientific literature which abundantly documented the high normative expectations for women to continue performing domestic functions in addition to their career roles. Women experience a proliferation of roles rather than an orderly transition from one role to another, and thus are vulnerable to role strain (Goode, 1960; Merton, 1957; Coser and Rokoff, 1971). We concluded that role strain is significantly higher for wives than for husbands and that these women are less successful at using the techniques for resolving role strain which are employed by men. For example, career women are less able to compartmentalize their roles in order to leave the demands of the career role at the doorstep or put the domestic role on the back shelf when career demands are most pressing. The delegation of some roles, another technique to reduce role strain, is more difficult for career mothers due to both psychological and social pressures which are gender specific.

The psychoanalytic literature on sex role identity, also reviewed in the earlier paper, has recently gone beyond earlier formulations on phallic envy to speculate on critical points in sex role identity in the developmental cycle (Lerner, 1973; Jaffe, 1968). In the process of ego individuation from the mother, a male child must, in one sense, devalue the female role to establish gender role identity. This devaluation continues to influence his attitudes toward women in later life. At the same time, he retains a dependency on a female to satisfy his needs for nurturance. The female child, on the other hand, undergoes the same devaluation experience in her ego individuation from the mother. Unlike the male, this devaluation cannot be projected onto the opposite gender, but instead is incorporated as a central component of her gender identity and later sex role. This literature is extremely useful in tracing the psychological origins of women's susceptibility to the conscious and unconscious need to satisfy the nurturant needs of others. When these psychological differences in the original formation of ego development are compounded with the sex-linked normative strictures on the female role, the results are frequently an asymmetry and unbalanced dependency in dual-career families which persists despite the best intention of couples to distribute workloads of the family.

Our later research on parenting roles in twenty-eight dual-career families tended to document these propositions (Johnson and Johnson, 1977). Women continue to bear primary responsibility for child rearing at the same time that they are actively engaged in careers. Their greatest problems are guilt and anxiety over perceived failures in mothering. In contrast, the husbands, while quite supportive of their wives' endeavors, approached these pressing demands from a more rational, nonemotional perspective, so they did not bear the emotional costs of role strain so prominent among the wives. In other words, individuals continued to act out the sex roles established early in life.

Nevertheless, dual-career families have developed strategies to meet the many constraints and strains, strategies which meet with varying degrees of success. In this chapter, we are priimarily concerned with these opposing ideologies on parenthood, marriage, and career and the pressure they place on these families. We will also examine the techniques needed to negotiate among these competing demands within the present social constraints of our middle-class family system.

THE FAMILY SYSTEM

An ambitious young woman who strives for career success has several initial options. She can determine the level of social complexity in her system of primary relationships, a decision which will later determine the degree that competing role demands will impinge upon her. At the minimal level of complexity, she can forego marriage and motherhood and concentrate her energies toward a career in an uncomplicated personal environment. This option was frequently exercised by professional women in the past, and recent demographic patterns suggest that significant numbers of young women are electing this option (Astin, 1969).

At an intermediate level of complexity, a woman may choose

marriage but decide against having children, so that the most serious problems facing her have to do with resolving competing career demands such as deciding which career takes precedence when one partner must change jobs and move to another city. While this situation can cause serious problems in a marriage, the stakes in the marriage presumably are lower in the absence of children. As the divorce rate suggests, individuals can, however, cycle in and out of marriages to resolve some of these issues, an option exercised more often in childless marriages.

As a third option, women who aspire to both marriage and motherhood simultaneously with a career are faced with the most complex personal environment unless they can sequence the most demanding events in their careers and their families. Sequencing means that women can cycle their roles by opting for an interrupted career when the demands of motherhood become compelling.

At the most extreme end of this continuum are those women who choose all three roles, career, marriage, and motherhood, and who reject role-cycling in and out of either their careers or their marriages. These women who have uninterrupted careers and marriages have the most potential demands upon them. Studying their adaptations should furnish insights into unusual adaptive strategies. The problem in doing so, as any researchers on the topic will attest, is that there are few such arrangements that have persisted throughout the child-rearing years. Most women have either lowered their career aspirations during the peak years of child rearing (Broscart, 1978) or have sequenced their personal lives over several marriages. This conclusion is supported by studies indicating that successful women today are more likely to be childless, divorced, or permanently unmarried (Astin, 1969).

This situation is understandable when one considers the dominant features of the upper-middle-class family system. For one thing, the family is more nucleated and isolated from the kinship unit than is the case in working-class families (Parsons, 1949). As a result, increasing expectations are focused on the marital relationship as a source for fulfilling emotional, intellectual, sexual, and social needs. This increasing specialization of the family as a unit for satisfying emotional needs is an unstable base upon which to build a marriage, for expectations between the husband and wife can be too high, and there are not always objective means by which they can be met (Rostow, 1965).

This situation is accentuated in dual-career families we studied (Johnson and Johnson, 1977). The majority turned to their spouses rather than other relatives to meet many of their emotional needs. One explanation offered centered on the greater need to exclude those relatives whose norms on the family favored a more traditional gender-based division of labor. These couples tended to associate with others who shared their views on family life. Grandparents and other older relatives who potentially might have been a good source of support in child care were often excluded because they resided away from the nuclear family or because they expressed disapproval of the wives' absences from the home. One way that some dual-career couples resolved this guilt-laden situation with their parents was to exclude them from close participation in their lives, in the process also excluding any support they might have given.

Irrespective of work commitment, this type of family system has fewer resources, because there are only two adults to meet the needs of children, rather than an array of auxiliary relatives who can help in the event of an emergency. When both these adults also have high career commitments, there are slender resources to meet unexpected needs of children. Most two-career families are competent in working out methodical arrangements for domestic work and child care. However, non-familial child care resources are minimal. If the family's social networks also do not have backup personnel to meet unanticipated situations, the dual-career family can easily become overextended.

In our research, we found that role strain, while pervasive, is situationally induced. Life might proceed smoothly as long as no additional demands are placed on the family. Because there is little leeway in their time and energy resources to meet additional demands, however, even a relatively unimportant event can overload the parents—particularly the mother (Rapoport and Rapoport, 1969). A school strike or snow day or a babysitter who comes down with the flu can raise havoc at breakfast. More serious problems at work or illnesses at home can cause the most carefully planned arrangements to disintegrate. It is at this time that the division of labor in the family is called into most serious question and, of course, we find that women are the ones who usually revert to the traditonal role arrangements at the expense of their careers.

THE MARITAL ROLES

Clearly, dual-career families with young children need an inter-changeable role system, particularly when they have few surrogates to perform domestic functions. This system refers to a *symmetrical* relationship, where both partners alternately perform the same roles and share them on an equal basis (Lederer and Jackson, 1968). Ide-ally, either a husband or a wife could handle an unanticipated domes-tic need depending on their work demands at the time. Despite this "ideal," no research to date documents the prevalence of such a role allocation (Clark et al., 1978). The norms on gender roles appear to be so pervasive that it is the wife who usually succumbs to the domestic role priority, while the husband continues his career role. Traditional arrangements, in fact, are apparently so durable that even among unmarried couples living together the females have primary responsibility for domestic roles (Stafford et al., 1977).

Although the need for equality and role interchangeability is pro-nounced, one cannot overlook the functionality of the more conven-tional, *complementary* role relationship present in many marriages. In contrast to the sharing and equality attempted in supposedly sym-metrical relationships, the more complementary union maximizes the differences between partners who perform different functions, but those which fit into a totality of family needs. In conventional mar-riages, this arrangement usually means that the man is the primary wage earner and the wife, the housekeeper and mother. An interde-pendent relationship results which can be quite efficient in fulfilling the basic functions of the family. Similarly, certain chores within the home are allocated on the basis of traditional gender norms, an ar-rangement which is more strongly endorsed by our normative sys-tem. It also receives more social approval than the symmetrical rela-tionships which are often the brunt of jokes on the castrating woman or the henpecked husband.

In dual-career families, however, the traditional division of labor is impractical, because the demands from work and home fluctuate and simultaneously affect both partners. More typical arrangements among career parents include role interchangeability and usually a day-to-day allocation of domestic responsibilities, depending upon each one's career responsibilities. Hence, the most mundane matter, such as who takes a child to a dentist or waits in the morning for the late babysitter to arrive, is potentially negotiable. Practically all areas of family life can be intermittently subject to surveillance and arbitration about "who does what," since all functions with the house are hypothetically assigned to both partners. Even with nonconflictual issues, such negotiation takes time. On conflictual matters, the negotiation may degenerate into petty arguments about who has the busier day, who is more "important," or who is wearier.

Unlike the separate-but-equal myth, which sustains more conventional marriages, dual-career partners may be faced with continual conflict over power, so that competition becomes quite pronounced. In themselves, high commitment careers are learned and conducted in a highly competitive atmosphere. Both participants must maintain a level of productivity which can equal or outdistance their colleagues. To have both marital partners engage in these careers often extends this competitiveness into the intimately and reciprocal interaction in the marriage.

Obviously, in such a situation, competitive strivings cannot be blandly neutralized at the doorstep. From the point of view of the career, competition might center on who has the higher degree of prestige, who is publishing more articles or making more money or even who is aging more gracefully. Since the principles of homogeny in mate selection predict that these couples have similar types of careers, the potential for conflict is heightened (Kerkoff, 1964).

This formidable but often covert conflict is compounded by competition, rivalry, and negotiation associated with conceivably every function within the family, since so many functions are at least hypothetically shared. Competition is latent or imminent in each partner's competence in budget management, meal preparation, consumership, the quality of parental nuturance, and sex. (A clinical view of sexual functioning in dual-career families has been reported by Johnson et al., 1978.)

Both social and psychological mechanisms are available to handle this ambivalent situation in order to minimize conflict, and we will turn to these in our conclusion. At this point it is only appropriate to conclude that a major reason that the conventional complementary role system persists to some degree despite the best intentions of both husbands and wives in two-career families has a great deal to do with the characteristics of the "symmetrical" relationship and its potential for producing conflict and competition. Neither partner is usually prepared for—nor can tolerate—the potential conflict which accompanies a marriage where roles are not clearly allocated. Unfortunately, however, the constraints imposed usually impede the career advancement of the wife, not the husband, because of the endurance of norms on gender roles.

THE FEMALE ROLE AND CONSTRAINTS
UPON CAREERS

Career women who also have families have some constraints imposed upon them over which they have little control, for they cannot be solved by rearrangements of roles within the family. The institutional constraints are the most prominent area where prejudice and discrimination impede women's advancement. The exclusionary policies which impede access to and advancement in high-status careers have not yet been visibly affected by strong affirmative action programs. Women continue to work at lower-level jobs and at less pay, while opportunities for advancement still seem to elude them. Although there has been a significant increase in the percentage of young women in professional and academic positions, it is too early to tell whether they will go on to compete on an equal footing with men in terms of promotion and economic reward.

One can assign blame to the victim (because "women are different") or onto the society (because "men are chauvinistic"), but neither projection appears to be an adequate explanation, for apparently there are numerous social and psychological factors operating together to impede the advancement of women (Bryson and Bryson, 1978). The women's movement has certainly furthered their interests, but it also has created as system of rising expectations because of the wide-spread assumption that women today can do anything. In dual-career families where there are young children, the women are likely to experience more strain than the men not only because of the additive nature of their role set, but also because of the incongruence between assumptions of equality and the reality of achieving career goals. Such a woman must accommodate not only the demands of her career needs, but also those of the needs of her husband and her children. She is a member of a family system which has a minimal natural support system, while her marital role has only vague definitions of how tasks should be allocated. In this ambiguous situation, she is more likely to face prejudice, discrimination, and delayed career advancement. It is no wonder, then, that the problems of dual-career families are basically problems for women. It should be re-emphasized, however, that the many sources of strain are most prom-inent during the peak years of child rearing, so that there is usually a diminishing potential for role strain as children mature and become independent.

PARENTAL ROLES AND CONTEMPORARY CHILD REARING

The past twenty-five years of child rearing have sometimes been termed the Spockian Era because of the popularity of one school of child-rearing advice. Dr. Spock and other child-rearing experts have popularized a watered-down rendition of psychoanalytic theory, which reflects changing attitudes and behavior toward the developing child (Wolfenstein, 1955; Slater, 1974; Storr, 1972). Unlike guides at other points in history, these manuals have had much influence on attitudes and behavior toward child rearing, since techniques are not generally transmitted in an orderly process from mother to daughter. Instead, the educated mother is more likely to turn to "expert" opin-ion and to seek an intellectualized approach to child rearing. Such a discontinuous process has enlarged and complicated the content of the mother's role (Rossi, 1968), since mothers in each new generation must fashion their own techniques with the help of the experts, rather than from their personal experiences or on advice from their mothers.

In addition to an array of options, each mother faces child rearing today with an ideology which is complicated by the current conception of human nature. As Wolfenstein (1955) has pointed out, the conception of a child's nature has radically changed in the past 100 years. In contrast to an earlier view in which the child was a "bundle of impluses" needing parental control, the current view is that there is "rich potential in every child." Hence, the modern mother has the complex task of molding and developing this bundle of potential into a future president, a scientist, and an academician, most importantly, a happy, well-adjusted adult. Additionally, the mother today must accomplish these difficult tasks in the atmosphere of "fun morality" where she must enjoy every aspect of her relationship with the child (Wolfenstein, 1955).

The result has been a professionalization of motherhood, in which the role has been expanded and hence has been made more time consuming. Since the blame for a child's failures cannot be assigned to the foibles of human nature or to some outside force, the doctrine of parental responsibility weighs heavily. When failures occur, the blame is typically assigned to the mother, a situation which is likely to produce guilt. It seems unlikely that the career woman who is also a mother can escape or ignore the expectations and pressure which are imposed by the current child-rearing philosophy. In fact, the nature of her busy life only adds to the difficulties (Johnson and Johnson, 1977).

One might ask why the husband and father does not share these vicissitudes. For one thing, despite changing views of women's roles, societal expectations on child rearing allocate responsibility to the mother irrespective of her work or social statuses. In fact, researchers rarely study the effects of the fathers' work role on child development, nor do they ordinarily study the role of the father in general (LeMasters, 1970). One can conclude that motherhood in most segments of society remains a sacred task demanding high dedication and commitment. In those circles, where two-career families are admired and emulated, alternate definitions of parental roles are being evolved. However, these families must come to terms with the omnipresent normative expectations of the maternal role and the effects it has on the mother with a career.

Working mothers appear to be more afflicted by self-imposed guilt than by objective evidence from empirical research. Hoffman and Nye's comprehensive review (1974) points out that the effects of mothers' working depend upon the nature of their employment, their family circumstances, their social class, the age and sex of their children, and the kinds of child care arrangements employed. Most importantly, the effects are associated with women's attitudes toward their work. As to the effects on children, Hoffman concludes from a summary of a large number of studies that the working mother provides a largely positive role model for her children. This positive model includes less-traditional gender role concepts, more approval of women's employment, and a higher evaluation of female competence. Women college students are also more prone to have higher career motivations if their mothers work. Also, there is a positive relationship between the mother working, level of intelligence, and academic performance of children.

There is some evidence, however, that the working mother experience significant guilt and anxiety (Birnbaum, 1971; Hoffman, 1963). One result of this guilt—at least among mothers who like their work—is that they make increased efforts to make up for the time they work, sometimes to a degree which might be considered overcompensation (Hoffman, 1963). Other research indicates that, when the children are adolescents, the role strain and anxiety decreases for these working mothers. In summary, despite the popular myths on the possibility of maternal deprivation in families where mothers work, there is no solid evidence that the mother's employment status leads to juvenile delinquency or other forms of social problems, at least for school-age children (Hoffman and Nye, 1974).

The dual-career parents interviewed in our study (Johnson and Johnson, 1977) raised their children by techniques usually described for upper-middle-class families. For one thing, they were more concerned about the quality of the relationship than with objective behavior. Almost all mothers rationalized their busy schedules with the much-used phrase, "It's the quality of the time spent with children that counts, not the quantity." Thus, parents devise *activities directed toward enhancing the environment of the children* both within the home and in educational settings. Family activities such as skiing, camping trips, bedtime stories, or dinner and movies out as a family were common. One mother summed up this technique, "When we have to juggle, it is a strain and I feel emotionally what I am missing. So I have to make up for it by conjuring something special to do." In addition, mothers of school-age children participated as parents in their children's school through supervision of their progress and involvement in some school activities. Concerns for achievement also received high priority, as did the emphasis on good psychological adjustment of the child. Such compensations for the competing commitment to their careers are most likely compatible with the characteristics of high-achievement women in general. The high potential for energy, high aspirations for self, career, and other family members, the commitment to the arts, learning, and self-actualization can all be directed toward both career and family, given the resources of time and energy.

With the high aspirations for children along with an ideology stating that the mother is so crucial in molding successful children, it is not surprising that role strain is high among career mothers. Nevertheless, the modes of managing role strain involve both subjective patterns of rationalization and objective modes of compensation. Additionally and on a more important level, the patterns of child rearing were geared to techniques which eventually could alleviate some role strain. Parental goals centered on *training children to be self-reliant and independent,* qualities that would adapt well to the two-career family.

These techniques give high priority to those values which reflect the internal dynamics of the child—namely, self-reliance, independence, consideration, self-control, and curiosity. This contrasts considerably to working-class mothers who give high priority to values that reflect behavioral conformity, such as obedience, respect, and neatness, the enforcement of which demand more parental vigilance. As Kohn (1969) has pointed out, such emphasis on self-direction in the middle class focuses on internal standards of control which are generally instilled by such indirect disciplinary techniques as reasoning and isolation.

Within our sample, the values of self-direction and independence, along with an emphasis on interpersonal relationships, were repeatedly espoused. Disciplinary techniques, at least as described by the parents, were neither punitive nor unpredictable. Furthermore, the children occupied the focal point in the family during nonworking hours, when generally both parents devoted much attention to the child's inner state and external behavior.

The point of this finding, that the two-career parents express the values of their class, centers on the impact these patterns of child rearing have on the career mother. The patterns, which emphasize the internal world of the child and attempt to instill sensitivity along with independence and achievement through more indirect disciplinary techniques, in one sense make child rearing more time-consuming, since problems are less likely to be approached directly—namely, parents are more likely to ask "why" rather than to spank. These patterns involve a higher degree of reflection and sensitivity on the mother's part than if she were using time-tried, more traditional values, which could be instilled directly by the "back of the hand." Since more mothers also espouse the high societal expectations for dedicated mothering along with the assumption of responsibility for the child's success or failure, her responsibilities do not always lessen even in adolescence. Hence, one tentative conclusion arising from this research is that the career mother has not devised new child-rearing techniques which are more compatible with her busy schedule and competing commitments. Since the effects are diffuse and subtle and not associated with specific behaviors, the psychological costs are also probably higher.

Another factor of middle-class families which can be accentuated in dual-career families is the allocation of responsibilities between the parents. In an earlier section, we discussed the attempted inter-changeability of marital roles in dual-career families. This character-istic is also found in parental roles where there is less specialization of female expressive functions and male instrumental functions. Nor-mally, parents' roles in most families today overlap into expressive and instrumental areas, a process which is particularly prominent in the modern family of the middle class, which has made more changes by minimizing the differentiation between both a mother's and a father's child-rearing role (Slater, 1974; Coser, 1974). This process, often called de-differentiation, probably has caused more change in the father's role, for he has become more active in the expressive functions of the family. The mother always has had some authority in the home, and she has always had dominance over expressive functions. However, women seem to carry their expressive functions over to the work situation more than men do, so they are more likely to perform dual functions. At the same time, they bear major responsibility at home. It is not surprising then that their role system imposes some strain on them. In any case, such a family system is more complex and perhaps confusing to the child; nevertheless, it reflects a relational pattern suitable for the fluid family structure needed for dual-career couples.

The problem arises, however, when both parents are involved in the child's emotional life and are simultaneously in authority roles, as then there are fewer opportunities for the child to establish some distance from either parent. Since there is also a high degree of internalization of parental values in this family type and fewer overt social controls to enforce these values, the parent-child relationship has a pervasive psychological dimension, for it is based on motivating the child to *want* to do what must be done rather than enforcing parental wishes by direct means. Coser (1974) describes the structural ambivalence stemming from this lack of differentiation of parental authority by pointing out that it could lead to personality absorption of the child. This process, originally described by Green (1946), conceptualizes a physical and emotional blanketing of the child, which leads to an increased psychological dependence upon the parents, a dependence which is continually threatened by the withdrawal of love. Since these overlapping functions are directed at internal attitudinal conformity as well as behavioral conformity, it is more difficult for the child to establish some psychological autonomy from the parents' influence.

This family type, consequently, is characterized by an emotionally intense environment where only two adults, the parents, are directly involved in both the external and the internal world of the child. Since both behavior and personality are of concern to both parents, conformity is expected not only in what a child *does,* but also what he or she *thinks,* yet it must be enforced indirectly.

There is a need for children at some point to establish social distance from the parent to dilute the emotional intensity of the nuclear family (Slater, 1974; Coser, 1974). Usually this is accomplished as part of the maturation process, when adolescents become more independent. Yet the psychodynamics of the situation usually impede total independence of the child or a lessening of the parental responsibility for the child's well-being. Since children rely on both parents for their emotional needs and both parents can exert authority upon them, there is an overwhelming amount of social control, however indirect, intertwined with affection. We can see how different this is from traditional segregated roles where expressive and instrumental functions are usually distinguished. Stern parental authority also makes it easier for the child to establish more distance from the parent.

Children in dual-career families are usually at an advantage, however, in comparison to those raised by full-time mothers. Because of the inevitable time demands upon dual-career parents, there are few all-attentive mothers—or fathers, for that matter—who are continually involved in all dimensions of their children's lives. However dedicated they are to parenting, they simply do not have the time to quiz their children upon their return from school or attempt to know everything about their friends. Furthermore, they generally raise their children to be independent, and research indicates that they have been quite successful in this goal. Last, if the mother's career has been uninterrupted, maternal surrogates have had to be used. Thus, the intrusion of parents into the internal world has probably been lessened, and the needed distance between parent and child accomplished. If one agrees with the propositions outlined above, one can conclude that this arrangement has been beneficial to both parent and child.

ADAPTIVE STRATEGIES

There is clearly a need to reduce the role strain imposed on women in dual-career families. While many of the techniques that could be used are easier said than done, they nevertheless should be mentioned. For example, the impediments to women's advancement should be abolished. Adequate and inexpensive child care should be made available. Career requirements should make allowances for women with children, so that they can design a schedule that is more flexible and without penalties to their career advancement. These suggestions continue to receive lip service from all quarters; we hope they will remain in the forefront of the women's movement.

Other impediments stem from the restricted resources of the middle-class family system and can be less easily solved. One cannot create a kinship support system where relatives do not exist or live too far away to be of real assistance. Fraiberg (1977) refers to these relatives as the "tribal guardians"—the aunts, grandparents, and neighbors who rise to the occasion to support a busy mother. Perhaps, however, if careers did not demand continual mobility, more guardians would be available. Also, if there is a continued evolution in the normative expectations of women's roles, there may be less disagreement between conventional and modern family styles, so that disapproval from relatives does not impede their support.

The strongest resource a dual-career family possesses lies in the marriage relationship itself—barring divorce, the husband is potentially the greatest support a woman has. It must be remembered also that husbands in dual-career marriages usually espouse norms on women's equality and are usually rather supportive in terms of concrete assistance. However, since they usually place a higher priority on their own career and since they are likely to make more money, their careers are rarely sacrificed for the family or for their wives' careers. Role-cycling, where alternating time periods are set aside for the ascendency of one partner, is difficult to accomplish. Nevertheless, if societal expectations favored the ascendency of women's careers, it would be easier for husbands to also cycle their careers. More young professionals are attempting such arrangements today; perhaps this will be a more frequently chosen option in the future.

The most immediate and feasible approach to the problems of dual-career families centers on the recognition of competitive strivings and the objective means by which they can be reduced. The egalitarian norms repeatedly espoused—that male and female roles should be interchangeable—should be recognized for what they are—norms which are difficult to translate into the realistic situation of family life. When the norms are so valued, yet not realized, competition is not always dealt with directly, since it is not supposed to exist.

It is also useful to examine the division of labor within a family both for its potential as a source of conflict and competition and for the possible inequity it imposes on the wife. Conventional arrangements, with their clear delineation of male and female roles, have some advantages, because functions are complementary. While division of labor realistically means that career wives have a proliferation of roles, working to their disadvantage, the principle of division of labor has many advantages. For one thing, complementary roles, where responsibilities are delegated for a fixed time period, essentially define certain areas of marital life as nonnegotiable and, hence, removed from the arena of conflict and competition.

Experience has taught many career wives to be skeptical of any suggestion which favors conventional role arrangements, for they well know that they are the ones who must make some sacrifices at the expense of their careers. Likewise, institutional changes in the nature of work itself and the penalities it imposes on women and men will be slow in materializing. For this reason, it is the family where some accommodations can be made. Young career couples are attempting numerous alternate arrangements which have not yet stood the test of time. It is to them that one must look for innovative changes. For dual-career families with young children today, there appear to be no easy solutions except for the passage of time. Children do grow up, and most careers reach a pleateau or an acme when rising aspirations do not always push the partners to further heights. Until that situation is reached, a nonidealistic approach which recognizes that children do usually flourish in dual-career families is to the family's advantage. Also, it is useful to be aware that the costs and strains are largely borne by women—and that, where husbands are not supportive, the whole arrangement is exceedingly fragile.

REFERENCES

ASTIN, H. (1969) The Woman Doctorate in America. New York: Russel Sage.
BIRNBAUM, J. A. (1971) "Life patterns, personality style and self-esteem in gifted family oriented and career committed women." Ph.D. dissertation, University of Michigan.

BROSCART, K. R. (1978) "Family status and professional achievement: a study of women doctorates." Journal of Marriage and Family 40, 1: 71–76.

BRYSON, J. and R. BRYSON (1978) "Dual-career couples." Special issue, Psychology of Women Quarterly 3 (Fall).

CLARK, R., F. I. NYE, and V. GECAS (1978) "Husbands' work involvement and marital role adjustment." Journal of Marriage and Family 40, 1: 9–21.

COSER, R. L. (1974) "Authority and structural ambivalence in the middle-class family," in R. L. Coser (ed.) The Family. New York: St. Martin's.

———and O. ROKOFF (1971) "Women in the occupational world: social disruption and conflict." Social Problems 18 (Spring): 535–554.

FRAIBERG, S. (1977) Every Child's Birthright: In defense of Mothering. New York: Basic Books.

GOODE, W. J. (1960) "A theory of role strain." American Sociological Review 25: 483–499.

GREEN, A. (1946) "The middle-class male child and neurosis." American Sociological Review 11 (February): 31–41.

HOFFMAN, L. (1963) "The decision to work," pp. 126–166 in F. I. Nye and L. Hoffman (eds.) The Employed Mother in America. Chicago: Rand McNally.

——— and F. I. NYE (1974) "Effects on children," in L. Hoffman and F. I. Nye (eds.) Working Mothers. San Francisco: Jossey-Bass.

JAFFE, E. (1968) "The masculine envy of woman's procreative function." Journal of American Psychoanalysis Association 16: 521–548.

JOHNSON, C. L. and F. A. JOHNSON (1977) "Attitudes toward parenting in dual-career families." American Journal of Psychiatry 134, 4: 391–395.

JOHNSON, F. A. and C. L. JOHNSON (1976) "Role strain in high-commitment career women." Journal of American Academy of Psychoanalysis 4, 1: 13–36.

JOHNSON, F. A., E. KAPLAN, and D. TUSEL (1978) "Sexual dysfunction in the dual-career family." Human Sexuality 13: 7–17.

KERKOFF, A. C.(1964) "Patterns of homogeny and the field of eligibles." Social Forces 42 (December): 289–297.

KOHN, M. (1969) Class and Conformity. Homewood, IL: Dorsey.

LEDERER, W. and D. JACKSON (1968) The Mirages of Marriage. New York: W. W. Norton.

LeMASTERS, E. E. (1970) Parents in Modern America. Homewood, IL: Dorsey.

LERNER, H. (1973) "Early origins of envy and devaluation of women: implications for sex role stereotypes." Bulletin of Menninger Clinic 37: 538–553.

MERTON, R. (1957) "The role set: problems in sociological theory." British Journal of Sociology 8: 106–120.

PARSONS, T. (1949) "The social structure of the family," pp. 173–201 in R. Anshen (ed.) The Family: Its Function and Destiny. New York: Harper & Row.

RAPOPORT, R. and R. N. RAPOPORT (1971) Dual-Career Families. London: Penguin.

ROSSI, A. S. (1968) "Transition to parenthood." Journal of Marriage and Family 30 (February): 26–39.

ROSTOW, E. (1965) "Conflict and accommodation," pp. 211–235 in R. Lifton (ed.) The Woman in America. Boston: Beacon.

SLATER, P. (1970) The Pursuit of Loneliness. Boston: Beacon.

———(1974) "Parental role differentiation," in R. L. Coser (ed.) The Family: Its Structures and Functions. New York: St. Martin's.

STAFFORD, R., E. BACKMAN, and P. DiBINA (1977) "The division of labor among cohabiting and married couples." Journal of Marriage and Family 39, 1: 43–58.

STORR, C. (1972) "Freud and the concept of parental guilt," pp. 173–192 in J. Miller (ed.) Freud: The Man, His Work, His Influence. Boston: Beacon.

WOLFENSTEIN, M. (1955) "Fun morality: an analysis of recent American child-training literature," pp. 168–178 in M. MEAD and M. WOLFENSTEIN (eds.) Childhood in Contemporary Cultures. Chicago: University of Chicago Press.

8

TIME MANAGEMENT AND THE DUAL-CAREER COUPLE
Anne M. Seiden

INTRODUCTION: TIME ALLOCATION AS VALUE CONFRONTATION IN COUPLE LIFE

Issues in the management of time are important in any couple's relationship. After all, everything that a couple does together is done in finite periods of time, and many of the issues which potentially or actually divide couples center on conflicts about the allocation of time. Time is, after all, the only one of a couple's resources which is totally inelastic. Goods, money, education, and marketable skills can all be increased (at least sometimes), but nothing gives anyone more than twenty-four hours a day. Changes can be made in how time is spent, or which time-saving services are purchased, but the total amount can never be increased or decreased.

Furthermore, there are almost always more competing ways to allocate time than there is time to be allocated. Final choice of how to spend time ultimately emerges as an issue of relative values and relative choices among competing priorities. The two individuals who make up a couple may rank these relative choices differently.

Indeed, many value conflicts in other arenas involve a large element of sometimes latent conflict about allocation of time. For example, an apparent conflict about visiting with in-laws or certain friends may occur, not because one or the other spouse is absolutely opposed to seeing the persons involved, but rather because each assesses differently the value of spending time this way as opposed to some alternative. Conflicts about the spending of money may latently involve either the obligation to spend time to enjoy the recreational value of an expensive item (such as a boat), or alternatively may involve a differing value assigned to the time which would be spent on washing the dishes if a new dishwasher is not purchased. Even conflicts about such issues as the tolerable level of dirt and disorder may not involve an absolute fondness for filth so much as a different evaluation of the priority of spending time to clean up. And even such apparently elemental passions as sexual jealousy sometimes center as much on the amount of *time* one partner spends with other persons as on the question of whether sexual intimacies occur.

If these issues are part of the fabric of life for all couples, they may be many times more so for dual-career couples. There are several reasons why this may be so.

First, most employment occurs during fixed "work hours," and when one partner is employed and the other is a homemaker, it has often been possible for the homemaker to diminish couple conflicts about time use by virtue of the ability to reschedule homemaking tasks. Although this occurs because the homemaker has greater control of her (or his) work schedule than many employed persons, the employed partner's *lack* of control over working hours may be translated into a *greater* degree of control over time allocation at home by insisting that couple time utilization be organized around his (or her) smaller amount of discretionary time. Time allocation issues can thus easily fit into a somewhat traditional power structure in the home, in which it seems natural that the employed partner have more control over the couple's allocation of shared time, just as the employed partner often assumes more control over the use of the couple's money.

Second, "careers"—as opposed to "jobs"—typically imply greater prestige in the extrafamilial world, and usually imply increased time demands as well. For many a true "careerist," the job is so closely identified with the self that the careerist is virtually always at work. Many such careers have been traditionally organized as male occupations, with the expectation that a support system, typically including the spouse, would be always flexible enough to organize other priorities around the time demands of the career. Persons with demanding careers quite often have stronger than average needs for rest and relaxation (which may be unduly postponed because of the demands of the career), coupled with smaller than average spans of time in which to satisfy these needs. For the partner to participate in these restorative needs may seem virtually to require the partner's ability to drop other time commitments at a moment's notice and seize *this* moment for participation.

Third, the very fact that the career and self, work and personal life are more closely merged in careers than in many "jobs" has other implications. The fact that the career demands and sharpens one's own personal energy is often invigorating, and in fact this kind of vigor may be part of the attraction that members of dual-career couples have for each other. Thus, the real challenge of time management for a dual-career couple may lie in the wish to have one's cake and eat it too; that is, to preserve the vigor and challenge which careers bring to our lives while negotiating the vulnerable personal time and space which are needed to maintain oneself and the couple.

Fourth, among the risks are the possible issues of competition in time allocation and prioritization. "Whose career is more important?" gets played out, often, in "whose time commitments are more pressing?" Should work on one's dissertation be postponed for this evening in order to attend the other's office party? Should one's important professional meeting be cut short because a sick child would otherwise require the other to miss an important conference? Can the sick child humanely or safely be left with the relatively new babysitter?

TIME MANAGEMENT AS A SKILL AREA

Current practical and popular literature, directed at business executives and, more recently, at the general public, provides a number of excellent books on time management skills (MacKenzie, 1975; Bliss, 1976; Lakein, 1974; Rutherford, 1977). Most of these books are quite sophisticated in dealing with the complex interrelationships between time allocation as a value issue and as an issue of developing skills to maximize one's achievement of cherished values. Skills, as opposed to values alone, enter the time allocation equation because of observations like the following:

(1) Many people find that they fritter away much of their scarce time in activities which they do not define as important, and conversely they never find time to do things which they regard as really important.

(2) Some people appear to achieve much more of what they regard as important than do other people with apparently equal resources, in ways that appear to be logically related to use of time as a resource.

(3) Some people are much more successful in achieving their goals in one area of life (such as work) than in other areas (such as personal or family concerns), and attribute their relative lack of success in neglected areas to "lack of time" even though they deplore the fact. Other people seem to be able to balance their achievements in various areas in a way that seems at least partially related to their skill in allocating time.

Historically, time management literature has emerged from the business literature, where it has long been noted that the effective executive is one who is skilled at deriving maximum benefit from his and others' time. Many of the skills which are stressed derive directly from a rather traditional male hierarchical view of organizational structure. Time is to be "saved" by delegating "less essential" tasks to the "lowest possible level," thus freeing the executive to concentrate on the "really important" tasks which he alone can do (male pronouns are used intentionally). The basic principle is a reasonable one; the general manager who used to be a salesman may *need* to be advised that sales issues which formerly preoccupied him should now be left to the current crop of sales personnel; that his promotion implied leaving old issues behind in order to spend time on new ones. The secretary who became an office manager, and then a high-level administrative assistant may *need* to be reminded that supervision of the clerical coffee breaks should be left to the new office manager (Henning and Jardim, 1978).

There are, however, a number of potential hazards in simplistically following this kind of advice. If less-important tasks are to be delegated, it is easy to assume that tasks which are delegated are by definition less important. The (often male) executive who "delegated" child care responsibility to the homemaker (usually female, often his wife) tended to regard the "delegation" itself as evidence that the task was less important. This reciprocal function of delegation and value assignment in time management will be further discussed below, but it is important to recognize that a realistic skill issue exists here, as well as a value one.

The general skills emphasized in most popular works on time management include the following: delegation, prioritizing, anti-procrastination techniques, techniques for breaking up large tasks which seem foreboding into small ones which are manageable. Or to recapitulate:

—Who should do the task?

—How important is it in comparison with competing time demands?

—If it is important but hard to do, how to overcome the barriers?

—If it is too large to fit into a daily schedule, how to divide it?

—If it seems important but is not getting done, what to do?

—If it seems trivial but is taking up too much time, what to do?

A major issue in addressing these important questions is how to properly relate the value issues to the skill issues. It is clear that many people quite frequently feel that their value preferences with respect to time and accomplishments are not being achieved. That would seem to indicate a skill problem.

Many of the time management skills advocated in this literature are similar to those involved in popular literature on assertiveness training (Smith, 1975; Fensterheim, 1975, for example). One is advised to be assertive about interruptions, people who want to delegate *their* time-consuming tasks upward or downward to you, your own tendency to procrastinate. Certain problems in couple and familial relationships emerge which are similar to those raised by all assertiveness training: One wishes to appropriately be assertive with respect to one's intimates, but there are limits. One does not handle an intimate in the same way one handles a used-car salesman (even if one's intimate *is* a used-car salesman).

Assertiveness is different in the situation where one has a single commercial goal from the role relationship, from situations in which one has the dual goal of fostering *both* one's own interests and those of the partner. An interruption from someone you love who wants to share a precious transient moment may break your train of thought at least as much as a routine telephone call, but the kind of program which is effective in postponing the latter may have devastating effects on an intimate relationship.

An extremely well-balanced approach to measuring one's wish to be assertive about one's own needs against one's wish to be sensitive to the needs of children is provided in the Parent Effectiveness Training series (Gordon, 1974, 1975, 1977, 1978), of which the most recent (Gordon, 1978) is by far the most sophisticated theoretically. This approach has been extended into other areas such as business management (Gordon, 1977) and special issues for women, including work and couple relationships (Adams, 1979). While none of these books deals primarily with time management as such, their more complete approach to assertiveness in intimate relationships is quite salient to such dimensions of time management as assertiveness, authority, and control. With deceptive simplicity, these really quite sophisticated approaches to caring human interaction advocate a "no-lose" method of attempting to resolve conflicts which helps avoid many power struggles often seen as inevitable.

PHILOSOPHICAL AND GENDER ISSUES

WHAT IS TIME?

There are a number of important philosophical treatments of the nature of time, which can only be noted here and not fully explored. It is well known that Western and Eastern views of time traditionally differ, and that within the Western tradition there are some traditional differences between American and European views. There are also some differences which are associated with religious traditions.

I think it is fair to say that our "official" Western philosophy of time is most closely associated with that philosophy which is generally referred to as the "Protestant Ethic." In this viewpoint, it is commonplace to say that "time is money," a metaphor referring not merely to the fact that time can be converted to money when one sells one's time for salary or pays compensation for someone else's time. It also conceptualizes time as a "substance" like money, which comes in units: small and large denominations that can be interconverted, added, subtracted, saved, and spent.

The monetary model of time is in sharp contrast to the time philosophy of some traditional cultures which are closer to nature. In agricultural or hunting societies, especially in temperate or cold climates, the unit of time during the busy growing or hunting season is simply not the same as the unit of time during winter. Many traditional proverbs express this point of view ("Make hay while the sun shines"; "A stitch in time saves nine"). Time can be organized around the rhythms of sunrise and sunset, summer and winter, special anniversaries, the religious week and day and year, with its specified times for ritual observances. Organizing time around religiously invested rituals can give deep symbolic meaning to the passage of time, and can even seem to slow its passing by maintaining contact with the past. Of course, the rituals themselves also can require considerable time for their performance.

In our contemporary industrial world, in temperate climates, it is clear that both philosophies about time express some essential truths, and for most people neither is quite complete without the other. Offices may expect uniform attendance between nine and five, during winter and summer, but this homogeneity of time is purchased at the cost of artificial lighting, heating, and perhaps air conditioning. Nevertheless, the outer environment has its impact. Getting to work at nine is not the same proposition when snow must be shoveled from the driveway, brushed off the car, when the motor club may be needed to help start the car, when traffic is slow and accidents are more frequent, when children have to be dressed in cumbersome snowsuits and perhaps driven to school instead of walking, and so on. In other words, the seeming homogeneity of the time unit in the work environment is purchased through some combination of technically modifying the physical environment, and/or some degree of delegating the responsibility of dealing with that environment to other persons. And even when this is successfully done, the physical environment tends to be brought back in symbolic ways. In the centrally heated office, someone no doubt will hang plastic or tinfoil icicles around Christmas, or spray some artificial "snow" on some of the window panes.

In examining the impact of these different time philosophies on couples, it is interesting to underline some traditional gender differences. The homogeneous, monetary model of time has been more associated with the industrial workplace and male world views (regardless of how many women work there). Conversely, the traditional, seasonal, religious, or quasi-religious view of time is often associated with female interests and obligations. In the office, the person who hangs those icicles is most likely, often, to be a woman. In the home, the daily rituals of bedtime and breakfast, birthday celebrations, holiday planning, and preparation of seasonal clothing are all often associated more with the mother's role than the father's. "I'm too busy working—don't bother me now" tends to be a more acceptable view of male work than of female work, especialy vis-à-vis children.

Of course, within a family, a husband might value Christmas but expect the wife to orchestrate it, or value neatness in the home, and certain kinds of dinners, while expecting the wife to provide those things. Some traditional wage-earner husbands have tended to define "work" as "what you do on the job" and "home" as "where you relax." Unconsciously it was all too easy to assume that the wife who stayed home all day therefore really did not "work." It was possible to grossly underestimate the time-consuming nature of housework, child care, purchasing, and the general complexity of the job of home management. It has become a commonplace observation that when housewives take jobs, let alone have careers, some husbands may support their doing so, and then be honestly astonished at the amount of household management and household work which has to be shared, or left undone, or added to her work week. A commonplace observation is a willingness of husbands to share work aspects but not managerial aspects of the housework.

TIME AND HOUSEWORK

It has become commonplace for wives to make observations such as, "When I returned to work, I thought I had a wonderful husband because he strongly encouraged me to work, and was always willing to help me with the housework, whenever I asked" (e.g., Morgan, 1978; Mainardi, 1970). It took several years to realize the philosophical and gender role implications hidden in those words "help me." Minimally, these two words imply: (1) The domestic work at which he is "assisting" is still defined as her responsibility. (2) If it is not entirely done, or not done well, this allocation of responsibility will make it more likely that she feels guilt or a sense of inadequacy than that he does. (3) If it is done to the satisfaction of both, it is more likely that she will feel gratitude to him for his participation which is defined as "help," than that he will feel similar gratitude for her participation. (4) Both members of the couple are emphasizing the labor aspects of household management far more than the executive functions of planning, organizing, and control. The amount of time, knowledge, alertness, and monitoring which go into the latter are denied, as is the extent of its potential intrusiveness on other activities. It is unlikely that it is shared.

Nadelson and Eisenberg (1977) tell a seemingly amusing anecdote: A distinguished woman professional, about to give a scientific paper, suddenly is distracted as she sits on the podium by the thought, "Oh, my God, I forgot to buy toilet paper." They did not find male professionals of similar rank who as often felt a sense of personal responsibility for remembering, scheduling, and orchestrating the purchase and maintenance of routine or unusual domestic supplies.

Thus, both the *value* aspects and the skill aspects of time management are intimately intertwined with other aspects of skill and values in couple life. A particularly salient aspect of values, often particularly troublesome in couple relationships, enters to the extent that there is potential encroachment from attitudes of perfectionism. This is a real problem in time management, because there are very few tasks for which the expenditure of considerable time might not improve the product, at least a little. Judgment in almost all kinds of nonmechanized human performance is needed to determine just where one meets the point of diminishing returns. There is a cutoff point beyond which more time invested in a project does not justify taking the time away from other projects. And, conversely, the demands of other projects may lead one to set that cutoff point earlier, before reaching what would have been the true point of diminishing returns, taking this project in isolation.

Couples may differ as to what level of nonperfection is acceptable in various areas of mutual responsibility. Basic values may be involved, as when a certain level of cleanliness is felt to be required for health. Or a certain level of neatness may be felt as a minimum requirement to consider oneself civilized. A higher level may be required to feel assured that one is meeting middle-class standards. "Ring around the collar" would not work as a message in advertising if it did not have the capacity to evoke some primitive and powerful feelings of self-definition. People who work at intrinsically dirty jobs have traditionally felt it worthwhile to invest considerable time and effort in order to be spotless, in their Sunday best, while, conversely, a desk worker may find Sunday the very day of the week it is enjoyable to lie back under a car and get covered with grease. Couples coming from different class backgrounds, or different ethnic groups, may have extremely strong value differences with regard to time allocation that are not necessarily consciously perceived as time issues.

Eisen (1971), in a book directed partly at overcoming perfectionism in housekeeping provides a keen and profound philosophical analysis. In housekeeping, she points out, there are three potential values: economy, ease, and elegance. It is one of the tragedies of life that no more than two of these values can be achieved simultaneously. Thus, a housewife can achieve elegance and ease by hiring good household help—at the sacrifice of economy. A skilled housewife can achieve elegance and economy by working her fingers to the bone. Economy and ease can be approximated if one is willing to live with less elegance.

It is important to realize that Eisen is writing from a *wife's* point of view. Traditionally, there have been husbands who in their domestic lives expected to achieve elegance, economy, and at least personal ease by expecting their wives to do the hard work required to achieve domestic elegance, economically, unobtrusively, and at times when they are out of the house—in much the same way that they might admire a wife's curls but expect her to use the curlers at times when they are not around. For such a husband to enjoy domestic elegance may require considerable denial of the amount of inelegant work his wife is doing, out of his sight. *Some* women have become quite skillful at doing housework unobtrusively, playing down the kind and amount of effort which is really involved. It may then come as quite a shock to him, if her hours of outside employment become similar to his, to observe just what is actually required to maintain the home.

Conversely, as Ehrenreich (1979) has observed in an extremely thoughtful paper on housework, many women in the past have elevated the levels of housekeeping far above those preferred by their husbands and families in an attempt to regain control and authority denied them in other spheres of life. "Stay off my clean floor" may not be perceived as the aggressive and controlling message that it can be, because it is conveyed in a spirit of dutiful deference to a higher value of cleanliness which is not to be questioned. The daughter who internalized the felt "rightness" of her mother's standards may have difficulty feeling fully comfortable with more relaxed standards in her own household. This may be so even though she knows intellectually that a career housewife might be more reasonably expected to gild the lily in the home, her only area of major occupational competition than would someone else for whom housecleaning is only one part of work life.

BIOLOGICAL TIME RHYTHMS AND TIME MANAGEMENT

Some people are "early people," reaching their peak energy early in the day, tending to wake early, get a great deal done early, and to be tired by nightfall. Other people are "late people," tending to wake with difficulty, require a longer period of time to "warm up," get moving effectively, and think clearly, perhaps tending to be more difficult to get along with in the morning. By late in the day, and on into the night, they have hit their peak energy and intellectual effectiveness, naturally wanting to work just when some other people are wanting to go to bed.

Differing biological time clocks can pose problems in couple relationships, although it has been suggested that courtship patterns may have a certain tendency to increase the probability that people with similar rhythms will marry. This is because energy rhythms for recreation are likely to be similar to those for work. A late person is more likely to be attracted to a partner who is vivacious and full of ideas for fun far into the night, and conversely an early person is more likely to be comfortable with a partner who does not pressure him/her for activity when sleep begins to seem more attractive. However, the excitement of a new relationship or courtship can lend energy temporarily to a fundamentally early person, providing a seeming time compatibility which is eroded when the novelty wears off. These problems are probably more soluble if they are understood for what they are, rather than interpreted as a possible waning of interest and love.

The biological *manifestations* of peak times are clear. Body temperature rises slightly, alertness and response speed are measurably increased, and problem-solving ability is demonstrably better. Susceptibility to irritation, fuzzy thinking, and quarreling as opposed to mutual problem-solving are all greater at nonpeak times. Couples who are attuned to each other tend to work around their knowledge of each other's peaks, knowing when to introduce a potentially charged topic or an onerous task.

The biological *bases* of these differences in peak times are not yet completely understood, although present-day sleep research, elegantly summarized by Hauri (1977) is beginning to provide some answers. All of us have a spontaneous *circadian* rhythm (from the Latin "circum dies," or around the day) with characteristic energy peaks and valleys which vary for individuals. For most of us, the spontaneous rhythm can be "trained" to fit a schedule, just as our spontaneous rhythms of hunger or urination can be "trained" to fit a schedule of mealtimes or availability of food and of toilets. External cues are a major factor in this entrainment process: light, noise, and activity tend to support waking during daylight hours, and dark, quiet, calm, a full-enough stomach, and a warm-enough environment all tend to support sleep during nighttime hours. But for some people, the circadian rhythm is either longer or more resistant to environmental entrainment, or both. Such people, in the absence of competing demands, would tend to stay up a little later every night than the night before, and sleep a little later every morning than the day before, ultimately getting their time quite out of synchronization with usual work schedules. People with short circadian rhythms would tend to doze off before bedtime, but they are more easily entrained to a schedule, since it is far easier to wake someone up than to force them to sleep.

There are, of course, a number of other reasons for sleep problems. People who are depressed, as a part of the biochemistry of depression, tend to lose aspects of their circadian rhythm and may both sleep poorly and experience loss of energy and alertness during the day.

Many people who work at high-level careers have some flexibility in adjusting their work schedule to fit their biological rhythms, but not all do, and if there are children, their school schedule tends to be inflexible. Couples where both parents are "late people" may have great difficulty in getting the family organized in the morning, and there can be considerable competition about whose responsibility it is to initiate the organization.

Basic issues of fitting biological rhythms to work rhythms can be compounded by moral attitudes toward these issues. "Early" people often tend to feel superior to "late" people, to regard themselves as more disciplined and harder workers. This is supported by the fact that they will less often have been criticized for tardiness in school, and by such maxims as "the early bird catches the worm." (It is obvious that in agricultural societies before effective artifical lighting, particularly for outdoor work, the person who was able to get up early and make use of all available sunlight was at a real advantage.) Conversely, "late people" often tend to regard themselves as more creative than early people, and certainly many creative careers than routine jobs are more flexibly adaptable to the energy rhythms of a late person.

MOVING FROM THE THEORETICAL
TO THE PRACTICAL

First, some axioms.

(1) Time management skills are likely to be important to anyone aspiring to a high-level career.

(2) They are particularly important in the dual-career situation, because the dual-career family does not have a traditional "wife" to take up some of the time-consuming slack which allowed career patterns to develop as they historically have.

(3) Some high-level careerists intuitively hit on effective time management skills, but many do not. Many of us may in fact have *less* effective time management skills than the average person. As in the tortoise-and-hare nursery fable, many of us bounded ahead during our early schooling on the basis of being very bright, having extra energy, having perhaps absorbed many ideas around the home which others had to extract from their education. As we progressed in our careers, we may have grafted on some useful tortoise-like habits of harder work and persistence. But many of us did so without going back and developing disciplined habits and skills of time management, even though such skills become increasingly important as our work and personal commitments increase.

(4) To become a good manager of time is not done all at once; it requires considerable practice. A few basic skills can be picked up in a week, but making it a way of life can require considerable time—perhaps a year or two (depending on the extent to which a backlog of consequences of prior disorganization continues to impact on the present).

(5) The approach outlined here is directed at the serious hobbyist—someone for whom time management offers practical benefits, but also becomes something of a game or interest. As in going on a diet, there are considerable difficulties regardless of how great one's motiviation, and success is much more likely if one can make an enjoyable game of it.

(6) The game aspects of time management derive part of their appeal from the self-discover aspects which are intrinsic to the process. It is extremely important to make this fun, not a process of self-blame. Ferreting out just what it is that is preventing you from instituting some seemingly desirable improvement in your time management skills can be extremely rewarding if you use it as an occasion to

discover something fascinating about yourself. It can be extremely painful if you use it as an occasion to blame yourself, as for failure to carry out yet another New Year's resolution.

(7) Like any hobby, doing it as a couple can double the fun and triple the rate of effectiveness.

(8) Management of time and management of space are interrelated. If things are disorganized in space, it will inevitably cost time to find papers and materials that you need.

(9) The serious student will clearly not be satisfied with the few ideas which can be outlined in this chapter. There are a number of excellent books and I particularly recommend Lakein's (1974) How To Get Control of Your Time and Your Life as the most comprehensive treatment for the general reader. It is well written, fun to read, and deals much more clearly with the interrelationship between personal and professional goals in use of your time than most other books on the subject. Winston's (1978) *Getting Organized* is a useful companion volume, directed perhaps primarily at women, and treating the organization of space and possessions more than time. The interested time hobbyist will find other books available in the psychology, self-improvement, and business sections of bookstores. Most of these books contain a certain core of general principles.

BASIC SKILLS IN TIME MANAGEMENT

First, most writers on time management emphasize the value of the daily prioritized "to-do" list. Essentially, this is a list of tasks one hopes to accomplish during the day, *ordered in terms of importance*. You make a list early in the morning, or the day before, of everything you realistically expect to do, and then you indicate A, B, or C by each according to importance, and you *rank order the As*. In whatever discretionary time you have, you start with the A-1 task, continue with it until it is done before tackling anything else on the list. When interruptions occur, you keep weighing their importance against that of the A-1 task. If you get nothing done in a day other than the A-1 task, you do not despair, because no other system would give you more yield in terms of your own definition of what is important.

Second, most writers in this area emphasize a difference between *importance* and *urgency*. There are some tasks which have a time

limit. If you do not submit your abstract before the cutoff date for the
program committee, it will not be considered this year. If you do not
file your income tax by the deadline, you face penalties. The income
tax may not be your personal highest priority, but the consequences of
missing the deadline could be serious. In terms of your *own* goals,
tasks may be urgent but not important, important but not urgent, both
urgent and important, or neither. Tasks which are both urgent and
important (getting your appendicitis treated before the appendix rup-
tures) will tend to be done. Tasks which are neither urgent nor important will tend to be postponed, as well they might. The crunch comes
with tasks which are urgent but unimportant, which tend to get over-
attended to ("Three day sale; this offer will never be repeated"), and
tasks which are important but not urgent ("Someday I really badly
want to write a book about that") ("I really want to spend more time
with my children") ("We should be having more fun").

Third, basic skills therefore center on:

(a) accurately identifying your long-range as well as your short-range
    priorities;
(b) determination to enter long-range, important/but not urgent tasks into
    the daily list rather than postpone them indefinitely;
(c) balancing *your* priorities against those of people who are important to
    you—your partner, children, boss, co-worker;
(d) seizing the initiative as much as is compatible with your other goals,
    which is particularly tricky in intimate relationships. The business-
    oriented time management literature suggests that you, for example,
    let telephone calls be screened, and group them for returning at a time
    convenient to you. But does your three-year-old child understand or
    respond well to this principle? Or indeed your lover?
(e) recognizing the time requirements of different kinds of tasks. Some
    tasks can be accomplished in ten minutes. Others (getting the outline
    of a controversial paper to jell) may require two or three hours of
    concentration, and *any* interruption could cost at least half an hour to
    get back into the proper frame of mind to continue. Sometimes one
    never recaptures the interrupted creative momentum, as illustrated by
    Coleridge's (1797) famous experience in writing the poem Kublai
    Khan;
(f) assertiveness, or having the courage of your convictions, and being
    able to enforce what you need to do to accomplish the other goals. This
    requires being able to say "no" to low-priority demands on your time.

Fourth, it is important to realize that skill-building takes time and practice, and is not accomplished at any one moment. A common time-management mistake is to make some degree of effort, find it frustrating, blame oneself, and give up in an orgy of guilt or self-blame.

Fifth, in a couple relationship, especially when dual time-consuming (or even time-voracious) careers are involved, *joint* time management planning is virtually essential. This is especially true with regard to long-run planning. Short-run planning is exemplified by the to-do list. Long-run planning involves the items you might have left off that list, and also considers long-run shifts in your priorities. It is particularly well done as a couple because some of the "growing apart" in life which some couples experience comes from shifts in priorities, which may occur so slowly that you and your partner are unaware of them.

Sixth, we will give more on long-range planning: you-initiated versus other-initiated tasks. Examples of long-run priorities might be: You have been wanting to write a book for a long time, but never seem to find time to sit down and get started outlining the research you need to do. You feel you would like to be getting more exercise, or more recreation, but somehow you never get around to starting. There are certain old friends, or family members, with whom you are losing contact. You are not doing certain kinds of things with your children that you would like to, and you are afraid that before you know it they will be grown and it will be too late.

All these examples share the characteristic that they are things *you* very much want to do, but which require you to initiate action. And there is nothing particularly urgent about doing any of them on any particular day. Rutherford (1977) calls these "Hipos" or high-priority, low-urgency items, and points out how easily displaced they are by other things that come initiated by others, with perhaps their deadlines attached. Filling out your IRS forms probably holds few rewards for you, but you will do them because it is urgently presented with a deadline and consequences, a low-priority (to you) but high-urgency item. These things tend to get done, and there are usually few alternatives. High-priority, high-urgency items also tend to get done and pose no problem: When you go into labor, the chances are you will drop other commitments and go on to give birth.

The problems and potential solutions in time management come from three main sources:

(1) the elimination of low-urgency, low-priority items—things which are done simply because they have always been done, and they really are not needed;
(2) the insertion of high-priority but low-urgency items from your long-range planning into your daily schedule (because unless they get done on some particular day, they will never get done);
(3) increases in efficiency of accomplishing all items actually done, and in *appropriate* delegation of some tasks to appropriate others.

Seventh is efficiency. One might think that efficiency would come first. Lakein (1974), like others, emphasizes this is not so. One can work very efficiently at doing tasks which really are not worth doing. The first principle lies in determining what is really most important to you to do. Having done that, however, there are a number of ways in which efficiency and effectiveness can be increased.

(a) Paperwork and planning. Keep all your to-do lists, phone numbers you want to remember, notes to yourself and so on, in one place, well-organized for the purpose. (Daytimers, 1980, pocket and desk calendars are superbly suited for this purpose, are *much* better organized than your average pocket calendar.)
(b) Delegation. Try to determine with every task whether you should be doing it at all—either because it may not be worth doing, or because someone else can do it better, more efficiently, or at lower cost than yourself. People tend to get caught in their own past histories. Perhaps making your own clothes was an economy when you were a graduate student. Just because you still possess the skill does not mean it is an economy now—perhaps someone else would love to have that job, and you can afford to pay to have it done. You might be invited to give a talk or write a paper that is no huge challenge to you—letting your graduate student write it under your supervision, and be senior author, could contribute much more to his or her career than to yours, save a considerable amount of your time, and still satisfy the audience that wanted your ideas.

Eighth is interruption management. Some kinds of tasks require at least several hours of sustained work in order to accomplish anything;

a two-minute interruption can cost a half-hour getting restarted.

These tasks need to be rescheduled in appropriate blocks of time with safeguards against interruption. You can use a secretary to screen phonecalls, or an answering machine, or work in the library, or much earlier or later in the day than potential callers would feel free to intrude.

Small tasks—e.g., returning phonecalls—can be grouped; you are less likely to be tempted to make them long-winded if you are making several in a row. When you leave a telephone message, it is only fair to recognize that the person you call may also want to group return of calls; you should indicate several times when you could be reached.

An astonishing amount of time is lost over incomplete telephone messages. Once an important NIMH official and I exchanged six phonecalls over three days, never reaching each other; when we finally connected, I discovered that what she needed was my social security number, information which my secretary could easily have provided if she had asked for it instead of me.

Ninth is procrastination management. There are some tasks, of course, for which procrastination is the perfect solution—Lakein (1974) identifies these as "C-Zs" and suggests that you keep a bottom drawer for all the things you cannot quite throw away but to which you will probably never respond. At the end of a year, you can look through and rejoice at all the unnecessary things you did not do.

Other procrastination comes from perfectionism, or intimidation by large tasks; the remedies are to develop skills in breaking large tasks into small ones, and adjusting levels of expected output realistically.

TIME MANAGEMENT AND CHILDREN

In most societies, children are incorporated more into the mainstream of adult life than is the case in ours. Small infants are carried on or near the mother's body as she goes about her other business; older infants and toddlers may be cared for by young children, at a distance close enough for an adult to supervise, but not requiring moment-to-moment adult attention. The relatively complete segregation of children from adult activities is a phenomenon that has occurred in rather recent historical times, since the Industrial Revolution, and is currently receiving some reexamination; it is not clear that it is good for children and their parents.

CHILDREN AND WORKING AT HOME

Small children generally expect their caretaker to respond to them whenever they wish. It is easier to be working at a task the child understands; he or she is not as likely to interrupt your making peanut butter sandwiches as your working on your dissertation. "Why read that book when you could be reading one of mine to me?" is a frequently expressed attitude.

If one is attempting to simultaneously care for small children and do complex intellectual work, some special juggling is in order. It is possible to block off those several-hour stretches of uninterrupted time for hours when you expect the child to sleep, and to do smaller tasks, less vulnerable to interruptions, when the child is awake.

CHILDREN AND WORK OUTSIDE THE HOME

It has become commonplace to say that it is not the quantity of time you spend with your children, but the *quality* of that time that counts. While this may be true, the phrase itself provides little guidance on how to do it.

Children appear to pose many of the same time requirements as do other creative endeavors—they need some uninterrupted time of their own, some protection against procrastination about their needs and wishes, and some sense of appropriate control over your time use (i.e., a sense of being prioritized very high).

Careful attention to transition times of day is one secret. Taking time to get your child off to school in a reasonably content way in the morning may represent a high yield for a relatively small amount of time. In some families, mornings are full of tension because of the difficult logistics involved in getting a large number of people dressed and ready for where they are going, all at the same time. Having one parent get up before the children do and dress first before dressing them can help; both dressing oneself and dressing a child proceed much more rapidly if the one task does not keep interrupting the other.

Dinner hours are disasters in some families; everyone is tired, hungry, irritable, and competing for attention at once. Some couples simply dispense with family dinner hours on weekdays; others would be horrified at the idea.

It is worth considering, though, that the family dinner may be one of those things that you tend to do simply because it has always been done that way. Actually, asking hungry children to wait for their dinner until an hour late enough to allow parents to come home from work, have a reasonable period of time in which to unwind, and then perhaps to prepare dinner may simply be too much to ask of the children. The old English custom of serving "tea" in the late afternoon (actually, for children a simple supper) can permit them not to be hungry while parents eat (and perhaps prepare their own dinner).

"Special" times alone with you for each child is another secret. The English religious leader John Wesley remembered from his childhood that his mother was extremely busy raising a large family—but she always scheduled one hour a week that belonged to each child alone, to spend with her in the way that was most meaningful to that child.

A somewhat similar suggestion has been made by Harrison-Ross (1974) but on a daily rather than weekly basis. She recommends finding at least fifteen minutes each day that each child can count on to have with a parent alone as his/her special time. Just before bedtime could be a natural time for this, or early in the morning if one of your children is an early riser, or after school or dinner if these times fit your schedule and your child's. Again, "transition" times of day are often a comfortable and spontaneous time for this. The essence is that the child knows that the time can be counted on and will be generally free of interruptions. In a few settings, a child can drop by a parent's lab or office on the way home from school, and this has many advantages.

Access to you, and a degree of control for the child is yet another secret. Part of what children want when they want their parents around is not a constant presence (which can even be intrusive), but the knowledge that they can reach you if *they* feel the need. They may want to check something out, make sure something has not been forgotten, and so on. If at all possible it helps to give even a young child your telephone number at work, and some idea of when you are most free to be called. If there is a bulletin board at child height where the child can leave a note *and be sure you will get it,* many "reminder" calls are not necessary; even a child who cannot write can enjoy dictating a note to a babysitter. (Magnets on the refrigerator door will serve the same purpose.)

CHILDREN AND CHORES

In any given instance, it is almost always more efficient to do the task oneself than to teach a child to do it, and supervise while she or he does it. Young children love to imitate adult behavior, including that which will later be called chores. Unfortunately, this interest in imitation peaks at an age earlier than the age at which the child's labor is really useful in accomplishing the task. Parents generally enjoy the child's identification enough to make a game of this shared participation, which forms a basis for the child's having some later pleasurable feelings about work around the house. Housekeepers often do not have the same incentive to share work with the child. In the interests of efficiency, they may simply do all the work themselves, discouraging the child from participating. Children raised in this way can develop the idea that work around the house is beneath them, an unfortunately elitist attitude. It is a good investment of some of your leisure time to spend it in doing work with children, not just recreation. The household itself can be physically arranged to facilitate self-care rather than dependence on being "served" (Howell, 1977).

SOME PERSONAL EXPERIENCES

This section might be subtitled, "How a ninety-eight pound weakling who never could find her other sock ultimately learned to juggle a house, husband, three children, chairing a department, writing papers, and participating in professional societies." It is rather personal and idiosyncratic, and based on my personal experiences. It is presented here in this way because of my belief that it might be useful to others in similar situations, including the kinds of persons likely to be reading the present volume from personal as well as sociological interest.

When we married, we already had some major issues around man-agement of time/space/organization. He was neat; I was sloppy. Worse than that, my family background led me to identify sloppiness of all sorts with being a warm/loving/good person, while his led him to identify neatness with being a respectful/sensitive/caring person. He once told my sister that he wanted me to become neater and better organized and had a five-year plan (a good sign: any indication that these things take time is a sign of realism; actually, it took fifteen years, and in the meantime, he became more genuinely comfortable with some surface disorder).

We had an unspoken contract that genuinely respected each other's wish to accomplish major things, and we both highly valued domestic life. He was more concerned about neatness and cleanliness than I was, but I genuinely wanted to organize my space and time better, in order to achieve my own goals. Thus, a largely unilateral change was acceptable because it was not imposed by one partner in a tyrannical way. And we both realized that a major change could not be accom-plished by moral pressure or wishful thinking.

We both realized also that physical environment is important. We invested a down payment in a house that had two studies on the ground floor—not easy to find, but space organization turned out to be essential to our time organization.

We both respected prioritization of desiderata, and of onerousness. Once, as an exercise, we listed all the things that needed to be done to maintain the household (grocery shopping, car repair, laundry, iron-ing, and so on). We both listed the tasks as (1) terrible—do it only because it has to be done; (3) actually rather pleasant or acceptable if other things are equal; and (2) somewhere in between. We found that there was less conflict than we had expected. To his surprise, I said I actually did not mind ironing because it occupied the hands and freed the mind to think. To my surprise, he said he actually did not mind dealing with car repair people because his technical knowledge in this area made him able to show off. Both of us were a little chagrined at how traditional some of our role allocations were—but that was our actual background, and we realized it would be silly to dismiss it. I had had some sophisticated instruction in ironing which he lacked, and he did actually know more about car repair than I did. However we might deplore the traditionalism of that division of expertise, it saved time for us not to both have to become experts on everything. Some of our "traditional" areas of expertise had nontraditional consequences. For example, his superior knowledge of machinery made him better able to repair the vacuum cleaner, select which one to buy, and supervise the person who was using it. Conversely, my interest in some "traditional" women's concerns around home and family led to participation in women's movement and health consumer issues—and things I learned there had major impact on his as well as my approach to major administrative issues within our universities (such as approaches to genuinely equitable recruitment, channeling of patient and student grievances in a health care system, and the like).

Both of us found that some of the practical administrative devices we used at work helped in home administration, and that some of the human approaches we stumbled into in dealing with our bright and by-no-means-subordinate children helped us in dealing with graduate students and employees.

For example, if I had not had an answering service with a radio-page "beeper" for my practice, I never would have discovered how reassuring it is to children whose parents are overcommitted to know that in a pinch they can page you anywhere and reach you instantly.

Similarly, he took his portable microdictation unit from work to our grocery store one day and walked down the aisles dictating a list of what groceries are located on which counters. The geographically organized grocery list transcribed from that dictation was xeroxed, and we keep a copy on our refrigerator door. It saves an hour a week in planning shopping, and another hour in doing the shopping—not to mention the major convenience of eliminating forgotten items and extra trips to the store. Similarly, if neither of us had had a secretary at work, we almost certainly would not have thought of hiring a part-time home secretary, which has turned out to be one of our major timesavers. It literally might not have occurred to us that someone else can balance the checkbook, pay the bills, order the mail-order purchases, and return the ones that do not pan out. The student who does this work for us in our home is pleased to have a job which pays reasonable money, can be done conveniently at flexible hours, and is in a dual-career home setting for which neither of us had the benefit of role models.

ISSUES FOR FURTHER RESEARCH

It is of considerable interest that time allocation and management appear more generally in the business and popular pschology literature rather than as a serious topic of social science research. Where they do appear in the latter, they tend to be somewhat undimensional in the way they are discussed.

While there exists a moderately larger body of research on, e.g., employed husbands' or wives' participation in household tasks, that research typically provides a time count or a task list. It rarely considers such interesting questions as:

(1) What other possible time uses are sacrificed or not sacrificed in favor of household or child care or leisure activities?

(2) How does the individual and his or her spouse feel about this?

(3) How often do spouses feel that they are using their time according to their own sense of priorities as opposed to imposed priorities?

(4) If imposed, who has the power to impose them, and from whence does that power derive? Under what circumstances does that power carry a sense of felt legitimacy? Under what circumstances is it still a power, even when felt as "not fair," and why?

(5) In situations of culture change, under what circumstances do customary ways of time allocation come to be questioned? How usual, cross-culturally, is it for individuals of varying age and gender to have a sense of "discretionary time" or freedom to set one's own priorities about time use?

(6) In childhood socialization, are there periods during which children in a given culture or family have greater or lesser control over their own use of time? What are the implications for child development?

Similarly, in the psychiatric literature, difficulties in accomplishing tasks are almost always treated as neurotic conflict about the task in question (or projected onto it). One is perceived as having—e.g.—a success neurosis, a writing block, work inhibition, and the like. Difficulty, especially for women, in managing time demands of both work and family roles are usually interpreted as ambivalence about the latter. While it is certainly true that some individuals do have problems which are well described by such "neurotic conflict" models, it has been my experience that many more have personal skill deficits or interpersonal value conflicts (or both) which center in time management. In any individual case, attention to skill issues might logically precede psychotherapeutic interventions, since it is possible to determine rather quickly whether skills are being developed. If not, individual counseling may be needed. In my own clinical experience, the most frequent barriers to developing time management skills are:

(1) Not realizing there *is* a skill area here—treating time management moralistically: "If I'm a good person, I'll get all the right things done."
(2) Managing time according to priorities imposed by someone else, while *thinking* they are one's own priorities.
(3) Excessive puritanism or "superwoman" values leading to inability to assign recreation and "goofing off" the priority the individual really feels for them—thus, leading to a situation where recreation can only be had by procrastinating on another commitment.
(4) Trying to please everyone.

IN CONCLUSION

We have found that our hectic individual lives and our attempts to coordinate them more smoothly have been aided by explicit consideration of time as both a conceptual and pragmatic dimension of our lives, whose management helps hold the whole show together. We have found that specific skills in management of time, and examination of values which underlie these skill issues, have been both helpful and illuminating. The idea that such a commonplace dimension as time could have such far-reaching effects on our lives has appeared to us to be of both practical and theoretical interest. The sociology, anthropology, and psychology of time allocation accordingly appear to us to be areas which merit further attention—both personally and professionally.

REFERENCES

ADAMS, L. (1979) Effectiveness Training for Women. New York: Harper & Row.
ARIES, P. (1960) Centuries of Childhood: A Social History of Family Life. New York: Alfred A. Knopf.

BLISS, E. C. (1976) Getting Things Done: The ABCs of Time Management. New York: Charles Scribner's.

COLERIDGE, S. (1797) Kublai Khan.

Daytimers (1980) Catalogue. Allentown, PA: Author.

EHRENREICH, B. (1979) "How to get your housework out of your system." Ms. Magazine 8 (October).

EISEN, C. (1971) Nobody Said You Have To Eat off the Floor: The Psychiatrist's Wife's Guide to Housekeeping. New York: David McKay.

FENSTERHEIM, H. and J. BAER (1975) Don't Say Yes When You Want To Say No. New York: David McKay.

GORDON, T. (1974) T.E.T. Teacher Effectiveness Training. New York: David McKay.

_____ (1975) Parent Effectiveness Training. New York: NAL.

_____ (1977) L.E.T. Leadership Effectiveness Training. New York: Wyden.

_____ (1978) P.E.T. Parent Effectiveness Training in Action. New York: Bantam.

HARRISON-ROSS, P. (1974) The Black Child. New York: Berkeley.

HAURI, P. (1977) "The sleep disorders," in Current Concepts. Kalamazoo, MI: Upjohn.

HENNIG, M. and A. JARDIM (1978) The Managerial Woman. Garden City, NY: Doubleday.

HOWELL, M. (1977) Helping Ourselves: Families and the Human Network. Boson: Beacon.

LAKEIN, A. (1974) How To Get Control of Your Time and Your Life. New York: Signet.

MacKENZIE, R. A. (1975) The Time Trap: How To Get More Done in Less Time. New York: McGraw-Hill.

MAINARDI, P. (1970) "The politics of housework," pp. 447–453 in R. Morgan (ed.) Sisterhood Is Powerful. New York: Vintage.

MORGAN, R. (1978) Going Too Far. New York: Vintage.

NADELSON, T. and C. EISENBERG (1977) "The successful professional woman: on being married to one." American Journal of Psychiatry 134 (October): 1071–1076.

RUTHERFORD, R. D. (1977) "Time management for executive secretaries and administrative assistants." Pasadena, CA. (unpublished)

WINSTON, S. (1978) Getting Organized: The Easy Way To Put Your Life In Order. New York: W. W. Norton.

9

THE BALANCING ACT: COPING STRATEGIES FOR EMERGING FAMILY LIFESTYLES

Charles Lawe
Barbara Lawe

Major issues facing working couples today stem from a variety of change factors. Women now make up 40 to 60 percent of the work force, not only in the United States, but throughout the world (Blake, 1974). Working women with families and household responsibilities work approximately seventy hours per week (Gauger, 1973). Of primary importance is the simple fact that women have fewer hours for their basic needs for rest, relaxation, and leisure (Szalai, 1973). The existence of this situation illustrates the rigidity of sex role stereotypes. As an alternative to being tied to inflexible sex roles, couples may adopt flexible perspectives about utilization of each family member's skills and satisfaction of needs. (Giele, 1979).

In general, dual-career families suffer from a number of conflicts, such as making decisions on whose job warrants what specific compromises from the other (Elder and Rockwell, 1976)—i.e., will the wife give up her job to move to another city in order for the husband to achieve an increase in pay and a promotion? Should their son be allowed to stay in the high school he wishes because he's a senior and wants to graduate with his friends, rather than give up his emotional support systems and relocate with the family? These situations illustrate the problems of how and what decisions are made in terms of potential compromise and sacrifice by whom. Such problems frequently result in stress, conflict, and emotional turmoil quite capable of undermining the solidarity of the family structure.

Inherent in the issue of flexibility is balance. The willingness to accept changes in sex roles governing parent-child relationships is an illustration of change supporting balance in terms of an egalitarian family system. The increase in women's work responsibilities outside the home calls for a sharing of the nurturant parent role by the husband. It had been thought that nurturance is a sacred maternal role, but Levine's (1976) study indicates that men have the ability to fulfill the nurturant parent role which can provide for flexibility in shared tasks.

Another area suggesting imbalance and a need for change is the division of household tasks. Regardless of the assumed benefits of technological innovation and despite "labor-saving" appliances, women are actually doing more housework than they were fifty years ago (Vanek, 1974). In the emerging egalitarian families, husbands are taking more responsibility for performing household chores, but the wife is still carrying a much heavier load (Ericksen et al., 1979; Giele, 1979). The study done by Ericksen et al. (1979) suggests that the greater the difference in marital power (as measured by the differences in income and education between the spouses), the less likely the husband is to share in domestic chores.

Research by Gianopulos and Mitchell (1975) suggests that the husband's disapproval of the wife's working tends to increase conflict in other areas of domestic life. Much of this conflict seems to center on domestic economic issues. The economics of this conflict tend to be perceptually based; the husbands in this study perceived the goal of the wife's employment as increasing the standard of living, whereas the wife's perception of the goal for her employment was to provide necessities.

What seems to be happening in current family lifestyle patterns amounts to a cultural lag between the emerging values of democratic-egalitarian families and the more rigid, traditional norms characteristic of constrictive sex role stereotypes. Perhaps the lack of dual-career parental role models to represent effective problem-solving has resulted in many women carrying a heavier burden in their attempt to meet expectations based on traditional norms as well as values supporting dual-career relationships. Therefore, dual-career couples currently face the problem of coping with the effect of conflicting role demands that were not part of their parents' experience. They are experiencing what Kahn et al. (1964) suggest in their general theory of role dynamics, which is that dual-career couples may have interrole conflict as well as intrarole conflict. According to Kahn (et al., 1964), "the most prevalent form of role conflict probably is role overload, in which a variety of legitimate requirements make simultaneous demands." Probably the fewer role expectations and responsibilities experienced by the preceding generation reduced the possibility for role overload. Herman and Gyllstrom's (1977) definition of interrole conflict is illustrated by various role conflicts such as job versus family tensions, work and home maintenance, work and family responsibilities, and sharing time between personal and family activities. Intrarole conflicts include such facets as job-related tension, motivation and involvement with the job, promotional opportunities, and work and pay satisfaction. Hall (1972) hypothesized that "women should experience greater inter-role conflict than men experience because women's multiple roles are likely to be salient simultaneously, and men's multiple roles are more likely to operate sequentially." The effect of such circumstances may be to create pressure for the woman to be "superwoman," the competent professional at the same time that she is a wonderful wife and mother. A survey of the emerging lifestyles for men and women suggests the desire for social systems that provide for flexibility and balance in the areas of career opportunities for both males and females, shared responsibilities in household duties, and innovations in parenting and child care (Cogswell, 1975). The focus of this chapter will be to provide strategies and methods to promote balance and flexibility.

THE STRUGGLE OF BALANCING

Most of the problems facing dual-career couples involve some form of conflict. The popular assumption is that conflict is negative and should be avoided, but conflict may be beneficial in the sense that it can expose issues, increase effective problem-solving, bring about emotional involvement, sponsor creativity, clarify objectives, and increase cohesiveness (Palomares, 1975). A state of imbalance in a couple's relationship may be a result of conflict in work roles. Issues commonly facing couples with role conflicts may include what is to be done, when the task is to be done, and who is to do what. Disagreement may result from philosophical and perceptual differences—i.e., the husband believes that the wife's responsibility is to take care of the household chores, regardless of any additional responsibilites she may have in the work world.

In addition, conflict may be due to the lack of satisfaction of emotional needs, whereas one party is attempting to deny the other party the right to fulfill personal needs—i.e., the woman's right to have a career versus the husband's refusal to "allow his wife" to work. Discord may arise when the two people have incompatible needs or when the partners see different solutions to the problem. In general, conflicts may originate because of discrepancies between goals, values, interests, and desires. Conflicts may also reflect underlying issues or pressure conditions such as lack of money, time, or space (Frey, 1979). The psychological predispositions of the individuals in conflict influences the amount and duration of the conflict. For example, rigid and aggressive individuals tend to elicit conflict, whereas individuals having characteristics considered trusting and egalitarian tend toward cooperation (Terhune, 1970). It may be important to note that the variety of combinations of the previously mentioned characteristics influence the nature, duration, style, and outcome of conflict.

A typical conflict for many dual-career couples may be one of accomplishment of household chores. For instance, Sam may feel that it is acceptable for Jane to have a career as long as no imposition is made on him, meaning that he should not have to take on any additional responsibilities. Jane feels that she has as much right to a career as Sam does and that domestic tasks should be shared. She wants to negotiate, but he will not even talk about the conflict and is angry that she brought it up. In this instance, the surface issues of household chores may seem to be the major source of the conflict. However, other underlying issues such as power and control, values and beliefs, and the like may, in effect, be the root sources promoting continuous conflict, even after the couple has resolved their differences on the issue of household chores. For example, Sam may continuously strive to control what he believes to be appropriate behavior for Jane according to his values, whereas Jane continuously strives to invalidate Sam's position. How this conflict continues may be determined by the nature of the communication flow between the two. If each attempts to manipulate and maneuver the other covertly, then it is likely that the focus of their conflicts will take the form of surface issues such as household tasks. The duration of their conflict is also likely to be extended. If, on the other hand, the communication is more overt, greater understanding and potential resolution should follow, based on the assumption that more direct communication reduces the likelihood of manipulation.

It is important to understand that some conflicts cannot be resolved, but couples can learn more effective strategies to manage them. According to Palomares (1975), various strategies for managing conflict exist, one of which is negotiating or asserting one's wishes and expectations concerning the conflict rather than blaming and demanding that the other concede. Couples may choose to compromise, both demonstrating a willingness to give as well as to receive. Effective listening is also extremely helpful in bringing about the resolution of a conflict. Frequently, an individual in conflict is convinced that he or she is right and that the other person is wrong, and sees only the underhanded and vicious acts of the other, while ignoring or denying similar self-made behavior. Such thinking and behavior tend to result in communication blocks (Johnson, 1972). To resolve the conflict, conditions such as openness to communication and willingness to trust need to be established. The process by which these conditions can be established is through active listening. There is an exercise that couples may engage in to establish effective communication. They agree that, before further action or consideration may be taken with regard to the conflict, each person must state perceptions of what the other is thinking, feeling, and doing to resolve the conflict to that other's satisfaction.

Other strategies, shorter-term in nature and benefit, may be used to resolve conflicts. For example, time out or any strategy that involves getting away from, avoiding, or defusing tension-provoking or conflict-engendering situations may render a potential short-term benefit. However, it is important to keep in mind that such strategies are not resolution based, but are energy renewing and tension releasing in nature.

Several steps seem important in learning to manage conflicts. The first step is careful definition of what the primary sources of conflict are. The next step is to determine what the couple is mutually willing to do to resolve the conflict. The third step is selecting precisely defined methods concerning each member's proposed part in resolving the conflict (i.e., specific new behavior necessary to resolve the conflict). In order to strengthen and maintain the new behavior, couples need to develop procedures for rewarding each other for these changes and also to assess progress (Ohlsen, 1977).

In addition, couples may increase their potential for resolving conflicts by using general problem-solving strategies. Such strategies involve resolving the conflict by breaking the problems into smaller units, prioritizing or ranking these units in terms of most important to least important, and then beginning to implement a plan or strategy for resolutions while paying attention to facilitative conditions necessary to carry out any strategy (i.e., active listening, continuing to negotiate, compromising, and cooperating both in spirit and in actual behavior). After prioritizing and selecting the smallest unit of the conflict, and mutually negotiating and agreeing upon a definite plan of action, implementation of the plan is the next step. Prior to implementing, all tasks and role behavior should be clearly defined in terms of who is to do what and when and how this behavior will bring about a solution to the conflict. In other words, individuals involved in the conflict should be in agreement with the nature of the conflict, the purpose and objectives for managing the conflict, and what desired outcomes may be expected.

A good strategy and plan of action for resolving conflicts usually involves generating a list of alternative strategies and backup systems, thus reducing the potential for additional conflicts that may arise during the implementation phase. The stage of implementation is characteristic of experimentation in that new behaviors and problem-solving strategies are being tested to determine their relative effectiveness. It is important to gather observable data; these data can then be recycled during the next stage, which is an evaluation of the implementation.

The problem-solving process is a continuous cycle involving clear definition of the problems of conflict, development and selection of alternative strategies, implementation of the strategies, and evaluation and redefinition of the problem. However, conflict is an inevitable part of all intimate relationships; it is how conflict is resolved that influences the quality of the relationship. Effective problem-solving does not guarantee that the conflict will not recur or that other conflicts will not arise. Perhaps the main effect may be to improve the quality of the relationship by reducing the tension and anxiety surrounding the conflict, thereby allowing couples to go about meeting their needs in a more productive fashion. The ability of the couple to resolve their conflicts increases the potential for mutuality and balance in the relationship. The overall outcome of effective problem-solving is not only to reduce and manage conflict, but also to create an atmosphere which promotes psychological growth for all family members.

CASE EXAMPLE OF CONFLICT RESOLUTION

Sue and Bob have the problem of determining who is responsible for carrying out household tasks that seem to pile up and create conflicts continuously. Part of the conflict comes from Bob's perceptions of the roles men should play within the family system; he believes that he is responsible for financial support and the traditional male tasks of maintenance of the car and household repairs. He feels that it is unfair that Sue should ask him to accept additional tasks such as cooking, doing dishes, laundry, and cleaning. His protests come in the form of generalizations.

Bob: I always have to do everything around here and you get away with doing nothing.

Sue: I do most of the household chores as well as taking care of the kids, and you always get all bent out of shape when I ask you to do the dishes.

Bob: What do you mean, I always get bent out of shape? You never used to complain. You don't have to have that job, you know. I make enough money to take care of all of us. If you want that job more than being a mother, then, I guess the kids just don't mean that much to you, do they? Money is more important than your kids.

At this point, Bob may have adequately hooked Sue's guilt about traditional responsibilities, and she may go do the dishes even though she feels that her career is as important as Bob's and she wants an egalitarian relationship, which includes an equal share of domestic chores. She resents his lack of cooperation in performance of these tasks that benefit all of them. In the past, Sue and Bob have spent a lot of time quarreling over these issues, which took time and energy away from their relationship with the children, as well as time that could have been spent performing the chores. And, at the same time, Sue probably experiences an increase in conflict between what she feels she ought to do in terms of her role expectations as a mother and her obligations and responsibilities to the family and her job. She may also feel, on an intrarole conflict level, less motivated and less satisfied in her roles as mother and spouse.

There seems to be a lot of guilt and resentment from both Sue and Bob in terms of not being able to satisfactorily fulfill all of the roles each has (professional, spousal, parental). There are power issues of not wanting to give in or be controlled by the other. Each holds a set of beliefs, perceptions, and expectations about the other's behaviors which are not stated clearly, but which are frequently used to find fault and make judgments which continue to escalate the conflict. The differences in this situation lead to conflict in the sense that they are seen as insults and evidence of not being loved as well as threats to personal autonomy and self-esteem (Satir, 1968). Both Sue and Bob want the other to conform to their wishes and expectations and are unwilling to compromise. Both want to receive rather than to give, and both feel that they are giving more than receiving.

In prioritizing the issues involved in this conflict, the issues of perceptions and beliefs that each holds toward the other is the most complex and difficult to deal with, but also creates most of the difficulties involved in the conflict. The most immediate and smallest unit that can be dealt with at this point is for Sue and Bob to state the other person's viewpoint concerning the conflict (beliefs, feelings, and behaviors involved in the conflict) in a nonjudgmental and nonevaluative fashion. The following hypothetical dialogue may serve to illustrate what we are saying at this point.

Sue: My understanding is that you would like a traditional family system with you in your job and me as a housewife.

Bob: I think you feel controlled by me and that I will punish you by making you feel guilty for not being a super-mom.

Sue: I sense that you feel infringed upon when I ask you to share household chores since I used to do all of them before I started working.

Bob: I'm beginning to understand how my beliefs regarding what I think you should do as a mother come more from what my mother would have done, rather than what you should do. I think how you define yourself as a mother is up to you.

Sue: I appreciate hearing that from you, but I want you to know that my responsibilities are more than just being a mother and wife. I really like my job and feel good about my ability and skill, which are parts of me I really enjoy.

Bob: It's hard for me to accept some of the changes in our relationship. I have a lot of ideas and beliefs that conflict with how you are choosing to live your life. I want to make the right choices and decisions with you. I agree with you that you have the right to choose how you want to live your life, but I want you to be sensitive to my needs as you ask me to be sensitive to yours.

The effect of such communication is to foster cooperation, under-standing, and mutuality, and at the same time to encourage the couple to be reality-based, thus paving the way for future negotiations and compromise.

The next step may be negotiating. It may be helpful for Bob and Sue to make a list of what they are each willing to do to bring about a compromise—i.e., hiring some help to do housework, owning and accepting their own frustration instead of dumping it on the other, more open and direct communication, and division of necessary tasks among all family members.

The next step is to agree upon how they can reinforce each other for new behavior. Sue and Bob can engage in mutual support-giving and nurturing by attending to, recognizing, and complimenting one an-other for demonstrating such behavior. A designated time each week could be used for evaluation and maintenance of the processes in-volved in coping with the conflict.

In conjunction with the previously mentioned strategies, a check-list of specific goals for behavior change could be posted in an oppor-tune place. Couples could keep a record by checking the various behavior goals on the list. This record could serve as a method of keeping track of the frequency that the desired behaviors were engaged in, verifying concrete changes. This information could be used at the weekly meetings to assess the effects of the strategies being used.

CREATIVE EFFORTS FOR MAINTENANCE AND ENRICHMENT

As conflicts begin to be resolved, and more balance and mutuality is being achieved in the dual-career family, there may be time and energy to go beyond stability to some other creative modes of family maintenance and enrichment. Assuming that basic needs are now being met in a more satisfactory manner, family members can seek to fulfill some needs for personal growth. The spirit of what we are attempting to express here deals with the heart of the issue of balance in relationships, in that family members are free to give and receive rather than having to feel obligated and controlled.

Frequently family members feel that they do not have resources to meet the demands that are thrust upon them. When our society was less mobile, families often found other relatives to help with certain tasks or activities. Many families today feel a need for this kind of shared help, as well as the emotional support that kinship networks provided. Families may want to develop new "relatives"—close friends who can share work tasks as well as their joys and sorrows. They may join together for frequent celebrations of friendship as well as sharing child care, maintenance of cars, communal gardens, or putting on a new roof. One such multi-family cooperative is a group of families who bought a ranch together. There is a separate dwelling for each family, but the work and rewards of the ranch are shared and a sense of support and closeness are developing.

Relationships frequently become stagnant due to lack of maintenance. In general, people tend to be better at mate selection than at relationship maintenance, as evidenced by the current rate of divorce. Sustaining contact seems to be an important factor in relationship growth. There may be several ways that a couple may use to enhance their relationship, such as planning a monthly rendezvous geared toward revitalizing the marriage by talking about what they wish to recapture, what they hope for in the future, and what they value in each other and the marriage.

Relationships tend to go sour when the individuals hold back, retreat, and withdraw from each other. A method for dealing with this is to spend some time writing letters to each other expressing unshared feelings, hopes and aspirations, requests, and things that they felt especially good about that went unexpressed.

What was previously suggested in the chapter will be most beneficial if carried out in a spirit of honest intentions and genuine involvement. The rejuvenating encounters we suggest work best when couples speak to, look at, and contact each other directly, using "I" messages (e.g., "I appreciate your sensitivity to me when I'm down"). Physical contacts (caressing, holding, and touching) may be more powerful ways of expressing tenderness, love, and concern than words, are certainly part of genuine encounters, and definitely enrich relationships.

In order tó be able to give to another in a spirit of enrichment, one may first need to be good to oneself. Some examples of self-enhancing endeavors that may bring inner peace and a readiness to be positively involved with others are yoga, meditation, jogging, poetry, music, and art. The individual needs to participate in the selected activity on a regular basis in order to maximize its potential to relax and energize. There are many ways one can achieve self-renewal; the method should be directed toward tuning in to oneself, increasing one's sense of well-being, and ultimately leading to heightened sense of awareness of self and others.

SUMMARY

Many dual-career families are faced with an overload of roles, responsibilities, and expectations, often creating situations of imbalance and conflict. Individuals may experience interrole conflict and intrarole conflict. In addition, there seems to be a developing transition or an alternation between traditional sex role stereotypes and more egalitarian values supporting dual-career relationships. Such circumstances are likely to contribute to the decay of family morale and support, and even to divorce.

On the other hand, dual-career families appear to have the resources for pulling together to work as a unit in which family members can achieve self-actualization. If open communication and a spirit of cooperation develops, each person is more likely to meet his or her own needs, both basic and creative, and to feel willing to help others meet their needs. This is not to suggest that an idyllic situation will magically exist, because significant relationships that are meaningful continuously require maintenance and energy. However, dual-career families can do many things to enrich their relationships and to provide for flexibility and balance.

A major focus of this chapter is a model for conflict resolution, in which problems are defined in specific terms, various resolution strategies are reviewed and weighed, and selected strategies are implemented and then finally evaluated. In order for conflict resolution to operate smoothly and to cope with both surface and underlying issues, a commitment to the dual-career relationship seems to be necessary. If one of the members does not endorse the dual-career situation, that person is less likely to sincerely endeavor to use conflict resolution in a meaningful fashion.

Paramount in what we advocate is for dual-career couples to share in creating the kind of mutual lifestyle that provides support, satisfaction of needs, stimulation, enrichment, and continuous growth.

REFERENCES

BLAKE, J. (1974) "The changing status of women in developed countries." Scientific American (September): 137–147.

COGSWELL, B. E. (1975) "Variant family forms and life styles: rejection of the traditional nuclear family." Family Coordinator 24 (October): 391–406.

ELDER, G. H., Jr. and R. C. ROCKWELL (1976) "Marital timing in women's life patterns." Journal of Family History 1 (Autumn): 34–53.

ERICKSEN, J., E. YANCE, and E. ERICKSEN (1979) "The division of family roles." Journal of Marriage and Family (May).

FREY, D. (1979) "Understanding and managing conflict," in R. Eisenberg and M. Patterson (eds.) Helping Clients with Special Concerns. Chicago: Rand McNally.

GAUGER, W. (1973) "Household work: can we add it to the GNP?" Journal of Home Economics (October): 12–23.

GIELE, J. (1979) "Changing sex roles and family structure." Social Policy (February).

GIANOPULOS, A. and H. MITCHELL (1975) "Marital disagreement in working wife marriage as a function of husband's attitude toward wife's employment." Marriage and Family Living (November).

HALL, D. T. (1972) "A model of coping with role conflict: the role behavior of college educated women." Administrative Science Quarterly 7.

HERMAN, J. B. and K. K. GYLLSTROM (1977) "Working men and women: inter and intra-role conflict." Psychology of Women Quarterly 1.

JOHNSON, D. W. (1972) Reaching Out, Interpersonal Effectiveness and Self-Actualization. Englewood Cliffs, NJ: Prentice-Hall.

KAHN, R. L., D. M. WOLFE, R. P. QUINN, J. D. SNOEK, and R. A. ROSENTHAL (1964) Organizational Stress: Studies in Role Conflict and Ambiguity. New York: John Wiley.

LEVINE, J. A. (1976) Who Will Raise the Children?: New Options for Fathers (and Mothers). Philadelphia: J. B. Lippincott.

OHLSEN, M. M. (1977) Group Counseling. New York, Holt, Rinehart & Winston.

PALOMARES, U. (1975) "A curriculum on conflict management." Human Development Training Institute, La Mesa, California.

SATIR, V. (1968) Conjoint Family Therapy. San Francisco: Science and Behavior Books.

SZALAI, A. (1973) "The quality of family life—traditional and modern: a review of sociological findings on contemporary family organizations and role differentiation in the family." Presented at the United Nations Interregional Seminar on the Family in a Changing Society: Problems and Responsibilities of Its Members, London, July 18–31.

TERHUNE, K. R. (1970) "The effects of personality in cooperation and conflict," in A. P. Swingle (ed.) The Structure of Conflict. New York: Academic Press.

VANEK, J. (1974) "Time spent in housework." Scientific American (November): 116–120.

PART III

CAREER ISSUES

10

COORDINATED-CAREER COUPLES: CONVERGENCE AND DIVERGENCE

Matilda Butler
William Paisley

A couple in which both partners work outside the home may be referred to as a *dual-job* couple. If both partners are committed to the continuity of their work—that is, if the work is important for personal development as well as for household income—then we may say that they are a dual-*career* couple. If the couple chooses to work together in the same field or in another arrangement that causes their work activities to overlap, we may say further that they are a *coordinated*-career couple.

Special opportunities and constraints face couples who attempt to coordinate their careers. The maxim that "two heads are better than one" has added significance when the two heads are keeping up with the same field. Coordinated-career couples can maintain more extensive networks of associates than individuals can. Partners with coordinated careers can also exchange effort on behalf of each other's projects as needed.

However, most coordinated-career couples find it difficult to achieve their shared goals in a given place at a given time. They are more subject to the caprices of the job market than are individuals. They must also cope with the suspicion of employers who view them as a two-person clique whether they work in the same organization or not. The "effort elasticity" of their relationship disappears when job stresses (e.g., promotion reviews) coincide, as will happen to persons whose careers are "in step."

Since the uncertainties of employment make total coordination a quixotic goal, couples pursue career plans that allow for both convergence and divergence in their activities. Especially in their younger years, they must make career choices that promise only a limited degree of coordination. The synergy that flows from a high degree of coordination is usually reserved for older couples with many career moves and compromises behind them.

FORMS OF COORDINATION

The structure of occupations determines reasonable limits for coordinated activity in each case. Two persons who are both musicians can "make beautiful music together" in the same orchestra, but not if they are both conductors. Two persons who are both surgeons would probably not work together in the operating theater; two persons who are both pilots may not be allowed to fly together. However, two teachers, researchers, therapists, writers, and the like can readily work side by side, depending of course on their temperaments and preferred modes of working.

Close coordination in some occupations implies a status differential which some couples accept as natural because of ability or seniority differences but which other couples will not tolerate. An aircraft, for example, has only one pilot; the other person is a copilot. A laboratory typically has only one director; the other person is an associate director. Two persons who have taught together may eventually progress to the point where either of them, but not both, can be department chairperson.

Thus, while the closest form of career coordination is side-by-side collaboration on the same tasks, there are structural and status reasons why many couples do not regard such *alter ego coordination* as feasible or even desirable. Furthermore, alter ego coordination becomes less feasible as couples progress in their joint careers to a level where the positions are "one of a kind."

An arrangement often seen among older couples who have faced the problem of reconciling the commonality of their interests with the singularity of higher-level positions is that of *institutional coordination*. They work in the same institution but not on the same tasks. While still benefiting to some extent from each other's ideas and knowledge of events, they have gained more flexibility in responding to institutional opportunities than an "alter ego couple" has.

To other couples, it is more important to continue working on the same tasks than to be employed by the same institution. They pursue *specialty coordination* by working as researchers in different laboratories, as teachers in different departments, as editors of different publications. In the early stages of their careers they can shift to alter ego coordination by moving to the same institution. In later stages, after they have climbed closer to the top of the pyramid of positions, no institution may be able to employ them both in the same specialty.

A fourth and final form of career coordination can be called *complementary roles coordination*. In these cases, it is of secondary importance whether the couples are employed by the same institution or work ostensibly in the same specialty. What *is* important is the contribution of each career to the success of the partner's career or to the success of a joint venture. One person may teach a specialty, such as law or business, that the partner practices. One person may enjoy or excel in conceiving or creating; the partner may enjoy or excel in some practical follow-through. There are also "music and lyrics" collaborations—interdependent use of different training and skills.

The four forms of career coordination are shown graphically in Figure 10.1. Only one variety of complementary roles coordination, that in which the couple works in different institutions and different specialties, is shown.

BACKGROUND STUDIES

In the past several years we have attempted to account for differences in career activity and achievement among male and female

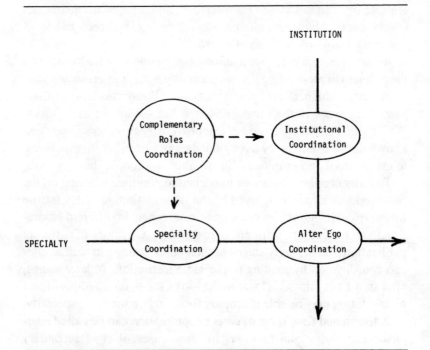

FIGURE 10.1 Four Forms of Career Coordination

NOTE: Complementary roles coordination can be worked out either with or without institutional or specialty coordination.

professionals, with emphasis on the activity and achievement of couples in psychology. Two studies of relevance to this chapter involved department chairpersons and couples in which both partners were members of the American Psychological Association.

(1) Survey of department chairpersons. Pingree et al. (1978) sent a questionnaire concerned with anti-nepotism policies to chairpersons of psychology and sociology departments in 2027 colleges and universities listed in the *College Blue Book* (1969). Only one department was randomly sampled in each institution. Questionnaires were returned by 329 (16 percent) of the departments, although 62 percent of 34 "major" departments (coded for separate analysis) responded.

The dependent variables of the study were perceived advantages or disadvantages to couples or to departments resulting from joint employment. Independent variables included the status of the department, its experience in employing couples, and its declared attitude toward hiring couples.

As might be predicted, most perceived advantages and disadvantages were converses of each other. That is, if a circumstance was expected to work out well, it was cited as an advantage. If the same circumstance was expected to work out poorly, it was cited as a disadvantage. For example, joint employment was viewed by some chairpersons as contributing to personnel stability in the department. Other chairpersons were more likely to see the disadvantage of two simultaneous vacancies to be filled if and when the couple moved on.

Table 10.1 summarizes the major advantages and disadvantages to the department and to the couple. In addition, supplementary data on the department's experience in employing couples and its attitude toward hiring couples showed the following differences in advantage/disadvantage responses:

(1) Departments with prior experience in employing couples were more likely to cite the "couple as clique" disadvantage than departments without prior experience (49 percent versus 35 percent). The converse was true of the "problems between spouses" and "administrative problems" disadvantages (20 percent versus 28 percent and 28 percent versus 34 percent).

(2) Departments favoring the employment of couples adduce more advantages and fewer disadvantages for themselves than departments that are opposed (27 percent versus fifteen 15 on advantages and 28 percent versus 42 percent on disadvantages). There were no substantial differences in the number of advantages or disadvantages cited with respect to the couples.

(3) The specific responses of "no advantage to department" and "no disadvantage to department" were given by 25 percent and 32 percent of departments favoring employment of couples and by 60 percent and 2 percent of departments opposing employment of couples.

Thus, the number of advantages and disadvantages cited by the department chairpersons was congruent in most cases with attitudes toward employing couples. Coordinated-career couples who are seeking joint employment in psychology and sociology departments

TABLE 10.1   Employing Professional Couples, as Perceived by
                         Department Chairpersons

	Advantages	Disadvantages
To the Department	Couple's unity between personal and professional lives enhances department (23%)	Faculty evaluations are more difficult (31%)
		Couple's marital and emotional problems upset the department (22%)
	Faculty professional and research activities can be coordinated better (14%)	Couple has a disproportionate influence on departmental politics (22%)
	Department has greater personnel stability (12%)	Couple's dissatisfaction may result in two vacancies at the same time (18%)
To the Couple	Couple is better able to unify personal and professional lives (27%)	Department influences couple's decisions and behavior (17%)
	Couple is better able to coordinate professional and research activities (27%)	Joint employment intensifies any competition or jealousy within couple (15%)
		Couple may be unable to maintain separate identities (10%)
	Couple saves resources, expenses, time (16%)	Couple may encounter problems (e.g., resentment) with colleagues (10%)

NOTE: Numbers in parentheses are the percentage of chairpersons making open-ended responses coded into each category.
SOURCE: Adapted from Pingree et al. (1978).

would be well advised to locate the 38 percent of all chairpersons who favor joint employment and have numerous advantages to cite, rather than the 37 percent of all chairpersons who oppose joint employment and have numerous disadvantages to cite.

(2) Status of couples in psychology. Butler and Paisley (1977) investigated the positions and affiliations of wives and husbands who were both members of the American Psychological Association in 1973, the year of the most recent biographical *APA Directory* available at the time of the study, or 1958, the year marking a fifteen-year comparison period. Analysis of the *Directory* uncovered 139 couples in 1958 and 322 couples in 1973. Mail verification of the marital status of the 1973 couples reduced that year's sample to 296. It was not feasible to verify, retroactively, the marital status of the 1958 couples.

The previously known fact that husbands are more successful than their wives who work in the same field (compare Clark, 1957; Fidell, 1970; Astin, 1972) was tested against three "folk hypotheses": (1) that husbands appear to be more successful than their wives because they are older, graduated first, and have more professional years; (2) that husbands are more successful than their wives because they graduated from higher-status universities; and (3) that husbands are more successful than their wives because they have higher degrees.

With regard to the first hypothesis, the median age in 1958 was forty-two for women and forty-three for men; in 1973, the median age was forty-five for women and forty-eight for men. In 1958, the median number of years of professional experience was eleven for women and ten for men; in 1973, it was fourteen for women and eighteen for men. Taking an average of both years, it may be said that husbands are somewhat older (about two years) and have a slight advantage in professional experience (about one and one-half years).

With regard to the second hypothesis, women were more likely than men to have graduated from a higher-status university, using the American Council on Education's rankings (Roose and Andersen, 1970). The differences are minor, however: 67 percent of the women versus 64 percent of the men in 1958; 43 percent of the women versus 42 percent of the men in 1973.

With regard to the third hypothesis, data on highest degrees were available for 1973 but not for 1958. In 1973, 89 percent of the men but only 75 percent of the women held doctorates. Since this difference agrees with the contention of the third hypothesis, further analysis of the educational data was required.

Table 10.2 summarizes the positions and affiliations of the 1958 and 1973 samples. Numerous differences are evident between women and men, adding up to the conclusion that men have been more successful than women even in these restricted samples of husbands and wives.

More-precise tests of the hypotheses resulted from measuring differences within each couple, then tabulating the difference scores according to the couple's professional age, highest degree, and university of graduation. For example, among couples employed in academic institutions in 1958, 82 percent of the husbands held higher-status positions than their wives, 8 percent of the wives held

TABLE 10.2   Positions and Affiliations of Psychologists in Samples of
              Couples, 1958 and 1973

	1958		1973		Both Years	
POSITION	Women	Men	Women	Men	Women	Men
Supervisor	5%	38%	14%	31%	10%	34%
Professor	6%	14%	7%	20%	6%	17%
Assoc. Professor	6%	6%	7%	12%	6%	9%
Assist. Professor	6%	15%	15%	10%	10%	12%
Lecturer	10%	3%	6%	1%	8%	2%
Researcher	18%	7%	7%	2%	12%	4%
Clinician/Therapist/ Counselor	36%	12%	34%	19%	35%	16%
School Psychologist	4%	2%	6%	1%	5%	2%
Other	9%	4%	4%	3%	6%	4%
	115	137	265	290	—	—
AFFILIATION						
Academic	45%	58%	49%	55%	47%	56%
School System	10%	2%	8%	2%	9%	2%
Hospital	14%	8%	8%	10%	11%	9%
Clinic/Group/Individual Practice	23%	15%	28%	19%	26%	17%
Government	2%	1%	2%	4%	2%	2%
Business/Industry	0%	3%	0%	3%	0%	3%
Research Organization	2%	5%	2%	2%	2%	4%
Miscellaneous/Other	4%	8%	3%	5%	4%	6%
	115	137	267	289	—	—

SOURCE: Adapted from Butler and Paisley (1977).

higher-status positions than their husbands, and 10 percent of the
husbands and wives held equal-status positions. In 1973, the corresponding percentages were 54 percent, 15 percent, and 31 percent—
distinctly better but still short of parity. Controlling for professional
age has the effect of increasing the number of couples holding equal-
status positions (from 10 percent to 18 percent in 1958, from 31
percent to 37 percent in 1973). However, controlling for the highest
degree and the status of the university of graduation has almost no
effect on the position status differential.

In the limiting case, husbands and wives who graduated from the same university in the same year and who were employed in 1958 or 1973 in the same university were compared. In 1958, 80 percent of the husbands held higher-status positions, none of the wives held higher-status positions, and 20 percent of the husbands and wives held equal-status positions. In 1973, the corresponding percentages were 60 percent, 5 percent, and 35 percent.

The conclusion of the Butler and Paisley study states that "differences in success between husbands and wives cannot be attributed to age, training, degree, or place of employment" (1977: 318). However, we have passed the point of research on the careers of professional couples where it could be said simply, "The remaining explanation is sex discrimination." Although sex bias and "anti-nepotism's ghost" are obstacles to women's progress, other determinants and decisions within each couple may also lead to these differences in success.

CAREER-COORDINATION STRATEGIES

A model of career coordination can be proposed in which couples begin their joint careers with little coordination, depending not only on the employment opportunities they encounter but also on the milestone in their training or employment when they begin to plan coordinated careers. The "balance point" in their careers is reached when they have achieved as much coordination as their interests and temperaments motivate them to achieve. Prior to reaching the balance point, they may change positions often in "coordination maneuvers." Once the balance point is reached, they may not change their positions again for many years.

Some assumptions of this model may be faulty. First, it is likely that couples meet partly on the basis of proximity and marry partly on the basis of common interests. If these premises are true, then the first years of marriage may mark the highest degree of institutional coordination or specialty coordination that they will achieve. Divergence from the high degree of coordination at the outset of their marriages amounts to a regression effect caused by biased sampling from the pool of all persons whose work is potentially coordinatable.

Second, time samples of the activities of couples may find some of them engaged in coordination maneuvers that cannot be interpreted by an outside observer. If one partner returns to graduate school or accepts a mid-career fellowship, he or she will appear to be uncoordinated with the working partner even though the goal of the move is to improve coordination thereafter.

Third, some complementary role coordination will be missed or misinterpreted by an outside observer. In a field like psychology, one partner may be a "soft" clinician while the other is a "hard" statistician; the apparent distance between their specialties may mask a successful collaboration involving the exchange of theories, examples, and methods. The outside observer's predicament is that another couple working in these specialties may not be collaborating at all.

Fourth, the "balance point" may be a false assumption. Even among couples who prize coordination and work toward it, other career-development goals may keep partners "off balance." Presumably, the goals of higher status, more responsibility, more income, more interesting work, and more congenial surroundings motivate couples as well as individuals; if so, tradeoffs between coordination and other goals seem inevitable.

This discussion gives rise to three research questions:

(1) Is there a conscious coordination strategy among couples whose work is coordinated or potentially coordinatable?
(2) How do couples articulate these strategies—does a system of strategies emerge?
(3) Can the indicators of coordinated-career strategies be found in aggregate data concerning couples, as well as in case history data?

THREE EXPLORATORY STUDIES

Three studies conducted during 1979 were focused on these questions. In the first study, case histories prepared by couples themselves were analyzed for coordination strategies. In the second study, the 296 couples found in the 1973 *APA Directory* (Butler and Paisley, 1977) were followed forward in time via the 1978 *APA Directory*, and

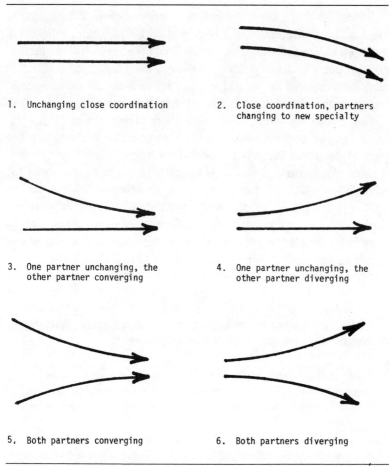

1. Unchanging close coordination

2. Close coordination, partners changing to new specialty

3. One partner unchanging, the other partner converging

4. One partner unchanging, the other partner diverging

5. Both partners converging

6. Both partners diverging

FIGURE 10.2 Models of Specialty Coordination over Time

their career shifts between 1973 and 1978 were tabulated. In the third study, the publication histories of forty couples from the APA sample were analyzed from 1968 to 1978.

The newsletter of an information service whose mailing list includes many professional women contained a request for brief case histories of dual-career couples, written by one or both of the partners. Forty-five case histories ranging in length from one to several pages were received.

For analysis purposes, the couples were categorized according to the kind of coordination they seemed to be pursuing, whether it involved their specialty, their institution, both specialty and institution, or complementary roles. Although the number of couples in each category was too small for quantitative analysis, the categories served to organize the qualitative analysis that follows.

Couples whose work is coordinated both in specialty and in institution (alter ego coordination) were well represented in the sample. In general, they had little to say about the dynamics of *becoming* coordinated (i.e., coordination maneuvers) and much to say about the advantages and disadvantages of *being* coordinated. They were not reflective (on paper) about compromises along the road to coordination. Indeed, their goal of doing similar work in a similar setting may have been simpler to plan toward than the goals of couples whose specialties or institutional preferences pulled in different directions.

Spokepersons for these couples made statements such as:

We not only have a dual career, we have a joint career in that we work together in writing and consultation. Our work and home life is very integrated, which we consider an advantage.

Being in the same field, we have the support of each other as colleagues as well. We find each other a good source of help, ideas, thinking about work, and frequently consult each other about professional concerns.

Because we are in the same field, we support and encourage each other and have developed an understanding regarding the pressures on the job and at home. We understand the fields [sic] each other is engaged in and function as positive critiquers for each other.

On the negative side, couples whose work is coordinated both in specialty and in institution most often complained of a lack of mobility:

[There is the] difficulty of finding jobs in the same location. I would like to move up and may need to move away from area to do so. Our mobility is affected.

The biggest difficulty is lack of mobility in regard to the job. We've both held each other back, I'm sure, because it's so hard for two people in the same field to get placed.

The task of finding two satisfying jobs in more or less the same place seems pretty overwhelming. We both have had to come to terms with the possibility that it might be the other one who gets a good offer, and that the one without a job . . . may be unemployed for a while.

Only among the doubly coordinated couples did a woman mention the following:

[Our] collaborative research efforts are generally successful. However, I've heard some (sexist) biologists say that they "couldn't evaluate" my research contributions since they were joint efforts with my husband.

Couples who share the same specialty but work in different types of institutions seem more relaxed about problems of mobility and of comparison with each other's accomplishments. One spokesperson summarized several advantages of this arrangement:

[There is] professional synergism. He does it; I teach it. So he gets tidbits from the academic world, pre-screened so that I pass on what will be useful in terms of the projects he has underway. I get "war stories" from actual companies, and I get his critique of which of those academic tidbits bear any relation to reality. Also each of us reads half the publications that we should, then point out to each other what's useful.

Among couples who work in the same type of institution but pursue different specialties, there is a surprising amount of reference to separation, past or present:

Both of us have limited job mobility if we want to live together. We have lived apart for two periods of time (2.5 years total) because of our careers, not because of our relationship.

The primary current disadvantage of our two professional careers is, of course, our separation [she is working at an East Coast university, he at a West Coast university]. It is difficult to find two fairly high level positions in an area. . . . We are able to get together approximately every six weeks.

Perhaps in contrast to couples who share both specialty and institution (alter ego coordination), couples who pursue different specialties at the same institution are concerned about receiving recognition for their separate work:

I must use my maiden name in order not to be viewed as his appendage.

When I consider that the two of us are virtually the same age and have worked the same number of years, it seems unfair that he is seen as Boy Wonder and I, as lucky to be on the Junior Varsity.

People see us as a "bloc." For example, we are both representatives to the college senate. We don't sit together at meetings to avoid looking like a voting bloc. No doubt, however, some of our colleagues think we're having marital difficulties.

Couples who differ both in specialty and in type of institution cite as advantages:

Differences in career choices provide cross-over stimulation.

More intellectual exchange and compatibility.

Both of us keep growing, but not at the expense of the other's career. . . . A sense of humor and a willingness to do more than our share, when it is needed, keeps [sic] things running fairly smoothly. . . . We have each had some honors from our respective professions.

As it happens, two of these three couples have geographically separated jobs and see each other only on weekends. The spokesperson for the third (unseparated) couple lists as disadvantages:

No "wives" to do the scut work. Difficulty in coordinating vacations and other leisure activities. Less time for sex and other interactions. Restricted opportunities for or with children.

The theme of too much work, rarely stated by other couples, recurs in the statements of couples differing both in specialty and in type of institution:

> There are many nights when the job has been draining and all we want to do is collapse, but one of our children [has a problem]. . . . I, the female, continue to carry the majority of the load at home. Although he shares more home-related chores than most men with non-working wives, he doesn't carry 50%.

> Persons find it convenient to make demands upon me on the basis of my husband's position, though we have not had any demands placed upon him by my employers.

The couples who responded to the invitation to describe the advantages and disadvantages of their dual careers may have been a biased sample, but within them not even one spokesperson expressed doubts about the career paths they had chosen. Older couples with senior positions and grown children said more about the advantages of dual careers than younger couples who are trying to establish their careers and their families at the same time. However, the latter did not question (on paper) the need to keep "juggling all of life's balls (children, house/home, career, community, et al.) while avoiding overload, frenzy, scheduling conflicts."

The most notable omission from these case histories of dual-career couples was the discussion of coordinated strategies couched in the general form of "five years ago we were . . . ; now we are . . . ; five years from now we shall be. . . ." Both older and younger couples, working in the same or different specialties and institutions, seem to be taking their dual careers one year at a time.

CAREER TRANSITIONS OF COUPLES IN PSYCHOLOGY

Coordinated strategies that were not mentioned in the case histories may still be indicated by the pattern of career transitions that are made by couples over a period of, say, five years. To test this possibility, the 296 couples that were previously identified in the 1973 *APA Directory* were followed forward in time via the 1978 *Directory*. Their careers in 1973 and 1978 were classified as either same or different in specialty and type of institution. Specialty was coded one level below the "major field" listed in the *Directory*. In the 1978 *Directory*, this level was labeled "specialty"; in the 1973 *Directory*, it consisted of a listing of subfields following each person's major field code. Six types of institutions were coded: (1) college or university; (2) hospital, clinic, or counseling center; (3) school system; (4) business or industry; (5) government agency; and (6) private practice or other self-employment.

Of the 296 couples identified in 1973, 38 were no longer APA members in 1978, 34 had reached retirement age, 6 had no employment history, and 5 were apparently no longer married, leaving 213 couples with active specialties and institutional affiliations in both 1973 and 1978. In both 1973 and 1978, about 35 percent of the 213 couples were coded as sharing both specialty and type of institution, followed by 27 percent pursuing different specialties at the same type of institution, 25 percent pursuing different specialties at different types of institutions, and 14 percent pursuing the same specialty at different types of institutions.

Figure 10.3 shows the sixty-eight transitions made by the 213 couples between 1973 and 1978. These transitions do not represent all the job changes that took place during the period. Changes that were made and then reversed midway between 1973 and 1978 would not have been coded. Changes that kept the couple in the same category (most commonly, changing colleges together) also would not have been coded.

Although the pattern of transitions appears to be balanced insofar as similar numbers of couples entered and left each category, three findings merit further attention:

(1) The number of couples sharing both specialty and institution declined over time.
(2) The number of couples sharing neither specialty nor institution increased over time.
(3) Almost all (93 percent) of the transitions involved only one change in the four attributes (two specialties and two institutional affiliations) describing each couple.

The first two findings agree with a divergence model of career coordination, which is predicated on an "artificial" degree of coordination when the couples meet and marry in graduate school or in their

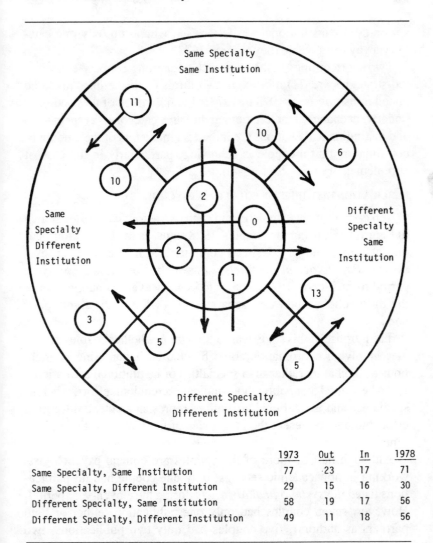

	1973	Out	In	1978
Same Specialty, Same Institution	77	23	17	71
Same Specialty, Different Institution	29	15	16	30
Different Specialty, Same Institution	58	19	17	56
Different Specialty, Different Institution	49	11	18	56

FIGURE 10.3 Couples' Transitions in Specialty and Type of Institution, 1973–1978

early careers. In other words, the requirements of positions and institutions tend to draw couples apart, into less-coordinated activities.

The third finding suggests that the majority of changes are not capricious. In 93 percent of the cases, one partner changed either his or her specialty or institutional affiliation, or both partners changed specialties of institutional affiliations but wound up only one category away from where they were in 1973.

Two shortcomings in this approach to charting couples' coordinated strategies are: (1) more than two-thirds of the couples made no coded transition from 1973 to 1978, although many of these couples underwent changes that left them in the same category; (2) specialties and institutional affiliations are imperfect indicators of the amount of coordination that a couple is achieving, particularly in the case of complementary roles coordination.

PUBLICATION HISTORIES OF COUPLES IN PSYCHOLOGY

Ten couples were sampled from each of the four categories shown in Figure 10.3, using the couples' 1978 status as the basis for assigning them to a category. Using a computerized information-retrieval system, *Psychological Abstracts* was searched over the eleven-year period from 1968 to 1978 in order to identify every copublication of the forty couples and every separate publication of the eighty partners.

The purpose of this study was to determine whether couples' strategies involving coordination could be charted better using publications as indicators rather than specialties or institutional affiliations. It can be argued that publications indicate actual joint effort, whereas specialties and institutional affiliations represent a potential for joint effort but also represent the exigencies of the job market at a given time.

Although half or more of the couples are clinical psychologists working in nonacademic settings, only one couple had no publications listed in *Psychological Abstracts* during the eleven-year period. However, seven couples had only one publication (either or both partners as authors), five couples had only two publications, two couples had three publications, and a total of eight other couples had fewer than ten publications.

Turning to the other end of the distribution, the most productive couple had sixty-eight publications in eleven years, followed by couples with forty-five, thirty-one, and twenty-eight publications and by two couples with twenty-two publications.

Wives and husbands were differentially productive across the four categories of specialty and institutional affiliation. Among couples sharing both specialty and institutional affiliations, the median number of publications for wives and husbands was 6.0 and 5.0, respectively. Among couples pursuing the same specialty at different types of institutions, the median number of publications for wives and husbands was 1.5 each. When couples differ in specialty, productivity favors the husband: 1.0 versus 3.5 publications among couples at the same type of institution and 0.5 versus 5.0 publications among couples at different types of institutions. These productivity differences are based on small samples and therefore cannot be regarded as reliable, but it is noteworthy that wives and husbands are so equally matched in productivity when they share the same specialty and so unequally matched when they are pursuing different specialties.

In order to be included in the analysis of copublication and separate publication over time, a couple had to have a total of ten publications with no fewer than three publications coming from the less productive partner. Eleven of the forty couples met this criterion. Table 10.3 shows the publication histories of couples sharing both specialty and institutional affiliation. Table 10.4 shows the publication histories of couples differing in at least one of these attributes.

TABLE 10.3   Copublishing and Separate Publishing by Couples in Same Specialty and Type of Institution (number of articles listed in *Psychological Abstracts*)

Year	Couple 1 W	J	H	Couple 2 W	J	H	Couple 3 W	J	H	Couple 4 W	J	H	Couple 5 W	J	H
1968	—	—	1	—	—	2	1	—	1	—	—	—	—	—	—
1969	2	—	2	1	—	2	3	—	1	—	—	1	—	1	—
1970	—	—	3	1	—	1	—	1	—	2	2	—	—	1	1
1971	1	—	2	—	1	—	—	—	1	1	—	2	—	—	—
1972	1	—	1	—	—	2	1	—	2	—	1	2	1	—	—
1973	4	—	2	—	—	—	—	—	1	—	1	—	2	1	—
1974	1	—	1	1	2	—	—	—	3	2	1	—	2	—	—
1975	2	1	1	1	—	1	3	—	—	1	2	1	1	—	—
1976	1	—	—	—	—	—	—	—	1	—	—	1	2	—	—
1977	2	—	1	2	—	—	—	—	2	—	—	—	—	—	—
1978	1	—	1	—	—	1	—	—	1	—	2	—	—	—	—
Total	15	1	15	6	3	9	8	1	13	6	9	7	8	3	1

NOTE: Key: W = published by wife; J = published jointly; H = published by husband.

TABLE 10.4   Copublishing and Separate Publishing by Couples in Different Specialties or Types of Institutions (number of articles listed in *Psychological Abstracts*)

Year	Couple 6			Couple 7			Couple 8			Couple 9			Couple 10			Couple 11		
	W	J	H	W	J	H	W	J	H	W	J	H	W	J	H	W	J	H
1968	—	—	—	—	36	—	—	1	3	—	—	1	—	—	—	—	—	—
1969	2	—	10	—	7	—	—	—	2	—	—	—	1	—	—	—	—	—
1970	3	—	10	—	—	—	—	—	3	—	—	2	1	—	3	—	—	2
1971	1	—	4	—	—	—	1	—	1	—	2	—	1	—	1	1	—	1
1972	1	—	6	—	—	—	—	—	—	—	—	1	2	—	1	—	1	1
1973	6	—	7	—	—	—	—	—	2	—	—	1	—	—	1	1	—	1
1974	2	—	3	—	—	—	—	—	4	—	1	—	—	—	2	—	—	3
1975	3	—	3	—	—	—	3	—	1	—	2	1	—	—	2	—	—	—
1976	—	—	1	—	—	—	—	—	—	—	—	—	—	2	1	—	—	—
1977	1	—	2	—	—	—	3	—	1	—	—	—	—	—	1	—	—	—
1978	1	—	2	—	2	—	2	—	1	—	—	3	—	—	—	—	—	—
Total	20	—	48	—	45	—	9	1	18	—	5	9	5	2	12	2	1	8

NOTE: Key: W = published by wife; J = published jointly; H = published by husband; Couples 6 and 7: Same specialty, different type of institution. Couples 8, 9, and 10: Different specialty, same type of institution. Couple 11: Different specialty, different type of institution.

Wives and husbands in couples like 1 and 3 appear to publish together by whim or by fortuitous circumstance. Their single co-publications do not occur at the beginning of the time period, indicating movement away from joint effort, nor at the end of the time period, indicating movement toward joint effort. Each partner is reasonably productive in separate publications throughout the time period, and the single copublications occur in the middle of sequences of separate productivity.

Couples 6 and 7 exhibit the extreme possibilities: high productivity without ever publishing together and high productivity without ever publishing separately (in 1968, couple 7 *did* copublish thirty-six articles together; these articles were mainly bibliographic reviews being published as a series by one journal). Couple 9 exhibits another extreme pattern in which one partner publishes separately but the other partner only copublishes.

If we can assume that one indicator of a coordinated strategy, whether or not the couple publishes together, is consistent productivity over the eleven-year period, then couples 1 and 6 exhibit coordinated strategies. Couple 4, which has the best balance of copublication and separate publication, also seems to be working within a coordinated strategy, although this couple does not publish in every year (a year off from publishing may, of course, be part of a coordinated-career strategy).

Patterns of discontinuity like those of couples 7 and 11 might tell us a great deal about the couples' strategies if we, as the outside observers, could interpret the patterns. Unfortunately, we do not know why couple 7 did not publish between 1970 and 1977, nor do we know why couple 11 published only between 1970 and 1974.

CONCLUSION

These data show us couples working together and separately, changing specialties and institutional affiliations, converging toward the "same-same" category of specialty and affiliation and diverging toward the "different-different" category, publishing with and without each other, and so on. What is not as apparent in the midst of all this activity is a system of career coordination strategies that the couples are consciously following.

The case histories infrequently mentioned multiyear plans or if-then contingencies. The transition data coded from the *APA Directory* showed slightly more movement toward divergence than convergence. The publication histories exhibit only a small number of archetypal patterns in which couples always or never publish in a certain way; most of the couples had published at least one article together, but copublishing is much less common than separate publishing.

Although roughly equal numbers of couples are moving toward convergence and divergence, there are indications in the data that convergence is a better goal if couples are temperamentally suited for it. All the case histories were positive about coordinated careers in principle, but couples sharing both specialty and institutional affiliation were more likely to mention the gratifications of their work and less likely to mention the exhaustion brought on by jobs, home, children, and the like. These "same-same" couples also had the highest joint productivity in the publication histories.

If not exactly a survival guide for young couples beginning coordinated careers, this study at least shows them that there are many ways to pursue such careers. The study also challenges other researchers who share our interest in the unfolding of career strategies, particularly with respect to sex differences in strategies and outcomes, to find indicators of career coordination that are less enigmatic than employment and publication histories per se.

REFERENCES

ASTIN, H. S. (1972) "Employment and career status of women psychologists." American Psychologist 27: 371–381.

BUTLER, M. and W. PAISLEY (1977) "Status of professional couples in psychology." Psychology of Women Quarterly 1: 307–318.

CLARK, K. E. (1957) America's Psychologists: A Survey of a Growing Profession. Washington, DC: American Psychological Association.

College Blue Book (1969/1970) New York: CCM Information Corporation.

FIDELL, L. (1970) "Empirical verification of sex discrimination in hiring practices in psychology." American Psychologist 25: 1041–1048.

PINGREE, S., M. BUTLER, W. PAISLEY, and R. HAWKINS (1978) "Anti-nepotism's ghost: attitudes of administrators toward hiring professional couples." Psychology of Women Quarterly 3: 22–29.

ROOSE, K. D. and C. J. ANDERSEN (1970) A Rating of Graduate Education. Washington, DC: American Council on Education.

11

EQUAL OPPORTUNITY LAWS AND
DUAL-CAREER COUPLES

Donna M. Moore

INTRODUCTION

The latest wave of the women's movement which began during the 1960s as well as the earlier civil rights movements left in its wake a series of laws which guarantee equal opportunity in employment for women (Friedan, 1977; Kanter, 1977). These laws have created a dilemma, however. While established to protect women's employment rights, they also sometimes establish career difficulties for women who are part of a dual-career couple.[1] Pogrebin (1975) points out that the dual-career family differs from both the two-person career—with both partners devoted to the career success of the husband—and the two-job family—where both partners work, but where the wife is seen as having a "job" which is dispensable and/or secondary while the husband has a career which requires everyone's support. The dual-career family is one in which the careers of both husband and wife are taken seriously; career commitment, motivation, and importance are attributed equally to both partners.

In addition to the legal issues, there are questions of alternative work patterns. Partly because the labor market has seen an influx of dual-career couples, partly because working women are making more demands for equitable sharing of household chores and child care, and partly because men are beginning to seek a more balanced combination of work and leisure, the search for optional work patterns has escalated in recent years. This chapter will give an overview of the laws related to equal employment opportunity, highlight the portions of those laws which are notably problematic for dual-career couples, and review the advantages and disadvantages of alternative work patterns being explored by employers and dual-career couples.

EQUAL EMPLOYMENT OPPORTUNITY: THE LAW

Title VII of the Civil Rights Act of 1964/The Equal Employment Opportunity Act of 1972 makes it unlawful employment practice for an employer (1) to fail or refuse to hire or to discharge any individual, or otherwise to discriminate against any individual with respect to his (sic) compensation, terms, conditions, or privileges of employment, because of such individual's race, color, religion, sex, or national origin; or (2) to limit, segregate, or classify his (sic) employees or applicants for employment in any way which would deprive or tend to deprive any individual of employment opportunities or otherwise adversely affect his (sic) status as an employee, because of such individual's race, color, religion, sex, or national origin [Section 703(a)].

Title VII was initially written to guarantee nondiscrimination on the basis of race and religion. The word "sex" was added by a Southern congressman who hoped that the inclusion of sex would take the pressure off employers who were discriminating on the basis of race. There is some indication that he had also hoped adding the word "sex" would insure the bill's defeat in Congress. Transcripts from the Congressional hearings tell us that including "sex" provided a great deal of comic relief to discussion of the bill—sex discrimination was clearly not seen as an important area of job bias (Friedan, 1977;

Pogrebin, 1975). The Equal Employment Opportunity Commission, which administers Title VII, indicates, however, that discrimination cases against women account for as many complaints as all the other categories combined. While women were almost excluded from this law, their inclusion and the ability it has given them to file discrimination complaints has expanded a philosophical and moral issue into a legal issue as well (Sandler, 1973).

Executive Order 11246 was issued in 1965 and amended to include sex by Executive Order 11365 in 1967. This presidential Executive Order carries the weight of law and requires all federal government contractors to have written affirmative action plans to include goals and timetables for hiring classes of persons who have previously been underutilized, notably women and minorities.

Title IX of the Education Amendments Act of 1972 prohibits discrimination on the basis of sex against students of any educational institution receiving federal financial aid. Recent court cases have held that Title IX does not protect employees of educational institutions but that employees must seek redress under Title VII.

While there are numerous laws protecting the rights of employees, Title VII and Executive Order 11246 as amended are the major ones protecting women from sex discrimination in obtaining employment and in receiving equitable treatment once they are employed. These, then, are the laws we will examine with regard to problems for dual-career couples.

THE LAWS: EFFECTS ON
DUAL-CAREER COUPLES

The major problem area in Title VII and Executive Order 11375 for dual-career couples is the area of *recruitment and selection*. Employers are required to analyze and review recruitment procedures for each of their job categories to identify and eliminate discriminatory barriers. Essentially, this means that employers are no longer allowed to seek employees exclusively or primarily through word of mouth or "walk-ins" which tend to perpetuate the present composition of a work force (if such composition is lacking women or other protected classes of persons). Such procedures have been ruled by courts to be "discriminatory practice" where females are not well represented at all levels. Further, employers are not allowed to advertise for persons of only one sex.

In recruiting applicants for jobs, then, employers are encouraged to utilize a wide range of sources, including but not limited to those places where one could expect to attract female applicants such as women's schools, women's organizations, media directed toward women, and by utilizing females currently employed by the organization to recruit applicants. The law does not require national searches, as some have implied, but simply states that employers must fill jobs in a non-discriminatory manner and must look for applicants wherever they might reasonably be found—for many positions, this will entail a national search, but certainly not for all positions.

While the law appears to be fair, it can be problematic for the dual-career couple, largely due to the requirement that persons be recruited in a non-discriminatory manner for positions and the requirement that employers select the best-qualified applicant for the job. For example, if an organization is recruiting for an engineer and a woman applies and is offered the position, she might begin negotiating for the company to also employ her husband who is an architect. While the company might wish to hire the husband, both because they want to keep the woman and because they feel the husband would be a valuable employee, they must be very cautious about offering the man a position which has either been created specifically for him or for which they have not publicly recruited applicants. Should they hire the husband without public advertisement, they run the risk of a female architect, who would very much like to have a job with that company, filing litigation charging that the hiring practice had been discriminatory, not allowing her to compete openly for work. If, on the other hand, they openly recruit applications for an architect's job, the female architect would apply and possibly be judged as much more qualified than the male applicant, and therefore be hired. As can be seen, the company has now gone through a delay while advertising for an architect, they have not hired the engineer's husband, and they may very likely lose both the female engineer and her architect spouse. This, of course, creates some anger in the company, which results in resistance to operating under good hiring procedures in the future—all of which gets blamed on Affirmative Action laws, and women and/or minorities.

These problems do not occur if the organization advertises for both an engineer and an architect simultaneously and the husband and wife are each the best-qualified applicant for their respective positions. The likelihood that such would be the case, of course, is remote.

Few couples will be fortunate enough to find a single organization, or two organizations within the same geographic location, recruiting for persons in both their professions at the same time. It is also unlikely, even if such simultaneous opportunities arose, that both husband and wife would be judged as the best-qualified applicants during such simultaneous searches.

Herein is the dilemma: Organizations are responsible for nondiscriminatory recruiting and for hiring the best-qualified applicants. This makes questionable the practice of hiring one spouse and creating a position for the second spouse, although presumably such practice could happen within the law if it was being done to correct previous discriminatory practices. It also creates difficulty if both partners are not judged the most qualified for their respective jobs. More importantly, perhaps, this often gives organizations excuses not to make affirmative action hires; e.g., "we would have hired a female engineer but we simply could not find a place for her husband."

A second problem for dual-career couples seeking work can be the *interview process*. Biased and subjective judgments during personal interviews have historically been problematic for women seeking jobs. Affirmative action guidelines indicate that interviews and interviewers' actions need to be carefully monitored. Data are abundant which indicate that women's skills and abilities are judged to be of lesser quality than those of their male counterparts (Pogrebin, 1975), which may be the reason some women in dual-career couples are not judged the best-qualified applicant while their spouses are so judged. It is important, therefore, that organizations interviewing both women and dual-career couples make every effort to insure that interviewers are as free as possible of stereotypes or prejudices about women's abilities for particular jobs or about dual-career families.

Further, a job application or employment interview may not seek information regarding the applicant's sex or marital status unless the inquiry is made in "good faith for a non-discriminatory purpose." Other questions are considered equally inappropriate during an interview. Any question regarding the applicant's personal life or history is unwarranted unless it is directly related to her/his ability to do the job for which (s)he is applying. While information about personal issues such as marital status or children might be shared voluntarily by the applicant during an interview, such information may not be used in making the determination regarding whether to offer the person a position. If a male applicant indicates during his interview that a major factor in his wanting the job is that his wife is also applying for a position with the organization, or already has obtained employment with the organization, it would be both inappropriate and illegal for the interviewer to base a judgment regarding the applicant on his marital status. This means that dual-career couples cannot appeal to an organization to hire them both on the basis of their marital status.

A third problem area for dual-career couples is *anti-nepotism policies*. This issue is perhaps best stated by the U.S. Department of Health, Education and Welfare (1972):

> Policies or practices which prohibit or limit the simultaneous employment of two members of the same family and which have an adverse impact upon one sex or the other are in violation of the Executive Order.

> If an institution's regulations against the simultaneous employment of husband and wife are discriminatory on their face (e.g., applicable to "faculty wives"), or if they have in practice served in most instances to deny a wife rather than a husband employment or promotion opportunity, salary increases, or other employment benefits, they should be altered or abolished in order to mitigate their discriminatory impact.

> Stated or implied presumptions against the consideration of more than one member of the same family for employment by the same institution or within the same academic department also tends to limit the opportunities available to women more than to men.

If an individual has been denied *opportunity* for employment, advancement, or benefits on the basis of an anti-nepotism rule or practice, that action is discriminatory and is prohibited under the Executive Order.

While this portion of the regulations would appear to support, rather than restrict, employment of dual-career couples within a common organization, research conducted by Pingree et al. (1978), as well as experiences of affirmative action officers and personnel officers, confirm that organizations are still reluctant to have both partners employed in the same institution. Therefore, while the law protects couples from anti-nepotism policies, informal operations would appear to be contrary to those laws.

The research conducted by Pingree et al. (1978), which included surveying academic departments regarding their attitudes about hiring dual-career couples indicated that people saw three major advantages to academic departments hiring couples: the couple's greater unity between personal and professional lives enhancing the department, the department's greater ability to coordinate faculty professional and research activities, and the department's greater stability of personnel. Advantages to the couple included their greater personal life/professional life unity, better coordination of professional and research activities, and the couple's ability to save expenses, resources, and time.

Disadvantages to a department hiring dual-career couples included difficulty in conducting faculty evaluation, marital or emotional problems of the couple upsetting the department, the couple's disproportionate or adverse influence on departmental politics, and the couple's dissatisfaction resulting in two vacancies in the department at the same time. Disadvantages to the couple included the department's effect on the couple's decisions and behavior, the couple's personal competition and jealousy, the couple's inability to maintain separate identities, and the couple's social problems with others (e.g., resentment from colleagues).

Overall, then, Pingree et al. (1978) indicated that the previously formal anti-nepotism rules which are no longer legal continue to operate informally. Only a third of the persons responding to the survey held positive beliefs about hiring professional couples within the same department. This means that couples seeking employment in the same organization would be well advised to stress the positive aspects of having both partners in the same employment location. It also means that dual-career couples might wish to know their legal rights in the event they believe they have been discriminated against and wish to act on those legal rights.

ALTERNATIVE WORKING STYLES FOR DUAL-CAREER COUPLES

Job sharing is defined as

> an arrangement whereby two employees hold a position together, whether they are as a team jointly responsible for the whole or separately for each half . . . criteria are that it (1) is voluntary—an option chosen by the workers; (2) involves the deliberate conversion of a full time position; (3) depends on the existence of a partner or other half; and (4) includes provision of fringe benefits [Meier, 1978: 2].

This, then, is not the same as a part-time job. When two people share a job, they are essentially working as a team to complete a job which would otherwise be done by one person. The team need not, of course, be spouses, but couples are increasingly looking to job sharing as a way to resolve the dilemmas of finding work in the same location.

The increase in job sharing is to some degree a response to the challenge of traditional life cycles and to seeking a better balance between work and the remainder of one's life. Not only are women demanding job equity, they are also asking for more flexible work schedules; conversely, men are demanding that they be given more leisure time to spend alone, in the rearing of children, or other individual pursuits. Advantages to job-sharing couples, then, include the ability to pursue a variety of personal and professional interests while also building a career, the ability to work with a spouse in a collaborative professional pursuit, and the ability to have open time to pursue individual professional goals outside job hours.

Disadvantages of job sharing to the couple, cited by persons and organizations who have actually worked in this manner, include the amount of time spent in a part-time job (hours expended always seem to exceed those contracted for), the overlap of work-related problems into personal time, the loss of individual personal recognition for jobs accomplished, the lack of understanding from colleagues regarding what shared jobs are, jealousy of other colleagues regarding what appears to be free time, the feeling that job sharers are seen as less professional than full-time workers, lowered job security in some instances, and the inability to schedule work hours (especially in managerial and administrative roles) when crises or important events are likely to occur, therefore leading to a feeling of being an outsider in the work place (Olmsted and Markels, 1978).

Advantages of job sharing for the organization include decreasing absenteeism because job sharers save their personal errands until after work and because when one partner is ill, it is more likely that the other person will cover for him/her; lower turnover since both partners have increased energy and greater flexibility which comes from being part of a team; the availability of more jobs, thus increasing the opportunity for an organization to make affirmative action hires; greater retention of employees who are happy with the shared appointment; organizational access to a wider variety of human skills; more energy devoted to each job, thus increasing productivity; the provision of a retirement option for older employees; and improved employee morale when persons do not feel overburdened by single-handedly performing duties during a long, tiring day (Olmsted and Markels, 1978).

In short, then, job sharing is one option for dual-career couples. Job sharing is more likely to happen in a small organization, and the job sharers are usually the only ones within the organization (that is, the organization is using one couple to "test" the viability of this option). Job sharers tend to be younger than average workers and usually share the job with a marital partner (Meier, 1978). While some companies, government organizations, and institutions of higher education are experimenting with job sharing, few institutions have actually written policies on the implementation of such positions. It would appear, however, that in higher education, where there are increasing costs, declining enrollments and an increased number of persons seeking employment, this might be one very creative way of meeting the needs of both the institution and the dual-career couple.

A second option for dual-career couples is *part-time employment:* each person working less than full time on their respective professional career, thus allowing each person the ability to have more freedom to engage in personal or professional activities of their own choice. Part-time work is different from shared jobs, in that the couple is not sharing the same position but is each working part time in different fields and perhaps within different organizations. The advantage of this option is the freedom it provides each person and the fact that part-time jobs in some fields are often easier to find within the same geographical location. The disadvantage, of course, is that if the couple is not in a profession which allows for development and/or recognition of part-time workers, this could have the effect of slowing one or both careers. This is particularly problematic for persons in scientific research, where part-time employment is generally not given credibility as dedicated professionalism—nor do most experiments allow the researcher much free time.

A third option for dual-career couples is to *take turns moving* for each other's career opportunities. The advantage of this option is that each person will have equitable opportunities to pursue her/his career possibilities. The disadvantage, of course, is that they will feel like they are always in transition and, more importantly, one person may be in a critical stage of her/his career when the spouse asks to move.

A fourth option is to *take turns working* in several-year cycles. Again, the advantage is that each person is given equal times to pursue a career and to be unemployed and free to pursue other interests. The disadvantage is obvious: Few professional careers can survive a several-year absence. Each reentry into the job market will be like starting the career over again. Also, fields change, and the person who has been unemployed for a period of time is presumed (true or not) to have "gotten behind." The option of taking turns working is more viable for couples where each person's field allows him/her to practice without being employed, such as the fine arts or human services. Again, this choice is probably least viable for persons in science and related fields.

A fifth option is for both partners to find *work within commuting distance* of each other. This gives several choices: The family can live between the two jobs and commute daily; they can live close to one person's work and only one partner commutes while the other takes responsibility for household chores; or if the distance is too great to be traveled daily they may maintain two households, commuting to spend only weekends together. The advantage of this choice is that it may be considered much more of a compromise than other options: Both people have their careers and they also work equally in contributing to the relationship. The disadvantage is that this almost necessarily limits dual-career couples to living in urban or higher population areas. A second problem is that if there are children, one of the partners will inevitably become primary caretaker while the other parent becomes a casual or weekend visitor. And, finally, this arrangement makes it difficult to see each other regularly, since most professions simply do not guarantee weekends free from conferences, reading and travel, or other job duties.

The final option to be reviewed here is that of *cross-country relationships,* in which couples have jobs which are too far away from each other to allow visiting more than monthly or quarterly due to time and cost. The advantage to this arrangement can be an increased freedom for each person to pursue her/his career and thereby establish solid professional reputations thus enabling the couple to select their next jobs in locations where they will be together. The disadvantage, however, is strong. Relationships take investments of time and energy, and this couple may relocate together a few years away only to discover that the years of separation have left a relationship weak beyond repair.

These options are not intended to be all-inclusive, but rather to be a sample of some of the options today's couples are trying—none of which is without disadvantages, pain, and often very high costs. One of the major difficulties of being part of a dual-career couple as we enter the 1980s is the proverbial lack of role models. As dual-career couples increase in number, find viable options, and share information regarding both successes and failures with each other, both personally and through the literature, it will become increasingly easier for young professionals to select options which make most sense for their careers and lifestyles.

In summary, while new laws have paved the way for women to enter nontraditional careers without the degree of resistance previously encountered by women, these laws have also been occasionally problematic for that new phenomenon in the world of work—the dual-career couples. This new market of employees will require that employers consider dual-career couples in ways which are nondiscriminatory, creative, and heretofore untried.

REFERENCES

CLARK, L. N. (1976) "Considerations for married career women." Journal of National Association of Women Deans, Administrators and Counselors (Fall): 18–21.

FRIEDAN, B. (1977) It Changed My Life. New York: Dell.

KANTER, R. M. (1977) Men and Women of the Corporation. New York: Basic Books.

McNAMARA, D. B., J. J. SHERER, and M. J. SAFFERSTONE (1978) Preparing for Affirmative Action: A Manual for Practical Training. Garrett Park, MD: Garrett Park Press.

MEIER, G. S. (1978) Job Sharing. Kalamazoo, MI: Upjohn.

OLMSTED, B. and M. MARKELS (1978) Working Less but Enjoying It More: A Guide to Splitting or Sharing Your Job. Palo Alto: New Ways to Work.

PINGREE, S., M. BUTLER, W. PAISLEY, and R. HAWKINS (1978) "Anti-nepotism's ghost: attitudes of administrators toward hiring professional couples." Psychology of Women Quarterly 3: 23–29.

POGREBIN, L. C. (1975) Getting Yours. New York: Avon.

SANDLER, B. (1973) "Sex discrimination, educational institutions, and the law: a new issue on campus." Journal of Law and Education 2: 613–635.

U.S. Department of Health, Education and Welfare (1972) Higher Education Guidelines: Executive Order 11246.

U.S. Equal Employment Opportunity Commission (1972) Guidelines on Discrimination Because of Sex.

——— (1974) Affirmative Action and Equal Employment: A Guidebook for Employers.

U.S News and World Report (1979) "Working women: joys and sorrows." January 15: 64–74.

NOTE

1. While the author recognizes that both blue-collar and white-collar persons may have dual-career relationships, discussion in this chapter will focus on dual-career professional couples. While most of the issues discussed will be the same for all groups, there is a need for research regarding where there are similarities and differences and how the differences might best be addressed for each group.

12

SALARY AND JOB PERFORMANCE DIFFERENCES IN DUAL-CAREER COUPLES

Jeff B. Bryson
Rebecca Bryson

Demographic and cultural factors that increase the frequency of dual-career couples as well as economic conditions that have begun to compel joint labor market participation have received much recent attention. In addition to examining the factors that account for an observed threefold increase between 1940 and 1976 in the percentage of working wives (Kolko, 1978) it is of interest to see how these couples fare in their occupations.

The present chapter will compare salary and, where available, other indices of job performance and job satisfaction for husbands and wives in dual-career marriages. When possible, these indices will be compared with similar measures on other members of the labor force: unmarried working women and working men. Where differences are observed, proposed reasons for the discrepancy will be considered. Elsewhere, distinctions between careers and jobs are made. Unfortunately, the salary data available to us seldom are accompanied by information that permits making such a distinction. We do, however, have one set of data collected on professional psychologists (Bryson et al., 1976; Heckman et al., 1977) where income productivity and career regard were assessed. These data will be presented in some detail after reviewing more general data on income differentials.

In terms of income (1977 census data), large differences are evident between husbands and wives who are employed full time. Median salary for husbands in these families is $14,286; for wives it is $8,696. Discrepancies increase with age, but it is not clear whether this is due to cultural change (implying that differences will in the future continue to diminish) or to greater promotional opportunities for husbands (implying that differences for the younger group will, as they grow older, become more exaggerated). Women working full time and married to men who work full time contribute 36.7 percent of the family income. However, only 23.2 percent of married women worked for all of 1977 in a full-time job. An additional 6.7 percent were continuously (through 1977) employed in a part-time job and 24.9 percent worked only during part of the year (in either a full- or a part-time job). Among husbands, 65.4 percent worked the full year in a full-time job, 1.9 percent worked continuously in a part-time job and 17.0 percent were employed, but not for the full year (1977 census data). Across all families, wives contributed 27.3 percent of family income. There is substantial disagreement about the major reasons for the difference in employment patterns and salaries. Variables that have been cited as contributing factors can be roughly divided into three categories: (1) differences in background and training; (2) differences in chosen work patterns and occupational roles; (3) institutional and employee discrimination.

DIFFERENCES IN BACKGROUND AND TRAINING

The extent to which differences in background and training explain differences in salaries has been considered in several studies. Sanborn (1964) observed that the ratio of female to male hourly wages was .67 in 1949. When these figures were adjusted for differences in education, age, urban/rural status, and race, the ratio was incremented to .76. Additional very detailed adjustments made to account for precise nature of work done resulted in a fraction of .87 (though these differences in type of work do not necessarily reflect differences in background and training.) While Sanborn did not look at different figures for married and unmarried women, it is interesting to note that in 1973 the identically calculated initial hourly wage ratio was .56. That is to say, females earnings were a smaller fraction of males earnings even disregarding proportion of time worked. While it is not made explicit, one reason for the change was, perhaps, the enormous increase in married women in the job market. Among full-time employed wives, the median income is more than $1,000 lower than for full-time employed female workers (a group that includes wives) and about $3,500 lower than that for female heads of households. It has been demonstrated that a rather powerful demographic predictor of income is marital status. These data and other studies show marriage is negatively related to income for women. It has, however, been found to be positively related to income for men (see Perrucci, 1978).

One comparison of experience-related factors among men, married and unmarried women found that amount of education is much more strongly related to income for males and unmarried women than for married women (Treiman and Terrill, 1975). Another background variable commonly used to predict income is college grades. Perrucci (1978) states that good college performance in terms of grades leads to higher 1964 income for men and never-married women, but the effect is not significant for married working women.

It appears, in short, that being married is predictive of lower income for women. Educational variables ordinarily used to predict salaries do to some extent explain differences among married women, single women, and males; however, they are of little use in predicting salaries within the married women group. It seems that differences in variables other than those ordinarily thought to reflect job qualification must be considered as factors that contribute to salary differences.

OCCUPATIONAL ROLES AND CHOICE BEHAVIOR

Many of the work patterns that have differentiated the female member of a dual-career couple from males and unmarried females have stemmed from conflicting claims on time. These tend to include working part time to accommodate spouse and children, absenteeism for illness of a family member, and career interruptions due to birth of children. There has been, in addition, a tendency to support the husband's career at the expense of the wife's. In addition to a disproportionate assumption of household responsibilities, this support has resulted in geographic constraints on the wife's initial job choice and career interruptions when moves were necessary to enhance the husband's career. Let us examine the extent to which these kinds of accommodations have tended to have been made by wives and ways in which such dimensions of choice (whether self- or other-imposed) appear to affect salary.

Obviously, the greater tendency on the part of the wife to work part time has resulted in less total salary. While persons may be concerned with the social pressures that dispose married women to work fewer hours than either their husbands or other women, it would be difficult to quibble with a time-adjusted payoff. The payoff does not, however, appear to be strictly time adjusted. Hill and Hoffman (1977) have observed that wives who work fewer hours are paid *less per hour* than wives who work full time. Men who work fewer hours are paid *more per hour* than men who work full time. These results suggest that wives tend to be hired to work part time when this option permits securing their services at a rate below market value. At the same time, husbands appear to be able to demand more for their services when working time is reduced.

The effect of wages on reduced working time due to other kinds of adjustments were examined by Corcoran (1978). These included absences due to own illness, absences due to illnesses of others, and career interruptions (labor force withdrawals). Irrespective of whether absenteeism was for self or to care for others, this type of reduced working time was not related to earnings.

Findings with respect to career interruptions were slightly ambiguous. In Corcoran's study, actual interruptions in career did not significantly affect wages, but delays in starting a career after school completion did appear to be associated with lower wages. The failure to find an effect of career interruptions on salary is discrepant with findings reported by Mincer and Polachek (1974) who found a substantial decrement associated with career interruptions. Differences in sample composition may, however, be associated with the differences in obtained results. While Mincer and Polachek's sample was a group of married women between the ages of thirty and forty-four, Corcoran's sample was a group of women who were not necessarily married between the ages of eighteen and sixty-four. It would seem that the proportion of career interruptions associated with having children (during which time investments in career-enhancing activities may be diminished) would be maximized in the Mincer and Polachek study. In the Corcoran study, child/family-related interruptions may have been offset by career interruptions associated with attempts to receive additional education and training, thereby enhancing job skills.

Mincer and Polachek also examined the effects of moves to new locations on salaries of husbands and wives. Moves for husbands were accompanied by higher salaries, whereas moves for wives resulted in lower salaries. In general, Mincer and Polachek have concluded that for each year of career interruptions associated with marriage or the birth of a first child, the net depreciation in earnings amounts to 1.5 percent. While the rate is small and insignificant for women with less than a high school education, it is rather large (2.3 percent) for those with sixteen or more years of education. That so much difference in salary is accounted for by difference in length, proportion of working time and discontinuity of work experience is challenged by Duncan (1974) and by Sandell and Shapiro (1978) on both theoretical and empirical grounds; yet they too agree that a substantial loss is associated with time factors.

That conflicting demands will arise seems inevitable. That domestic responsibilities should be shared in a dual-career marriage is commonly given lip service, but is not borne out by the previously cited data on percentage of work time or by data on self-reported household responsibilities and differential career regard that we shall consider subsequently.

An alternative to sharing responsibilities associated with entering the family life cycle is to reduce their likelihood of occurrence. This is an alternative that is chosen with increasing frequency. Women are postponing marriage and child bearing, and reducing family size (Van Dusen and Sheldon, 1976).

DISCRIMINATION

One difficulty in studying the effects of discrimination is defining what we are willing to regard as discrimination. Frequently positions available on a part-time basis to married women are structured in a way that makes them less desirable than the parallel full-time positions (e.g., the lack of tenure track part-time faculty positions, and the previously cited differences in part-time salaries). These situations result in unequal pay for equivalent work, yet there is no scarcity of persons available to fill the positions because geographical constraints tend to produce an abundant labor supply.

Another kind of institutionally imposed barrier has been institutional anti-nepotism policies. Such policies have been particularly bothersome in situations where husbands and wives are similarly trained and could find ideal employment in the same area only if they were hired by the same company or institution. Though affirmative action regulations now prohibit anti-nepotism policies, Morlock (1973) found evidence for large numbers of unwritten anti-nepotism policies in academic institutions.

The possibility of functional though inexplicit anti-nepotism and anti-women policies operating in the hiring and supervising of married female employees makes it very difficult to study the effect of these two major sources of discrimination against married women. The common practice of assuming that any difference in wages that remains after years of education, grades, and time on job are considered is due to employee discrimination results in an overestimate. There are a multitude of unmeasured potential contributors to the difference—e.g., difference in relevance of education to job, difference in willingness to assert and promote self, and difference in productivity on the job.

A STUDY

To examine in some detail the ways that dual-career couples viewed and enacted their roles in a situation where range of education and type of occupation was highly restricted, we examined productivity, salary, division of responsibility, and job satisfaction of husband and wife psychologists. In addition, couples were asked to describe how they would react to certain kinds of situations that could arise in developing their careers. The results of these analyses will now be considered.

What effect, if any, does the dual-career marriage have on the productivity and reported satisfaction of its members? This question does not have any simple answer, for the effects seem to depend in part on which member of the couple is being considered, and on the degree to which the partners have accepted an egalitarian model for their marriage.

One of the first problems that rises in attempting to consider effects on productivity is that husbands and wives who have distinctly different types of careers do not have a common metric for assessing productivity. We resolved that problem in our work by surveying what we termed "professional pairs," or couples who had similar training and professional identifications.

In the spring of 1972, we sent out an extensive survey questionnaire to 605 persons who were identified as members of the American Psychological Association but who were not receiving the *American Psychologist* (the "house organ" of the APA). This was possible only if that person had claimed "husband-wife credit" on the annual dues statement; therefore, this list ostensibly defined a set of psychologists who were married to other psychologists. Data collection was halted in January 1973, when a total of 200 completed surveys had been returned (few additional questionnaires were returned after that date.) Included in this packet were separate questionnaires for the husband and wife, and a third for them to fill out as a couple. An abbreviated form of this questionnaire was sent to a control group of 150 male and 150 female APA members who were randomly selected from the 1972 *APA Directory* but not married to each other. Initial reports from this research were presented in Bryson et al. (1976) and

Heckman et al. (1977). The following details some of the results relevant to the question of salary and productivity differences in these professional pairs.

Initial comparisons of the four samples on educational and demographic information revealed that the husbands and wives differed from controls in two ways: (1) They tended to receive their final degrees at an earlier age (Husbands = 30.2, wives = 30.6; male controls = 32.5, female controls = 32.0), and (2) this was true despite the fact that the final degree was more likely to be the doctorate for members of these couples (husbands = 90.5 percent, wives = 79.5 percent; male controls = 82.2 percent, female controls = 62.9 percent). Data for the control groups are quite similar to that for the APA membership at large (Boneau and Cuca, 1973).

Examination of data regarding type of employment and reported work activities also revealed some differences between groups. Males (both husbands and controls) were more likely to hold academic jobs (58 percent and 53.4 percent, respectively) than wives or female controls (46 percent and 43.6 percent, respectively). Also, wives were more likely than any other group to report being unemployed at present (husbands = 1 percent, wives = 10.5 percent; male controls = 2.7 percent, female controls = 4.8 percent).

Information regarding salaries, hours of work per week, and job duration is presented in Table 12.1. As may be seen, wives have held their present jobs for the shortest period of time, work fewer hours per week (26 percent were employed only part time), and receive less compensation for their work than any other group. Husbands, on the other hand, are essentially equivalent to their same-sex controls in terms of job tenure and hours of work per week, but their financial compensation is highest of the four groups.

TABLE 12.1   Present Job Status

	Husbands	Wives	Male Controls	Female Controls
No. of years held	6.1	3.8	6.4	5.4
No. of hours/week	39.4	34.0	39.8	35.5
Annual income (× 1000)	19.4	13.6	18.5	14.7
N	199	179	70	57

In summary, it appears that although both husbands and wives in the professional pairs had received more training than their same-sex counterparts, this served to benefit the husband substantially more than the wife. While husbands were more likely to be employed than male controls and reported higher annual incomes, their wives were less likely to be employed than were female controls (and more likely to be employed part time), and received less in annual income than did female controls.

In a separate analysis, we examined some selected correlates of the income differential between husbands and wives (which averaged $7,310). The two largest correlates, not surprisingly, concerned the wife's job history: The income differential was less the greater the total number of years she had been employed ($r = -.32$) and the greater the number of hours per week that she currently worked ($r = -.32$). However, the differential was not significantly related to husband's job history, although the difference tended to be greater the longer the husband had been employed ($r = .11$) and the more hours he worked per week ($r = .09$). The income differential was related to one measure of productivity, the difference between husband and wife in the number of publications ($r = .17$). However, the income differential was more highly correlated with the number of children in the family ($r = .21$), with the difference increasing with family size. It is also interesting to note that the income differential is more substantially affected by the amount of responsibility for household duties that the husband accepts ($r = -.28$) than it is by the amount of responsibility for these duties accepted by the wife ($r = .14$). The amount of responsibility assigned to professional help or others was not related to the income differential ($r = -.003$). This pattern of correlations is quite consistent with the progression toward the "symmetrical family" predicted by Young and Wilmott (1977): The income differential between husbands and wives diminishes most effectively as the wife increases her attention to her job outside the home and the husband increases his attention to his job inside the home, or, in Young and Wilmott's term, as the family becomes more symmetrical.

Evidence that we have not progressed to the point of the symmetrical family is abundantly clear in some of the comments written by wives and husbands in response to a request on the survey that they discuss the most significant problems they had encountered as a member of a professional pair. For example, one woman wrote:

> In spite of his enthusiasm for my professional development I have been completely responsible for child care and regular domestic-type things. I consider this to have been a major detriment to my career—I do not object strongly to having these responsibilities, but in viewing my husband's attitude toward my professional life I find it difficult to live up to his expectations in both areas.

The essence of this discrepancy was summed up by one woman, who noted that "when the children were small I cared for them; my husband, on the other hand, 'babysat.'"

Husbands, in general, expressed less concern with the inequities in the distribution of domestic duties. While few were as extreme as the husband who stated, "I know she is overworked, holding a three-fifths time regular job, doing private work, and doing essentially all the housework. However, she seems to enjoy it; I have tried, unsuccessfully, to have her cut back *on her professional work*" (italics added!), many husbands expressed an intellectual awareness of the inequity, but did not seem motivated to do anything about it. One husband mentioned "occasional feelings of guilt over what I deem differential home responsibilities but my wife insists that she prefers this arrangement." Indeed, it does appear that in our study, as in the report by Rapoport and Rapoport (1969), most of the wives in these couples accepted as inevitable that they would have to bear the major burden of responsibility for child care and domestic organization, resulting in more strain on their careers than on their husbands'.

PRODUCTIVITY

Indices of productivity included self-reports of numbers of articles published, papers presented at conventions, books published, and grants received. Median values for these indices are presented in Table 12.2.

TABLE 12.2   Professional Productivity

Group	Publications[a]	Papers[a]	Books[a]	Large	Grants[b] Small	None	N/A
H	10.1	4.2	0	42.0	14.0	24.0	20.0
W	2.3	.75	0	21.5	15.5	36.0	27.0
M	6.3	2.2	0	22.2	14.0	34.7	29.3
F	1.0	.0	0	14.5	11.3	33.9	40.3

[a]Medians.
[b]Percentage responding in each category.

Husbands were found to be the most productive group in terms of all measures (although the median number of books was zero for all groups, the mean was highest for husbands), with male controls second. Wives exceeded female controls in all categories, and were essentially equivalent to male controls in terms of grants received. However, it is important to note that their productivity failed to approach that of their husbands in any category, a fact that is considered in greater detail later in this chapter.

A further comparison of salaries and publication rates for the professional pairs is presented in Table 12.3. In order to eliminate some of the confounding caused by differences between husbands and wives in employment history and type of job, we examined only those persons who were currently employed full time and who had obtained the doctorate, and classified them on the basis of their reported major job activity (teaching, research, services). Also, we

TABLE 12.3   Professional Pairs: Salary and Productivity

Major Activity		Person-Years of Employment 1–5 N[a] S[b] P[c]			6–10 N S P			11–15 N S P			16+ N S P		
Teaching	H	10	14.0	6.5	17	15.0	8.0	6	16.5	13.0	29	22.0	32.0
	W	8	12.5	5.0	18	14.0	3.0	5	17.0	7.0	7	20.0	8.0
Research	H	6	16.0	6.0	6	20.0	16.0	12	24.0	18.5	15	23.0	32.0
	W	9	15.0	4.0	6	20.0	16.0	4	17.5	14.5	4	20.5	17.5
Services	H	2	—[d]—		6	18.0	2.0	14	21.0	2.5	11	24.0	2.0
	W	11	15.0	0.0	8	17.0	1.3	7	16.0	4.0	6	16.5	1.5

[a]Number of persons in cell.
[b]Median salary in thousands.
[c]Median number of published papers reported.
[d]Not reported because sample size was too small.

defined job experience in terms of person-years of employment, to adjust for periods of part-time employment.

Examining this table, one may see that, in general, wives both earned less and published less than husbands within the same category. However, both these differentials tend to be less at the younger person-years of employment index levels. The publication rate data are consistent with Guyer and Fidell (1973), who found that sex differences in productivity are less among more recent graduates. The present data also indicate that these relative increases in productivity are being remunerated. Alternatively, of course, it may be argued that any disparities in both productivity and salary are likely to be less evident in entry-level jobs. It would be necessary to conduct a longitudinal research program to determine if these apparent equalities are maintained.

SATISFACTION

Somewhat more subjective than salary or productivity, but equally important to the individual's sense of well-being, is satisfaction with one's current state, in terms of both domestic and professional duties, responsibilities, and achievements. In this area, the evidence is also relatively clear: Wives in professional pairs report less satisfaction with (a) the amount of time they have for domestic activities, (b) the amount of time available for avocational activities, (c) amount of time available for professional activities, (d) their rate of professional advancement, (e) opportunity to interact with their colleagues, and (f) freedom to pursue long-range job goals. They were also more likely to report problems stemming from differential achievement of self and spouse (Bryson et al., 1978).

Taken together, our findings regarding salary, productivity, and satisfaction form a rather complex picture. The effects of dual-career status for the husband seem uniformly positive: He tends to be more productive, to earn more, and to report a level of satisfaction with professional and personal life equal to or greater than that of any other group. For the wives, however, the effects of dual-career status are less uniform. Although they are, as a group, more productive than their same-sex counterparts, this productivity is not reflected in job stability or income. As a result, they report lower satisfaction than any other group.

The easiest advice we can offer, given this, is to suggest that, if you are a male psychologist, you should marry a female psychologist. However, if you are a female psychologist you should not even consider marrying a male psychologist. Unfortunately, the inherent asymmetry in this advice makes it less than helpful. A more useful approach is to examine the factors that seem related to this asymmetry—institutional constraints (especially the application of anti-nepotism policies) and personal constraints upon career development.

INSTITUTIONAL CONSTRAINTS

Encounters with anti-nepotism policies were common; 45.5 percent of the pairs in our sample reported one or more such encounters. However, these encounters seemed to affect the wife's career rather than the husband's. Questionnaire comments provided additional detail on these encounters: In all cases, it was the wife, rather than the husband, who was denied a position or requested to resign (in the case of marriage to a colleague). Although explicit anti-nepotism policies were declared discriminatory by HEW's Office of Civil Rights in 1972, such changes have come too late to alter their effects on many in our sample. Also, as Pingree, Butler, Paisley, and Hawkins (1978) point out, such policies still exist in the attitudes and informal hiring policies of many administrators.

Data comparing pairs who work in the same institution with pairs who are employed in different institutions (regardless of reason) argue against anti-nepotism policies, for pairs who are able to work together are more productive. Data relevant to these comparisons are presented in Table 12.4.

Working in the same versus different institutions had no significant effect on salaries, although husbands tended to be paid more, and wives less, when employed in the same institution. However, pairs who worked in the same institution were significantly more

TABLE 12.4   Professional Pairs Working in Same Vs. Different Institutions

	Husbands		Wives	
	Same	Different	Same	Different
Mean Salary	23.0	21.2	13.9	14.7
Mean No. Publications	21.5	17.1*	9.9	5.7*
Grants Received[a]	67.7	50.4*	55.4	28.6**
% Ph.D.	95.4	88.0	83.1	77.4
N[b]	62	131	62	131

[a]Entries are percentages reporting receipt of either small (less than $5000) or large grants.
[b]Total not equal to 200 because of 7 blanks.
*Difference significant at .05 level.
**Difference significant at .001 level.

productive than their same-sex counterparts, in terms of both publications and grants received.

While a portion of these results may be attributed to selection factors (e.g., a [nonsignificantly] greater proportion of those working in the same institution have obtained Ph.D.s), it appears that, in general, working in the same institution facilitates professional productivity for both members of the pair. When one considers that many couples refuse, as a matter of principle, to seek employment for either at institutions with anti-nepotism policies, the consequences of anti-nepotism policies become clear: Institutions that fail to hire both members of a professional pair risk failing to hire either of these highly productive people, and even if they do hire one, they may restrict the productivity of both.

While institutional policies such as anti-nepotism practices or rules would be expected to constrain the joint career development of a professional pair, there is no necessary reason for these constraints to be imposed solely upon the wife. The undeniable fact that such policies are disproportionately applied to the detriment of the wife's career can only be explained by considering other, more personal constraints, either self-imposed or imposed by other family members.

PERSONAL CONSTRAINTS

Primary among these socially or personally imposed constraints is the deeply held belief in the primacy of the husband's career. Even when the dual-career couple attempts to reject such beliefs in their own thinking it is imposed upon them by others. As Bailyn (1965) has noted, the professional woman must always contend with the thought that retreating from work is an option that is as likely to win praise as disapproval. The constant imposition of such attitudes can subtly but pervasively alter even the most adamant attempts at opposition. As a result, the couples themselves may begin to place differential value upon their two careers.

One area in which differential values may be noted is in the allocation of responsibility for household tasks. In our survey, wives had the major responsibility for cooking, marketing, child care, and laundry. The only stereotypically female activity for which they did not bear the majority of responsibility was housecleaning, but this was because outside help was employed, not because husbands shared the responsibility. In fact, the only difference between the professional pairs and the married male controls was in the likelihood of employing outside help to perform some domestic activities: The husbands in both groups took on approximately equal (and small) shares of responsibility for household tasks. Equivalent findings have been reported elsewhere (e.g., St. John-Parsons, 1978).

In another series of questions, professional pairs were asked to indicate the degree to which spouse's employment would constrain their acceptance of a substantially better position in another town, and to indicate the degree to which they would expect their spouse to consider their employment in accepting another position. Responses by husbands and wives to these two questions are presented in Table 12.5.

Responses to these questions indicate two things: (1) both husband and wife tend to consider the wife's employment as secondary, but (2) wives tend to subordinate their career even more than husbands do. As may be seen, the proportion of wives reporting that they would accept the position only if their husband received a satisfactory offer (68 percent) was matched by the proportion of husbands reporting that they would expect their wives to accept such a position only if they also received a satisfactory offer. However, while 41 percent of the husbands stated that they would accept a position only if their wife received a satisfactory offer, only 26 percent of the wives expected this degree of consideration from their husbands.

TABLE 12.5   Professional Pairs: Perceived Relative Career Importance and Value

Questions and Alternatives	Husbands	Wives
If you received an offer of a substantially better position in another town, under what conditions would you accept?		
1. Regardless of spouse employment	7.5	1.5
2. If spouse could probably find employment	28.0	4.5
3. Special conditions	18.0	19.0
4. Only if spouse received satisfactory offer	41.0	68.0
If your spouse received an offer . . . under what conditions would you expect him/her to accept?		
1. Regardless of my employment	5.0	17.0
2. If I could probably find employment	13.0	36.5
3. Special conditions	10.0	16.0
4. Only if I also received satisfactory offer	68.0	26.0

The tendency for wives to subordinate their careers to their husbands' is also seen in response to a set of questions regarding (1) who had attained and (2) who merited the greater professional recognition. Although both samples reported that the husband had attained the greater recognition, wives were more likely to report this (W = 67.5 percent, H = 56.0 percent, z = 2.75, p < .01). Even larger effects were found in reports of who merited the greater recognition. Although the absolute number of attributions to the husband were less for both groups, the difference between husbands and wives increased; while 59.5 percent of the wives felt that the husband merited greater recognition, only 31 percent of the husbands agreed (z = 5.72, p < .001).

In sum, the professional pair is not egalitarian. Instead, like other dual-career couples, they tend to divide household responsibilities along sex-stereotypic lines and to place differential values on their careers. It also seems clear that the pressures for such differentiation fall disproportionately upon the wife.

CONCLUSIONS AND IMPLICATIONS

The prior discussion seems overwhelmingly negative, leaving one to wonder why and how a professional pair can continue to exist, given the constraints placed upon the wife's career development. In fact, some of our couples expressed surprise at how negative things seemed in terms of responses to the survey, for things did not seem that bad to them personally. There are a number of advantages to being in a professional pair. Those most frequently mentioned by our respondents included having a resident colleague available for support, consultation, and understanding, that the combined income served to remove many financial pressures, and that each spouse could take pride in the accomplishments of the other, as well as one's own.

It seems reasonable to view the professional pair as a mutually supportive and facilitative unit whose goals may come into conflict with external pressures. Within the family unit, each member of the pair is motivated by the presence of the other and derives satisfaction from the other's accomplishments as well as from his or her own. However, the shared and individual goals of each member of the pair conflict with the external realities of institutional policies, societal expectations, and domestic demands.

These conflicts must be resolved in some way. Typically, this resolution is based at least in part on traditional sex roles, for this is, quite simply, the easiest road to take, given society's pressures and the force of one's own beliefs, which are a product of that society. As a result, when employment pressures require, the wife's career is more likely to be considered as secondary, her job is more likely to be part time or non-tenure-track, and her pay and level are likely to be less than her husband's. It is important to note that this division typically is accepted by both members of the pair, probably because in most cases it occurs as a series of small steps, each taken without considering their cumulative effect. And, in turn, these decisions serve to support and maintain the stereotypes to which they were initially perceived as a necessary or rational response.

There are several different implications of these findings, for the professional pair and other dual-career couples, and for their employers. First, the couple should be more aware of the significance and potential ramifications of each career decision for both of their careers. If a decision is made to subordinate one career, it should be made consciously, with both members aware of the potential effects of this decision on career development. It would also seem valuable for the couple to focus on intrinsic qualities of their respective jobs, such as productivity or performance, rather than extrinsic rewards, such as income or promotion, as the bench mark for satisfaction and success, for the former are more directly under their control.

Employing organizations should be more aware of the potential and the needs of professional pairs. First, as such couples seem to be more productive than their more traditional colleagues, they should be viewed favorably as employees. Employing institutions (and professional pairs) should resist the tendency to "take advantage" of these pairs by hiring only one, then treating the other as a sort of captive permanent part-time employee. And finally, efforts should be made to provide more flexibility in working hours for such couples, recognizing their shared responsibility for the demands of domestic duties.

The current trend in American society is toward an increase in the number of dual-career couples, as economic demands and changing cultural norms bring more and more women into full-time, career-oriented jobs. However, the present data suggest that the mere fact of dual employment is not, by itself, sufficient to cause a shift away from the tendency by both spouses to subordinate the wife's career. The development of more enlightened and egalitarian attitudes within the dual-career couple depends instead upon the prior development of supportive attitudes within the larger society. In this sense, the dual-career couple is better considered as a reflection of its cultural context than as a force for change.

REFERENCES

BAILYN, L. (1965) "Notes on the role of choice in the psychology of professional women," in R. J. Lifton (ed.) The Woman in America. Boston: Houghton Mifflin.

BONEAU, C. A. and J. M. CUCA (1973) "The APA's Manpower Data System: inventory of member responses to individual questionnaire items." JSAS Catalog of Selected Documents in Psychology 3: 115.

BROSCHART, K. R. (1978) "Family status and professional achievement: a study of women doctorates." Journal of Marriage and Family 40: 71–76.

BRYSON, R. B., J. B. BRYSON, M. H. LICHT, and B. G. LICHT(1976) "The professional pair: husband and wife psychologists." American Psychologist 31: 10–16.

CONTE, M. (1977) "Labor market discrimination against women," in G. J. Duncan and J. N. Morgan (eds.) Five Thousand American Families: Patterns of Economic Progress. Ann Arbor, MI: Institute for Social Research.

CORCORAN, M. (1978) "The structure of female wages." American Economic Association 68: 165–170.

DUNCAN, O. D. (1974) "Comment (on Family investments in human capital: earnings of women)." Journal of Political Economy 82: 109–110.

GUYER, L and L. FIDELL (1973) "Publication of men and women psychologists: do women publish less?" American Psychologist 28: 157–160.

HECKMAN, N A., R. B. BRYSON, and J. B. BRYSON (1977) "Problems of professional couples: a content analysis." Journal of Marriage and Family 39: 323–330.

HILL D. and S. HOFFMAN (1977) "Husbands and wives," in G. J. Duncan and J. N. Morgan (eds.) Five Thousand American Families: Patterns of Economic Progress. Ann Arbor, MI: Institute for Social Research.

KOLKO, G. (1978) "Working wives: their effects on the structure of the working class." Science and Society 42: 257–277.

MINCER, J. and S. POLACHEK (1974) "Family investments in human capital: earnings of women." Journal of Political Economy 82: 76–108.

MORLOCK, L. (1973) "Discipline variation in the status of academic women," in A. S. Rossi and A. Calderwood (eds.) Academic Women on the Move. New York: Russell Sage.

PERRUCCI, C. C. (1978) "Income attainment of college graduates: a comparison of employed women and men." Sociology and Social Research 62: 361–386.

RAPOPORT, R. and R. N. RAPOPORT "The dual career family: a variant pattern and social change." Human Relations (1969) 22: 3–30.

ST. JOHN-PARSONS, D. (1978) "Continuous dual-career families: a case study," in J. B. Bryson and R. Bryson (eds.) Dual-Career Couples. New York: Human Sciences.

SANBORN, H. (1964) "Pay differences between men and women." Industrial and Labor Relations Review 7: 534–550.

SANDELL, S. H. and D. SHAPIRO (1978) "The theory of human capital and the earnings of women: a reexamination of the evidence." Journal of Human Resources 8: 102–117.

TREIMAN, D. J. and K. TERRILL (1975) "Sex and the process of status attainment: a comparison of working women and men." American Sociological Review 40: 174–200.

U.S. Bureau of the Census (1977) Current Population Studies. Washington, DC: Government Printing Office.

VAN DUSEN, R. A. and E. B. SHELDON (1976) "The changing status of American women: a life cycle perspective." American Psychologist 106: 106–116.

YOUNG M. and R. WILMOTT (1977) The Symmetrical Family. London: Routledge and Kegan Paul.

13

GOING SHOPPING: THE PROFESSIONAL COUPLE IN THE JOB MARKET

Janet R. Matthews
Lee H. Matthews

A major issue for the new or recent graduate of any training program is whether or not a job will be available following graduation. Although the specifics of employment seeking may vary somewhat from one discipline to another, there are a number of issues which are the same. The following chapter deals specifically with the employment issues which may be faced by the dual-career couple within psychology.

Job placement issues have been a focus of interest to the American Psychological Association for many years (Cates and Cummings, 1970, 1972; Cuca, 1975; Cummings and Cates, 1971, 1973). Since each job seeker is in a somewhat unique position, the problems faced by the individual applicant (Perlman, 1976) and the dual-career couple (Madell and Madell, 1979; Matthews and Matthews, 1978) have also been addressed. Such articles have provided guidelines to the job seeker as well as the message, "I made it and so can you."

The present chapter will include data from two sources. The first will be the authors' experiences as a dual-career couple within the employment market. The second will be partial data from a survey of dual-career couples within psychology. This survey was an outgrowth of the authors' personal experiences and a desire to learn if these experiences were common among dual-career couples within psychology. Descriptions of experiences reported by other dual-career couples are integrated with the authors' experiences. Additional anecdotal reports appear in the section of the chapter dealing more specifically with the survey.

BACKGROUND

We had been led to believe by some former professors that we were in a unique position in terms of the job market—we were a professional pair. This unique position was described by them as rather unenviable. At first, such comments had come close to striking terror in us. Considering our employment situation from as calm a perspective as possible, we remembered similar comments which had been made when we were applying for our internships. In the case of the internships, we had no difficulty being placed in the same facility (we would gladly have settled for the same community) and even had a choice of where we would go. This internship experience may have made us more confident than the employment situation warranted, but also helped to counteract the negative remarks from others. Trying to find two jobs, especially in these times of employment slowdown, was an issue faced by many of the couples in our survey. Typical of the impact on professional couples was the response given by one couple when asked to list the disadvantages of seeking employment as a dual-career couple. They said, "Two jobs are harder to find than one." This statement was then repeated once and the third-listed choice was a "see above."

As far as our "uniqueness" as a professional pair, we really had minimal data at that time to either agree or disagree with the comment. We had two such pairs on our graduate training faculty and had begun to read about others (Bryson et al., 1976). In terms of numbers within any specific profession, we were at that time in the dark. Generally speaking, however, we entered the arena of the employment market with high hopes and optimism.

THE SEARCH

Not wanting to get a late start on the employment search, we submitted the first application in August for a position commencing in September of the following year. Although we realized that it is possible to apply too early for jobs, the academic market begins earlier than that for applied positions, so this move was appropriate.

At this point, our area of search for employment was highly restrictive, as we were interested in one particular southwestern state. Each month, we searched two psychology employment papers for potentially appropriate vacancies in that state. Although we did not realize it at that time, we were making our first mistake. While geographical preference by a job applicant is certainly understandable, such a lack of attention to appropriate positions in other parts of the country can lead to problems. Some people have said that the community, or part of the country, is a high priority for them (Madell and Madell, 1979). Several couples in our survey mentioned that from the list of eight items to rank in order of importance for a job change, five of the items were equally rated as the most important. These items included geographic location, both spouses' type of job, and that both of them had a job offer. Our reaction has been one of the job's appropriateness being of greater importance that the geographic locale. Thus, the issue of geography versus job type appears to be one of individual priorities.

As the year progressed, we became immersed in our internship duties and paid less attention to sending letters and curriculum vitae. Here was a second mistake. Jobs do not come looking for the applicant, except in rather unusual circumstances. It is important to be active rather than passive in a job search.

A third mistake can be seen in a hesitancy we felt in applying for jobs which requested letters of recommendation before the first curriculum vitae screenings. We found ourselves worrying about "bothering" our references too often until the "right" job appeared. There are several ways to deal with such an attitude. One is to establish a placement file at your university, but we hesitated to do that for a number of reasons. We were each applying for a variety of jobs. A general letter about our qualifications seemed inappropriate. Information which might be useful to a screening committee in an academic setting was not the type of information needed in an applied setting. We were also told that it could be helpful to have letters of recommendation which were obviously geared to the specific job. Thus, we ruled out the placement service of the university as a viable method of dealing with our applications.

Another method is to spread your requests around, if you have a sufficient number of faculty who are willing to write such letters. Even with a greater distribution, there were still certain faculty we felt we would need to lean on too heavily. An application packet which does not include references from the chairperson of your dissertation committee and your director of clinical training (if you are in such a program) could be taken as indicating that these people were unwilling to make a recommendation. Not being satisfied with either of the alternatives which we found for letters of recommendation, we decided to wait for the employment service of one of our regional conventions. Our rationale was that we would have an initial interview behind us prior to requesting letters. We believed that we would have some indication from such an interview of our employment chances and thus could limit the number of requests for letters.

Since we each were scheduled to present a paper at a regional convention, we felt that we were starting off well. We headed for that convention with high hopes. While we found the convention to be both intellectually and socially stimulating, the situation at the employment service was a real shock. A term which was frequently heard in reference to the service was "meat market." That phrase aptly described the feelings voiced by many applicants that they were like a piece of meat being passed from table to table for inspection. Unfortunately, it seemed to be a "buyer's market" in which the applicant either takes this impersonal attitude by employers or has no interviews.

Perlman (1976) has stated that conventions are not the places to find jobs. Although the atmosphere is not truly a comfortable one, we did not find that conventions were poor shopping markets. On the contrary, we found them to be fruitful sources of information.

From our first employment service experience of the year, we discovered a number of things about ourselves and "our situation." While these discoveries did not lead to employment offers at that time, they were quite useful in later employment service experience. First, we discovered that even "new" clinical psychologists were expected to have both publications and ongoing research projects. Prior to this, we had been under the impression that as "applied" psychologists we would not have these research pressures. Although we expected the need for publication records for large and/or graduate-level programs within the academic world, we did not expect them from liberal arts settings. Thus, our perspective on the viable openings was altered through this interview experience. At this point, we were still being rather selective about the type of job and the geographic location of that job and so we did not make complete use of this service. While we are not suggesting that you interview for any job for which you might be qualified just to get the practice in interviews, it is very easy to overlook jobs which could turn out to be appropriate. From a more positive perspective, we found that some employers in this setting tried to be friendly and make useful suggestions to us.

The issue of whether or not to mention the other member of the couple during a job interview is one which every dual-career couple should decide prior to actively interviewing. There are certain factors which need to be considered while making such a decision. If you are using the same employment service, especially a convention-type service which has open book listings of applicants, it is quite possible that the employer will have noted the existence of your spouse. Such listings are often in either alphabetical order or the order of filing. If you filed at the same time, you will probably have back-to-back listings. Since an interview was offered, the fact that your spouse is in the same profession has not harmed you up to that point. Even if the employer did not notice the existence of the other member of the dual-career couple prior to the interview, it is quite possible that if you made a sufficient impression for the employer to notice you in more social situations at the convention your spouse's career will become apparent.

A potential source of discomfort for the dual-career couple looking for jobs is that, if they have similar backgrounds and training, they may find themselves in competition for the same job. Several respondents in our survey indicated that this was a difficult situation to handle as everyone knows that "psychologists have a tendency to be very competitive." Although we had been told that prospective employers could not ask directly about the spouse and that person's employment situation, we found that they frequently did ask such questions. While that happened slightly more frequently for the female than the male, it was also often asked of the male. We responded to such questions as frankly as possible. It was our position that we would look for jobs mainly in communities of sufficient size that the person who did not have a job when we moved there would have a "reasonable" chance of finding one after arriving. Most potential employers appeared to take this information well, and in several cases they then provided the name of someone for the other member of the pair to contact about a potential position. Overall, we felt that we had more assistance in terms of leads for additional jobs than situations in which we were rejected because there were two of us in search of employment.

YOURS, MINE, OR OURS

Because we had decided to look for two jobs at the same time, our experience may have been somewhat different from that of other dual-career couples. There are many approaches to job applications and career decisions. Although our approach was based on decisions which attempted to give equal weight to each spouse's professional career, other couples mentioned different arrangements. One such arrangement, described with some regularity, involved giving major consideration to the career of one member of the couple (most often the male). Often this approach means that the other spouse has to leave a satisfying job or take a less fulfilling job because of the primary spouse's offer. Several women in our survey indicated that they viewed such a situation as more of a women's issue than a function of both partners being psychologists. They stated that this situation was likely to be found in dual-career couples from any profession and was probably the result of women's socialization process.

The issue of a couple seeking jobs at the same time is related to another concern which was consistently mentioned in our survey, lack of geographic mobility as an issue for the dual-career couple. Often, one member will commute long distances in order to obtain or maintain a job which s/he enjoys. Frequently, the distance driven and mentioned by respondents was in excess of sixty miles; often these were one-way distances and were driven on a frequent basis. Some individuals mentioned driving these distances at least three times per week. Several couples mentioned that although they were able to find satisfying jobs, the distance involved required that they not spend all seven nights of the week together. One respondent indicated that because she and her husband had academic positions in universities in different states many of the items typically asked of such couples really were either inappropriate or impossible to answer.

Although such disruptions in family life are not uncommon, many of the couples viewed these disruptions as challenges rather than as problems. One couple, when asked about their current state of residence, responded by saying, "together—Kentucky." Another couple responded to the same question by stating "Indiana—(or do you mean house okay, but sewers backed up this weekend)." While another couple responded "chaotic, but fun" and then listed their home state. Thus, humor appears to enter into dealing with a potentially disruptive situation.

In our own job-hunting situation, although we did experience some sex stereotyping (the female must be the child specialist, which was not true for us), we found very little of this issue. Perhaps we missed some of the more subtle points of interviewing, but we basically felt that our respective gender had a minimal effect on our job search.

A major problem area for us involved facilities which had two current openings for which we were qualified. We had no strong position, either positive or negative, regarding working at the same facility. Thus, we were open to interviews for such positions. In several cases, we had the impression that the prospective employer felt he or she was doing us a favor by interviewing both of us. We had several firm job offers following this type of interview. A major problem with these offers was that we were told that a specific sum of money was available for these positions. We were then told that we could divide it between us in any manner we chose. On considering advertised positions in comparable facilities in the same state, we found that these offers often were less money than would be paid to two comparably trained but unrelated professionals.

Reports from our survey revealed similar experiences for many dual-career couples. A number of couples appeared to have made a significant effort to find jobs in the same place. Several respondents indicated that one of the advantages is having a mutual "pool" of friends, books, and interests while knowing that you are also going to be working with someone you like.

One disadvantage of working in the same facility is a feeling about the organization in which you work if your spouse is "mistreated." This may be an accurate perception of an event which happens within the organization, or may be one spouse's perception of the other's treatment. It was noted by some respondents to the questionnaire that it is difficult to be completely objective when dealing with issues that may affect your spouse.

One of the major employment disadvantages consistently mentioned was the impact of nepotism rules and the failure of institutions to treat salaries, research grants, and consultant fees as applying to individuals, rather than to the couple as a "package."

Even within academic settings, where it would be expected that if the couple were hired there would not be as many difficulties, several respondents indicated that, due to early nepotism problems, one spouse interacts less with the other spouse during work hours. One respondent indicated that this was "sort of an overcorrection effect." One couple related an incident in which one member went to work in a facility where the other spouse had been employed in another division for some time. When he stopped by with a friend at noon to say hello, the wife assumed he was inviting her to join them for lunch. When the husband realized that she planned to come along, he insisted that she not do that. This couple went on to indicate that for a period of approximately one year, the male member of the couple was quite upset whenever they happened to come in contact with each other in the work situation. This often led to his literally avoiding her at work. They appeared to have difficulty separating office friendliness from more personal meaning.

THE SEARCH INTENSIFIES

We attended a second convention specifically for the employment service. While we had gained experience from the first one and had some promising interviews, no jobs had been forthcoming. This second convention provided a nice vacation, but little of relevance in terms of our job search. At this point, we made another discovery about convention employment services. Not all regional conventions have the same size employment service. It is important to consider the data on previous employment services for the convention you consider attending. The size of the employment service may be of greater importance than the geographic location of the convention.

As our internship year drew to a close, we had had both individual and joint offers for employment but had not accepted any positions. This, too, is a decision which is specific to each dual-career couple, and no general rules can be given. The question is whether to take a job which you do not really feel is right so that you at least have employment. For us, several issues were involved in the decision to decline offers which we felt we would view as temporary. First, we firmly believed that if either of us accepted a position (other than a stated temporary position), that acceptance should be made with the intention of staying for awhile. This is not to say that we would hesitate to leave a position which was not appropriate, but rather that we were not at ease in starting a job simultaneously with beginning a job search for another one. From a more practical standpoint, there are difficulties in trying to interview for potential positions when you are just starting a job. Time off can be a problem. Thus, distant positions may be eliminated from consideration. There is also the problem of letters of reference. It could be viewed as unfavorable if there were no recommendations from the current employer. Some jobs even state that at least one reference must be from the current place of employment. The current employer does not have an opportunity to get to know you before being asked to write a reference. In addition, the attitude which you have about this job could have a negative impact on your relationships with colleagues. They could hesitate to try to get to know you and help you become involved in the system since you will not really be there very long if you can help it.

Our final convention try of the year was at the American Psychological Association's national convention. By this point, our finances were running low, but we followed the advice of valued mentors who suggested that a visit to this employment service could prove to be beneficial. We found the "meat market" atmosphere to be a familiar one but there were more buyers than at the regional level. There were also more friends in attendance who could (and did) recommend us to their friends who "knew someone who knew someone" who was hiring. Here, again, is a tip about the employment market. We had been hesitant to approach too many people and ask if they had heard about a job that might fit one of us. That was a mistake. Many faculty, some of whom we knew only moderately well, were quite willing to introduce us to people who were in a position to point us toward jobs. Several trips for interviews and job offers resulted, and our current employment are an outcome of our trip to that last convention placement service.

Using such a large employment service brought some new rules to the game of job seeking. One was to plan to spend as much time as possible at the employment service. New job descriptions were posted throughout the convention. Some notes from prospective employers required rather rapid response if an interview was to be made available. Listening to the conversations of other job applicants leads to possibilities for you. Another rule was to try to get an interview for any job which might be of interest. Since job descriptions are often quite brief, it pays to request an interview for all jobs which "might" be of interest. At the very worst, the person will reply that you are not qualified for the position and thus are not invited to have an interview. If an interview is offered, it provides an opportunity to deal with a variety of questions, some of which may be new to you.

Another point of advice, especially applicable to new or recent degree recipients is, "Don't be shy or undersell yourself." With the current buyers' market, the only person to sell you is likely to be you. It is easy to become overwhelmed in a large employment service setting and get the impression that you do not have much to offer a prospective employer. An interview given from that perspective is not likely to result in a job offer.

In terms of interviews, we found no standard format. In several cases, we had joint interviews, which in general were more frustrating than individual interviews. Many of the questions appeared more vague than those typically encountered in individual interviews. In addition, questions seemed to be asked of neither of us in particular. That can be partially a situational test. It can be done in an attempt to determine whether one member of the pair will lean on the other. Such information could be useful if the prospective employer is hiring a dual-career couple for positions which involve interaction. On the other hand, it may be the result of the interviewer not really being accustomed to interviewing a dual-career couple. It was our experience that it was difficult to balance our roles in such an interview. After our first joint interview, we found it necessary to discuss how we would handle such situations in the future. By prior agreement about areas of questions which we mutually decided belonged to one or the other, we made some movement toward balance. Since the types of questions varied to the degree they did from one interview to another, this procedure only partially handled the problem. Another potential pitfall of the joint interview involves one member of the couple getting into a good dialogue with the interviewer. In this case, it may be difficult for the spouse to ask some questions which are personally important. This problem can be handled in several ways. One is to prearrange some method of indicating to each other when you feel left out of a conversation or want some information. Another is to be assertive. We found that the fact that we were not newly married helped here. It required less conversation to handle these issues than it would have during the earlier years of our marriage. While the dual-career couple does not want to provide the impression in a joint interview that they are totally dependent on each other, they also do not want to convey the impression that they cannot work together. This tradeoff of questions and statements by each member can aid in giving a good impression.

Couples who apply for jobs together should be aware that one of the consistent disadvantages mentioned by couples who work in the same facility is a lack of diversity of experiences and often being under significant equivalent work strains. Because they share a common knowledge about the problems inherent in the job, this tends to give them a better base for communication, but, by the same token, because they are both so emotionally involved in the situation, it is often difficult for either of them to maintain sufficient distance to look objectively at what has happened in the work experience. A number of the couples mentioned the restriction of social contacts because they are both working in the same locale. Frequently mentioned was the fact that although it was nice to have a common "pool" of friends, there was very little interaction with individuals outside their professional contacts. This appears to be one hazard in accepting a position at the same facility and should be considered in going shopping for a job.

Although only mentioned occasionally for couples who work in different facilities, often there is considerable jealousy when the dual-career couple is employed at the same facility. Other staff members may resent the dual-career income and the personal support provided by such an employment situation. Another frequently mentioned disadvantage of couples who hunt for jobs and obtain them in the same agency is the tendency to involve themselves in too much "shop talk" outside office hours, including in social situations.

Some mentors suggested that if our final convention employment service did not provide the desired results, it might be best to simply move to the geographic location which we preferred and then try to make contacts. Since we have not tried that method, we can only say that it represented too great a risk and expense for us. Our personal search resulted in two jobs, at about the same time, which were close to the ideal which we sought. We did not obtain our geographical preference. We had never even been in our current state of residence prior to the job interviews. The end result, however, has been a good one. While there was probably a certain degree of luck in the outcome of our job search, we feel that our willingness to say "no" when the job was not right left us readily available when the "right" jobs were there.

After settling into these jobs, we began to discuss our experiences. We also met other dual-career couples who had similar questions about the types of unique problems and satisfactions of being a dual-career couple. Consistently the issues of too much focus on work and a lack of variety of nonprofessional friends were mentioned as disadvantages for the dual-career couple in psychology. Other issues included the expectations that one spouse or the other would be understanding about the need to work late hours, concerns over promotional considerations, and conflicting social values. Frequently, couples mentioned the "tendency to spend too much time working, and not enough time together on nonprofessional activities" as a major disadvantage. One result of such discussions was a survey we conducted to try to gain more information about these issues.

THE SURVEY

METHOD

The initial pool of potential subjects was obtained from the 1978 *APA Directory,* plus our acquaintances. The cover letter requested that if the respondent were aware of other dual-career couples within psychology who might be willing to participate in the survey, to please inform us. We were especially interested in those couples where the wife did not adopt the husband's last name and thus would not be obvious from an alphabetical listing such as the one which we used. Such additional names were supplied by some of the respondents to the survey. Through this procedure, we identified dual-career couples in psychology in forty-six of the fifty states plus the District of Columbia. A total of 503 such couples was contacted. This contact included a cover letter explaining the reason for the study and the anonymity of the results, a questionnaire for the male, a questionnaire for the female, and a stamped return envelope. The return rate for the questionnaires was 54.1 percent. Since an anonymous approach was used, no follow-up contacts were made.

The questionnaire requested one page of demographic data. These items could be answered jointly by the couple or by one member for the couple. These questions included age, length of marriage, number of children, and place of residence. Also included were items related to joint professional activity. The page to be completed individually by the male and female member consisted of fourteen items to be rated on a five-point Likert scale (1 = strongly disagree to 5 = strongly agree). These items included job satisfaction, social issues, interrelationship of job and home, and potential for job change. Additional items considered areas of specialization within psychology, work status, type of employment, a ranking of factors of potential importance in considering a job change, types of problems (if any) encountered in interviewing or working together, and several open-ended items on advantages and disadvantages of being a dual-career couple within psychology.

RESULTS

The median age of the female subjects responding to the survey was thirty-nine years, with a range of twenty-seven to seventy-three years. For the males, the median age was forty-two years with a range of twenty-six to seventy-five. In the majority of cases, the husband was older than the wife. The average difference was in the 1- to 3-year range.

The typical couple reported having married while still in graduate school and currently having been married for more than ten years. Thus, most of these subjects had faced some of the issues which we had during our job search. Although some respondents had only a master's degree, 83.7 percent of the respondents indicated that both members of the dual-career couple were doctoral-level psychologists. In terms of job hunting, it was interesting to note that 57.9 percent of the couples reported the male receiving the terminal degree first and 59.5 percent of the cases reported that the male had obtained the current employment first. While this pattern accounts for the majority of the cases who responded to the survey, it is certainly not an overwhelming part of the sample.

Although 95.2 percent of these dual-career couples reported that both members were currently employed, only 58.7 percent of them worked at the same facility. Although most of them engaged in some joint professional activities (87.2 percent of the respondents attended professional meetings together), the issue of leaning on each other or needing to work together was not an overwhelming one.

The job situation did vary when the male and female respondents were compared. Although 94.8 percent of the males were employed on a full-time basis, only 72.6 percent of the females were so employed. This work status was the choice of 77.6 percent of the females and 86.2 percent of the males. Thus, while the majority of the respondents were working to the degree they chose, there were also some who were not in a preferred work situation. Based on comments made to open-ended questions, it appeared that some of these dissatisfactions with employment status were the result of the need to obtain two professional positions. There was a tendency to feel that once good jobs had been located, it was difficult to move to another community which might offer better employment opportunities for only one member.

This hesitancy to move is not an indication that these individuals were unhappy with their current employment. Both male and female respondents indicated a moderately high (median = 4) degree of satisfaction with their current employment. They differed, however, on reported degree of personal involvement with their jobs. The males indicated a higher degree of personal involvement (median = 5) than did the females (median = 4). Neither group, however, supported the position of keeping work life and home life as separate as possible. Perhaps the fact that both members of these couples were trained as psychologists contributed to this pattern of responding. It has been the authors' experience that having a spouse from the same profession makes it easier to discuss job-related issues within the home setting. Such a situation can, however, lead to difficulties in keeping any time totally unrelated to one's profession.

The employment situation for the dual-career couple involves both initial employment and the possibility of a job change. A number of factors can be considered when a dual-career couple plans a job change. Table 13.1 presents eight such factors. The most important of these factors for the females responding to our survey was that both members of the dual-career couple have job offers. For the males, it was a toss-up between that item and their own job offer. The least important factor for both groups was working in the same place.

TABLE 13.1   Job Change Factors for Females (F) and Males (M)

	Median Rank	
	F	M
My job offer (type of job)	3	2
My spouse's job offer (type of job)	3	4
That we both have job offers	2	2
Geographic location of the proposed job(s)	3	4
My salary	6	6
My spouse's salary	6	6
Combined family salary	4	4
That we work at the same place	8	8

An integral part of the employment search is the interview process. As mentioned previously, there are certain unique experiences which may occur in this process for the dual-career couple. We were interested to see if our experiences were typical of what has been experienced by others in the same situation. A number of our questions dealt with interview and joint employment issues. The most prevalent difficulty our respondents reported relative to interviewing and/or working together was nepotism rules. This problem was reported by more than 40 percent of both male and female respondents. Although this issue has previously been addressed in the literature (Pingree et al. 1978), it has not been resolved. Dual-career couples need to be aware of this issue not only when applying for jobs but also in maintaining employment.

A number of illustrations of job-related advantages and disadvantages to being a dual-career couple within psychology were provided by the respondents to our survey. Selections from these comments

TABLE 13.2   Interview and Joint Employment Issues (in percentages)

	Female	Male
Nepotism rules	43.4	40.8
Lower combined salary than two comparable independent professionals	29.8	15.5
Not being treated as two independent professionals	35.8	24.9
Employer taking attitude of "doing you a favor"	23.6	16.9
One member essentially ignored during interview	14.6	11.7
One of the two positions really below your qualifications	17.5	15.5

can be used to illustrate the range of possibilities. Most of these anecdotes appear applicable to a variety of careers in addition to psychology. Some of the respondents indicated that, due to the job market being somewhat tight, they had changed careers. Typically, these situations involved one member obtaining a job in the preferred area and the other member taking a job in a less-preferred area. An example of this situation is provided below.

> Because of nepotism rules at two local universities with a federated program in psychology, I ventured private practice—which is currently highly successful and lucrative. This now seems really fortunate—the lack of a university position at the time of my graduation.

In this case, one member changed jobs and found the new position was a good one. Although this type of "happy ending" may not occur in all cases, it does seem to be an option which may be overlooked by the dual-career couple hesitating to make a job change until both have employment in their preferred areas.

A variety of types of situations can be subsumed under the title of interdependence of the two positions. This relationship may be from the point of view of the dual-career couple, the employer, or acquaintances. One type of acquaintaince reaction is provided below.

> Even my closest friends and colleagues do not think my wife and I should be paid according to equitable rules or be allowed to "officially" work together even though we have demonstrated productivity and meet the usual quality and quantity standards.

This question of interdependence may be raised by the potential employer during a job interview. Such an issue seems to be of particular importance to the dual-career couple considering employment in the same facility.

> For one job interview in which we would have been hired together, concern expressed that we need same vacation time—request that one of us take the month of July and one of us the month of August.

Whether a couple is willing to be employed with such a restriction is an individual decision.

Although nepotism rules are not found at all facilities today, they still apear to be a problem for the dual-career couple on the job search. Such rules can influence not only the initial hiring but may come into play later if one member of the couple is faced with a promotion which would require, or could be viewed as requiring, one member to supervise the other. From the perspective of initial employment, consider the following comment.

> We were told that although there were two positions in a certain place, and although both of us were the top candidates, we could not both be hired due to nepotism rules.

Another report indicated a potential nepotism problem after working at a university for a period of time. Such situations could limit at least for one member of the pair's advancement possibilities.

> Since my husband is chairman in the department in which I teach, the university wanted to transfer me to another department; now he has applied for the deanship, and if he gets it, I'll have to move to another college.

Other comments provided cases in which the dual-career status was viewed as a detractor in terms of one's changes of obtaining a particular job. In the following example, the dual-career status was seen as limiting the possibility of initial consideration for a job.

> Though qualified, we were both denied U.S. Civil Service classifications until contacting congressman, who expedited the appropriate ratings.

For this couple, the dual-career status appears to have limited the first step in the job search—the appropriate credential for the desired positions. Being a member of a dual-career couple may thus require a little special handling if the desired goal is to be reached.

In some cases, the blocking may be less obvious than in the previously cited example. It may be that overt reactions are dealt with more easily than covert ones. The following example illustrates the covert approach.

Covert prejudice when wife attempted to get job at same place. Took seven years although opportunities were available with regard to position openings for which she was skilled. This last time we would have sued, I think, if necessary since the selection committee placed her as their clear number one choice. It is horrible being not selected for something because you are married.

One reaction to such situations might be that they are highly unfair and should not exist; but the fact is that they do exist. It is fine to talk about changes and educating people to the real situation of the dual-career couple, but it is also important for the dual-career couple to be aware that these situations are prevalent. With such prior knowledge, the dual-career couple can better prepare for job hunting, make more informed decisions about such job situations, and realize that barriers should not be personalized.

Another group of comments deals with the dual-career status contributing to obtaining a job or increasing a job's potential. These comments seem to come mainly from psychologists in applied areas.

We find that as marriage and sex therapists (in addition to being psychologists) people, i.e. couples, will call us for an appointment simply because we are a married couple.

In the next case, the marital status has led to an unusual therapy situation.

We currently have an emotionally disturbed teenager, from a very influential family, living with us because of our profession and our marital status. This arrangement has lasted nine months and will probably last another nine months.

A final employment issue suggested by these respondents involves whether or not to accept jobs in distant communities. There appear to be several ways of dealing with this employment option. The following comment is an excerpt from a letter from one psychologist with specific locations deleted to maintain anonymity.

My spouse left for a job interview only a day before I was called on my first interview. We returned from both interviews and received offers for one-year positions within the week [a one-year postdoctoral position for the male in the midwest and a one-year replacement position for the female on the coast]. The decision was made to take both positions and to use that next year to search for those "two perfect jobs" again.

At the time this letter was written, the female was beginning her third year in a permanent position at the same facility where she had accepted a replacement appointment. The male was in his second year in a permanent position at a different midwestern facility. Their divorce had been final for about seven months at that time.

Another couple was able to find jobs which allowed weekend visiting but not during the week. Their comment was as follows:

Lived apart for two years and only saw each other on weekends in order to pursue job interests.

For this couple, the separation did not end the marriage. They indicated that they had finally been able to obtain positions in the same community and did not indicate regrets over having pursued independent positions when that had been viewed as necessary.

From these comments, it can be seen that there are a number of employment issues which are unique to the dual-career couple. There does not seem to be any good answer about how to handle these issues or even how to prepare for them. Perhaps the only preparation which is available at this time is to be aware that they exist and to know how some others have dealt with them. With that type of information, individual dual-career couples may be better prepared to face the employment market. Also, the potential employers and colleagues of dual-career couples may be made more aware of the role they play and to distinguish between myths and realities regarding dual-career couples.

FORECASTING THE FUTURE

To forecast the future in the area of dual-career couples and employment would be rather presumptuous. As more attention is paid to dual-career couples, it seems logical to expect that some of the current problems could be eliminated. Dual-career couples should be treated as independent professionals who happen to be married to other professionals. As long as the employment situation is a buyers' market, it will remain easy for potential employers to maintain some of the practices described in this chapter. Perhaps by the dual-career couple being more aware of potential pitfalls, they will be better able to deal with them. By being aware that they are not alone in their dual-career status, these couples may be better able to cope with the unique frustrations which they face in the job market.

One couple made an interesting observation: They see themselves not only as a dual-career couple but as having a joint career. They viewed their relationship in that light, and even noted that many of their publications were joint. Perhaps this is a concept which could be developed and elaborated further. We often point out the dual aspect of professional pairs, while paying much less attention to the positive interactional qualities of their joint relationships. We hope this approach will change in the future.

REFERENCES

BRYSON, R. B., J. B. BRYSON, M. H. LICHT, and B. G. LICHT (1976) "The professional pair: husband and wife psychologists." American Psychologist 31: 10–17.

CATES, J. and T. CUMMINGS (1970) "Placement report: 1969." American Psychologist 25: 778–782.

——— (1972) "Placement report: 1971." American Psychologist 27: 475–476.

CUCA, J. M. (1975) "Placement reports: 1973 and 1974." American Psychologist 30: 1176–1180.

CUMMINGS, T. and J. CATES (1971) "Placement report: 1970." American Psychologist 26: 503–507.

——— (1973) "Placement report: 1972." American Psychologist 28: 930–932.

MADELL, T. O. and C. M. MADELL (1979) "A professional pair at the job market: a reply." American Psychologist 34: 275–276.

MATTHEWS, J. R. and L. H. MATTHEWS (1978) "A professional pair at the job market." American Psychologist 33: 780–782.

PERLMAN, B. (1976) "The hunt: job hunting for the new Ph.D. psychologist." American Psychologist 31: 298–303.

PINGREE, S., M. BUTLER, W. PAISLEY, and R. HAWKINS (1978) "Anti-nepotism's ghost: attitudes of administrators toward having professional couples." Psychology of Women Quarterly 3: 22–30.

EPILOGUE

We now know that, as a result of the struggle for women's rights, a new social phenomenon emerged, the dual-career couple. We can predict with some certainty that the numbers of dual-career couples will increase as more women gain access to higher education and thereby increase their chances for employment advancement. In addition, equal opportunity laws as discussed by Moore earlier will help to insure that more women will be afforded parity with men in the hiring, firing, and retention process.

The dual-career structure epitomizes the concept of equity for the members within it, if it is to be truly egalitarian. Equity enables people to make choices based on preference, rather than on obligation. When one perceives that s/he has options, then it naturally follows that one would feel in control of one's life. This sense of control promotes a state of general well-being, and the lack of control promotes the opposite effect. However, equity is a continually changing notion which has to be constantly renegotiated, clarified, and developed. Priorities change. It is easy to get trapped into thinking that they are permanently fixed. For example, if a woman believes that her family should always come first, then she is apt to place her career second or third. Similarly, if a man believes that his career is first, then his domestic responsibilities will be put off until his career demands are addressed. The more helpful perspective may be to assume that career, family, or other aspects of the dual-career relationship, may shift depending upon one's energy level, time allotment, deadlines, preferences, and commitment.

This fluidity of priorities enhances equity and is the cornerstone of the dual-career relationship. Fluidity sets it apart from the prescription of roles of the traditional family. The dual-career relationship enables individuals to seek personal satisfactions in living, but requires a different kind of effort which may seem more difficult because it is new and untried.

What has become apparent in this book, however, is that—despite the efforts of dual-career couples—many things have not changed and will not change until there are major attitudinal changes in the dual-career couples themselves and in the major social institutions. The basis for change must originate within the thinking of both women and men. Obviously, if only women are willing to alter their attitudes, and men want to maintain the status quo, changes in roles will lag as they have. Attitudinal changes must occur not only at an individual level, but collectively within groups as well. Men and women can both benefit in the long run.

Lynn's chapter is a good beginning in the examination of attitude change. He has pointed out that only when parents of female children believe that their daughters should and can be intellectually and creatively independent will these daughters be able to break out of a traditionally feminine role. When parents of female children insist that their daughters follow traditional female development, it is the daughters who lose out and reduce their options. Traditional female development is based on passivity, dependence, and undue caution, and these traits are not likely to be compatible with intellectual strivings and achievements. Lynn clearly states that, in fact, when a child is prompted to investigate a myriad of curiosities, independence of thought is fostered. Lynn's study of women is crucial to the understanding of the developmental issues. Men's developmental issues should also be investigated with respect to their intellectual and creative achievements. How do parents encourage or discourage these pursuits?

In the section on marriage, our authors refer to the traditional female role reversion which is alluded to by Lynn. Hawkes, Nicola, and Fish's study of young marrieds pointed out that wives fell into traditional sex roles when there were children. These women maintained responsibility for domestic chores even when their husbands stated they were in favor of wives' employment. Clearly, the women could not or would not insist that their husbands assume these domestic tasks. Nor did the husbands take responsibility in this area.

Similarly, this theme was repeated in the Lopata, Burdeno, and Norr study of Chicago women. Their sample of women reported that husbands did not share household work. The wives, reporting their perceptions only, insisted, however, that they help their husbands with their job issues.

How does such an imbalance occur and continue? Nadelson and Nadelson addressed this issue poignantly and have told us about the powerful dynamics of guilt, anxiety, depression, and anger. They informed us about the universal emotional state, guilt, that takes its toll on women, and how it serves the individual.

Guilt is a feeling that is more prominent in women who choose to work, rather than working out of financial necessity. Several authors in this book point out that guilt seems to be a woman's issue, that men are more immune. Johnson and Johnson, Nadelson and Nadelson, and Hawkes, Nicola, and Fish all attend to this in their chapters. Guilt, experienced by the women in the dual-career relationship, most likely reflects the lack of role models available and the concomitant sense that one is betraying the full motherhood role by outside employment. This is a gnawing and uneasy state which accounts for the fact that women do not readily relinquish domestic responsibilities, even when husbands prefer to "help." Women speaking to themselves might say, "Since I have elected to work, I must compensate for abandoning my family by continuing to do all of the housework so that I can still be regarded as a good wife and mother."

When women's children or husbands succumb to school problems, occupational setbacks, life crises, depression, or general unhappiness, women assume that they are responsible for these events. "If Johnny gets a bad report card, it must be my fault since I'm working." "If my husband does not get his promotion, then I am responsible since I have not entertained enough or because I was not emotionally available to him." Women have erroneously assumed responsibility for others' unhappiness (but seldom for others' happiness).

This form of self-blame is again related to career achievement. Women are going against traditional role models when they accept outside employment, and suffer emotionally when external events are not perfect, as they never can be for any sustained length of time. As a result of not achieving perfection, women are inclined to berate themselves and believe that in fact they cannot succeed in many areas. Males, on the other hand, have been expected to succeed primarily within their occupational pursuits, which suggests the putting-all-their-eggs-in-one-basket phenomenon. As a result, males are defined as success or failures in terms of their occupational achievements. Unfortunately, men seldom get credit for being effective husbands or fathers. When men are attentive to their husbandly or fatherly roles, they are often perceived as "ne'er-do-wells," or shirking their occupational responsibilities.

The next section, families, underscores the marriage section by again identifying the state of "guilt" endemic to women. Johnson and Johnson addressed the crucial concept of role strain and pointed out that even in dual-career families, the person primarily responsible for the children's well-being is the mother. This responsibility is covertly agreed upon by both parents; we cannot assume that fathers have ignored this responsibility any more than we can assume that mothers have been willing to relinquish it. Seiden, and Lawe and Lawe clearly addressed the need to negotiate these key issues.

Seiden stressed the importance of understanding time management. She pointed out that time management is *not* bias free. It is closely associated with three paramount issues: struggles for dominance, expectations of role contingent upon gender, and interpersonal negotiations. In essence, Seiden told us that time and its management are associated with emotional and control states. Time is not managed outside an interpersonal sphere. Time clearly has many values and is significantly defined within a personal context.

Lawe and Lawe gave us prescriptions for conflict resolutions within the dual-career relationship. They stressed other key concepts, such as commitments to the dual-career philosophy and relationship which must be based on basic trust. Their prescriptions were complimented by similated dialogues, making clearer the realistic aspects of negotiated relationships. They emphasized the necessity for bearing in mind that dual-career couples have human, occupational, achievement, and interpersonal needs which should not be denied, lest the relationship become vapid and empty.

Taking a look at the employment issues, the next section addressed the inequities in the job market. Butler and Paisley looked at publication patterns among couples and centered their chapter on career coordination of dual-career couples. They noted that many of their couples did not seem to be making intentional systematic efforts to coordinate careers. Their chapter can be used as a "survival guide" for dual-career couples, particularly those in academia. Butler and Paisley have included data from department chairpersons, sex discrimination interferences, and publication productivity of dual-career couples.

Moore's discussion of equal opportunity laws is a good instructional section on knowing what the recruitment and selection consequences can be for dual-career couples. Although she cites the legal parameters of hiring dual-career couples, she also insisted that we understand that employment rights protected by law can manufacture new problems that may not necessarily be easily surmounted by the dual-career couple.

Bryson and Bryson posed the question of how it is that dual-career women continue to pursue careers in the face of severe occupational constraints. They told us also that when employment pressures bear upon the dual-career couple, the woman's career has a tendency to be viewed as secondary to her husband's. They informed us about the fact that many times the dual-career couple's goals will conflict with those of society, institutions, and domestic demands.

The final chapter by Matthews and Matthews was an eye-opener for any dual-career couple who is job searching. Not only did they describe their own experience in joint interviews, but they summarized their survey results from other dual-career couples. Their chapter is helpful in that it identifies important issues in the informed consent area. We were informed about the unequal subtleties that exist—such as nepotism, differential employment rates, and so on.

This book has been an endeavor into the understanding of the myriad of complexities inherent in the dual-career structure. If women's issues have been attended to more, it is only because the data have been there. Men in dual-career relationships have research value too, and perhaps more studies will be conducted with them in mind, though up to now the number of studies is lacking.

There are other areas of the dual-career family worthy of further investigation. Rapoport and Rapoport have called for more systematic studies with respect to the following:

—the quality of the marital role

—socialization effects upon the children

—the impact upon other social institutions

Rapoport and Rapoport are optimistic that "increasingly rational levels of discourse" can take place as we expand our understandings.

Finally, we must be mindful that in addition to these scientific issues, the dual-career family is a human enterprise. It embodies commitment, trust, caring, and regard. These qualities must be carefully and continually nourished and acknowledged. In fact, they are the glue, or the necessary cementing ingredients, for maintenance of the dual-career structure as it strives for full equity.

—*Fran Pepitone-Rockwell*

ABOUT THE AUTHORS

FRAN PEPITONE-ROCKWELL is a clinical psychologist with an appointment as Assistant Professor in the School of Medicine, Department of Psychiatry, and is also Director of the Women's Resources and Research Center, University of California, Davis. She received her Ph.D. in 1974 from the California School of Professional Psychology in San Francisco. She has since been actively involved in activities which combine her clinical training and her academic feminist interests—serving as a consultant and participant in community projects working with suicide, rape, families, and battered women. With her husband, she conducts couple therapy, and lectures, researches, and writes on issues which affect the attitutdes about and treatment of women by professionals who serve them.

RHONA RAPOPORT is Co-Director of the Institute of Family and Environmental Research. She received her Ph.D. from the London School of Economics in sociology, and she is also a qualified psychoanalyst. With her husband, she has authored numerous books and papers, including *Dual-Career Families Re-Examined* (Martin Robertson/Harper & Row); *Leisure and the Family Life Cycle* (Routledge & Kegan Paul); and *Fathers, Mothers and Society* (Routledge & Kegan Paul/Vintage).

ROBERT N. RAPOPORT is Co-Director of the Institute of Family and Environmental Research. He received his Ph.D. from Harvard College in social anthropology. Among his books and articles are *Communities as Doctor* (Arno Press); *Mid-Career Development*

(Tavistock); and "Transition Between School and Work" (Oxford Review of Education). He is currently doing research in the area of family breakdown and informal supports.

DAVID B. LYNN has since 1968 been Professor of Human Development in the Department of Applied Behavioral Sciences at the University of California at Davis. He received his Ph.D. in clinical psychology at Purdue University. His publications include *Parental and Sex-Role Identification: A Theoretical Formulation*, *The Father: His Role in Child Development*, and *Daughters and Parents: Past, Present, and Future*.

GLENN R. HAWKES is a developmental psychologist with an appointment as Professor of Human Development in the Department of Applied Behavioral Sciences at the University of California at Davis, where he also serves as Professor of Behavioral Sciences in the Department of Family Practice of the School of Medicine, and Associate Dean for Applied Economic and Behavioral Sciences. He received his Ph.D. in psychology from Cornell University.

JoANN NICOLA is a Ph.D. candidate in child/family sociology with an appointment as Assistant Professor of Child and Family Development in the Home Economics Department of California State University, Sacramento. Her special research interests are in dual-career families, nonsexist early childhood education, verbal and nonverbal creativity in preschool-age children.

MARGARET FISH plans to continue her graduate education in developmental psychology. She received an M.S. in child development at the University of California at Davis (while her husband was earning a Ph.D.), prior to which she was a social worker and assistant editor of an insurance publication. She is the coauthor of two research articles on mother-infant interaction.

CAROL C. NADELSON is currently on the Blue Ribbon Commission on the Future of Public Inpatient Mental Health Services in Massachusetts. She earned her M.D. with honors at the University of

Rochester School of Medicine, where she received the Benjamin Rush Award in Psychiatry. She also currently serves as an associate psychiatrist-in-chief at New England Medical Center Hospital, and as Professor and Vice Chairperson of psychiatry on the faculty of Tufts University School of Medicine.

THEODORE NADELSON is Director of the Psychiatric Consultation/Liaison Service at Beth Israel Hospital in Boston, Massachusetts. He received his M.D. from the University of California Medical School, San Francisco. He has completed courses of study at Brooklyn College, the University of California at Berkeley, and the Boston Psychoanalytic Society and Institute.

HELENA Z. LOPATA is Professor of Sociology and Director of the Center for Cooperative Study of Social Roles at Loyola University of Chicago. Her books include *Occupation: Housewife* (Oxford University Press); *Marriages and Families* (D. Van Nostrand); *Widowhood in an American City* (Schenkman); *Polish Americans: Status Competition in an Ethnic Community* (Prentice-Hall); and *Women as Widows: Support Systems* (Elsevier).

DEBRA BARNEWOLT is a doctoral candidate in sociology at Loyola University of Chicago. Her areas of interest include sociology of the family and women's studies. She has been involved in the project on changing commitments of women to work and family roles for the last three years, and she plans further research on the women's roles of employee, wife, and mother.

KATHLEEN NORR is the Deputy Director for the research on factory organizations in India. She is a member of the Center for the Comparison Study of Social Roles at Loyola University of Chicago.

COLLEEN LEAHY JOHNSON is an anthropologist in the Medical Anthropology Program of the University of California, San Francisco, where she is also Training Director of the Multidisciplinary Program in Applied Gerontology. She received her Ph.D. in 1972 from Syracuse University. She is currently completing an NIMH-funded project on family supports to the elderly, in which sex roles has been one of her major areas of interest.

FRANK A. JOHNSON is Professor and Vice Chairperson in the Department of Psychiatry at the University of California, San Francisco. He also serves as Chief of Psychiatry at San Francisco General Hospital and Director of the Social and Community Psychiatry Programs there. In addition to his work on dual-career families, he has published research in the areas of existential and cross-cultural psychotherapy.

ANNE M. SEIDEN is a psychiatrist with an appointment as Associate Professor in the Departments of Psychiatry and Public Health at the University of Illinois Medical Center, Chicago. She also serves as Chairperson of the Department of Psychiatry, Cook County Hospital. She has been actively involved in bringing her feminist and health consumer interests to bear on medical care and educational establishments, and has written and lectured extensively to psychiatric and other audiences about issues involving women and mental health.

CHARLES LAWE is a counseling psychologist serving a joint appointment between the University Counseling Center and the Counselor Education Department at Montana State University. He received his Ph.D. in 1976 from Indiana State University. With his wife, he has written and made presentations concerning dual-career couples, and participated as cotherapists for couples who face problems stemming from role conflicts.

BARBARA LAWE is a counselor at Bozeman Junior High School in Bozeman, Montana. She is active in volunteer community services, such as Family Planning and the Bozeman Battered Women's Network. She has collaborated with her husband in many professional endeavors, including giving stress workshops and acting as cotherapists for dual-career couples. Since she and her husband both have very busy schedules, they experience many of the struggles creating problems for the couples they counsel.

MATILDA BUTLER is Director of the Women's Educational Equity Communications Network, a nationwide information service sponsored by the U.S. Department of Education. She received her Ph.D. in psychology from Northwestern University. During previous teaching at Stanford University, she cofounded the Organization for Women in Communication, and directed the "Women in Advertising" project.

WILLIAM PAISLEY is a member of the faculty of Stanford University, teaching communication. He received his Ph.D. from Stanford in communication research. With Matilda Butler, he has coauthored *Women and the Mass Media* (Human Sciences Press) and has coparented several children. His research focuses on the flow of information in society.

DONNA M. MOORE is currently completing her Ph.D. in social-personality psychology at the University of California at Davis, while working as Human Resources and Affirmative Action Officer at Montana State University. She has been active professionally in developing and conducting programs to assist people in reducing sexism and racism, and in increasing positive communication skills and self-esteem.

JEFF B. BRYSON and REBECCA BRYSON became a dual-career couple while in graduate school at Purdue University. Having fought and won the battle for joint academic appointments, they are both currently on the faculty of San Diego State University. They have served as coeditors of a special issue of the *Psychology of Women Quarterly,* which was subsequently republished as *Dual Career Couples.* He is a social psychologist who is currently investigating the factors that influence the expression of sexual jealousy. She has previously trained in measurement and experimental psychology, and is examining cognitive and behavioral effects of nicotine.

JANET R. MATTHEWS is a clinical psychologist with an appointment as Assistant Professor in the Department of Psychology at Creighton University in Omaha, Nebraska. She received her Ph.D. in clinical psychology from the University of Mississippi. She has been a consultant and participant in community projects on mental retardation, second marriages, and homosexuality, and her research interests are in the area of student stress reactions and undergraduate education issues.

LEE H. MATTHEWS is a pediatric psychologist with an appointment as Assistant Professor of Medical Psychology in the Department of Pediatrics at the University of Nebraska Medical Center. He received his Ph.D. in clinical psychology from the University of Mississippi. He has served as a consultant to a state school of retarded children, a day care center for handicapped children, four Headstart Centers, and has been involved with hospital and community projects on child abuse and neglect, second marriages, and teacher education.